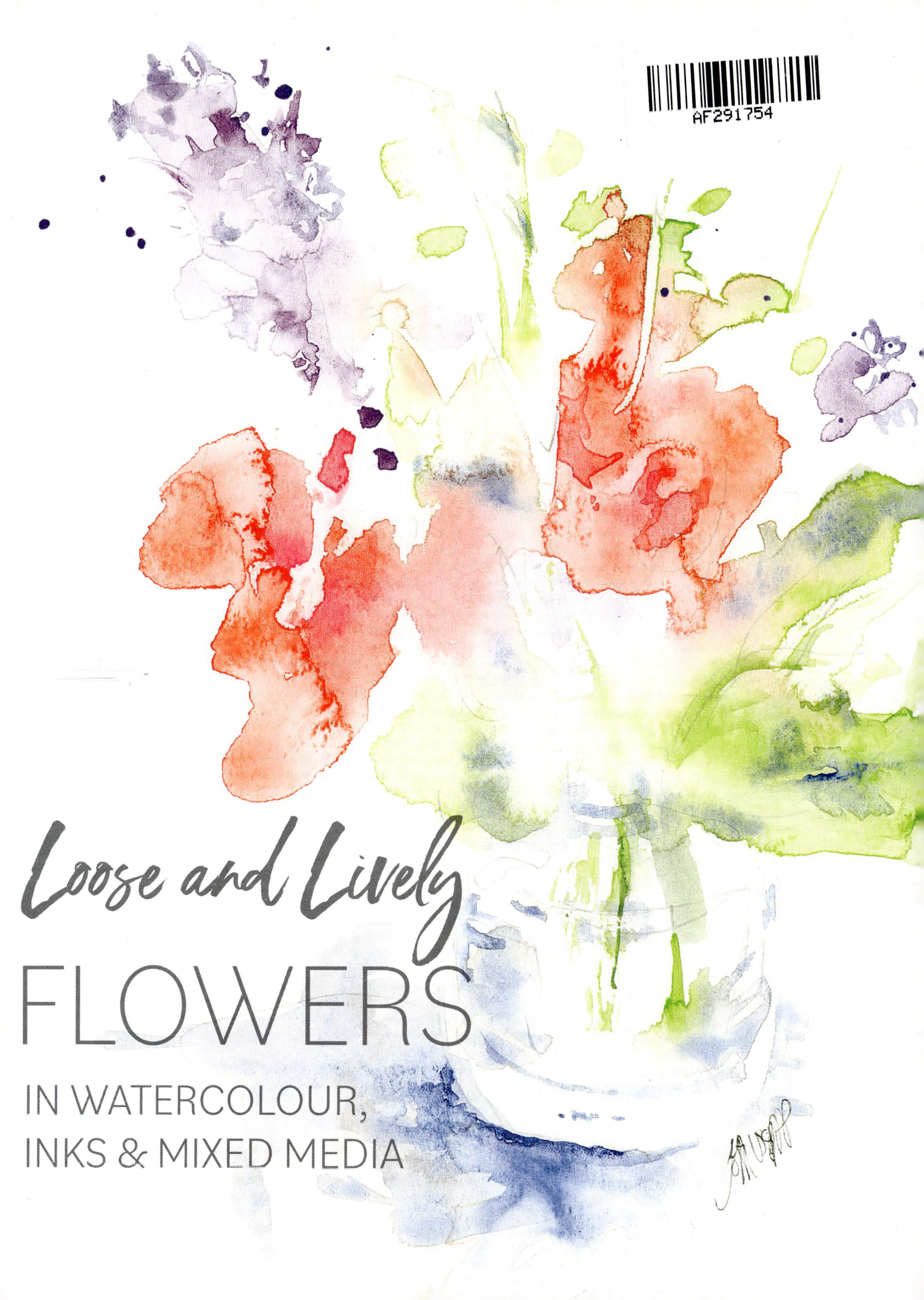

Loose and Lively

FLOWERS

IN WATERCOLOUR, INKS & MIXED MEDIA

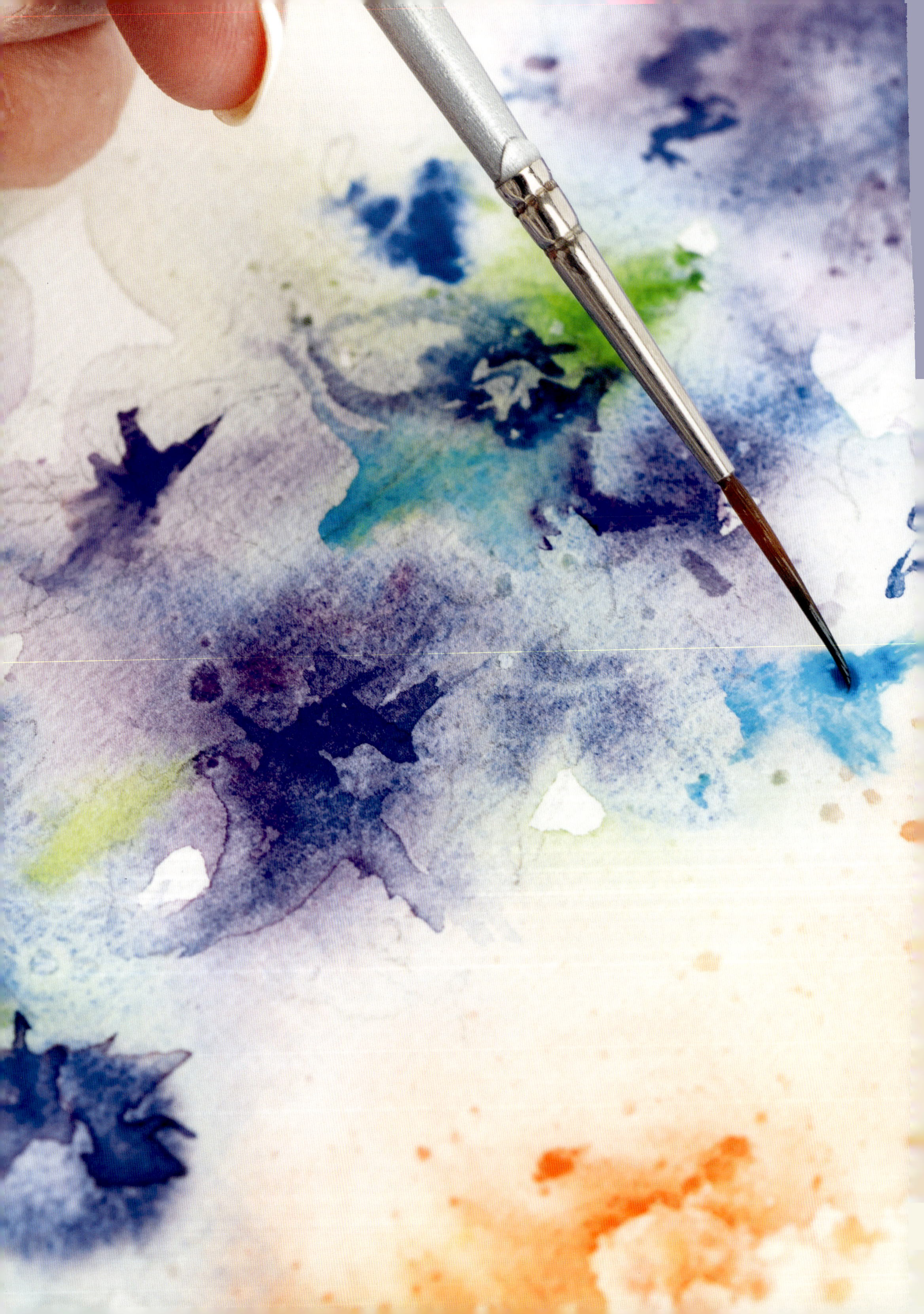

Jo Allsopp

Loose and Lively
FLOWERS

IN WATERCOLOUR, INKS & MIXED MEDIA

SEARCH PRESS

First published in 2026

Search Press Limited
Wellwood, North Farm Road,
Tunbridge Wells, Kent TN2 3DR

1 2 3 4 5 6 7 8 9 10

Text copyright © Joanne Allsopp, 2026

Photographs by Mark Davison at
Search Press Studios, except for pages 8,
36, 46 and 54, author's own; and page 38
(bottom left), by Neil Boynton.
Photographs and design copyright ©
Search Press Ltd. 2026

ISBN: 978-1-80092-337-9
ebook ISBN: 978-1-80093-324-8

Editor: Edward Ralph
Managing Editor: Becky Robbins
Designer: Emma Sutcliffe
Head of Design: Marrianne Miall
Publishing Director: Samantha Warrington

Bookmarked Hub
For further ideas and inspiration, and
to join our free online community,
visit www.bookmarkedhub.com

Publishers' notes
The Publishers and author can accept no
responsibility for any consequences arising
from the information, advice or instructions
given in this publication.

For errata, please visit our website
(www.searchpress.com) or the Bookmarked
Hub (www.bookmarkedhub.com).

GPSR information can be found
at www.searchpress.com

Printed in China, LP012026

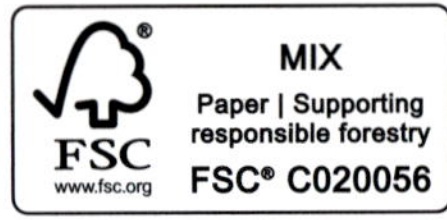

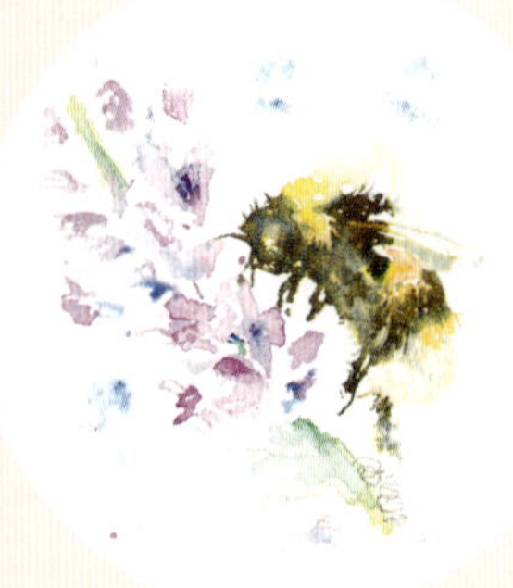

Dedication

I would dearly love to dedicate this book
to my girls, Jorgie and Geri: from little
buds have blossomed the most bright
and beautiful flowers. xx

Acknowledgements

Wow, my second book as an author! Firstly I would like to
thank my editor, Edward Ralph, who has assisted me on both
of my books and once again has shown such professionalism
and understanding throughout the whole process. Also,
Mark Davison for his excellent skills with our studio photography
– we three together had a great rapport, which made for the
most enjoyable and positive experience. All of the team at Search
Press are amazing and again I had the lovely Emma designing this
book for me and making it look absolutely stunning.

I thank too, from the bottom of my heart, my ever-loyal students,
readers, family and friends, without whose support and
encouragement I would not have been doing this. Great thanks
also go to those who kindly supplied their fabulous photographs
for me to use to create my artwork: Heather Allsopp, Louise Roe,
Sue Russell and Neil Boynton.

My biggest thanks must go to my greatest fan, the one who has
never doubted me, and that is Mr Allsopp. He has shown such
understanding and consideration throughout – even managing
to tip-toe around me in his size 9s whenever I needed to squirrel
myself away and concentrate. I really would not be where I am
today had it not been for his help and belief in me and so thank
you, Geoff, you have been a star. xx

Contents

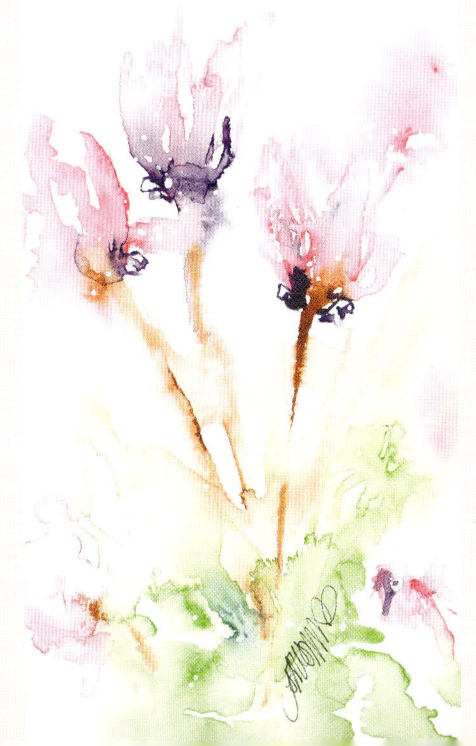

Introduction

Who doesn't love flowers? Whether carefully tended in a garden or popping up in the wild, flowers are always in fashion. I just love the beautiful sights and smells of flowers in all their many different varieties.

Nor are they simply decorative. The sight of yellow flowers can produce higher levels of serotonin (no wonder the yellow rose was my Nan's favourite flower) and boost our feelings of well-being. Many offer other medicinal benefits. Flowering plants also help our planet in so many ways: producing oxygen, food, purifying water, reducing pollution, and much more – it's no wonder we all appreciate the power of flowers.

How we feel is extremely important in helping us deal with everyday ups and downs. Since seeing flowers can release our happy hormones, painting them is a great way to slow down and spend time enjoying and appreciating their colours and shapes.

As an adult tutor, I teach most days and so feel blessed to be constantly practising and improving my painting skills. While I paint a range of subjects, I am often led by my learners and always elated when they suggest flowers – I never tire of painting them in all their endless variety.

I would love for you to feel the same enjoyment in painting flowers as I do. In this book we will be working in a very loose and relaxed way: think big, think bold and think bright. We are also going to be using lots of exciting mixed media along the way, which can give some amazing results when trying to emulate the varying textures of flora.

Let's go!

ALMOND BLOSSOM
A pure watercolour piece, using negative painting
(see page 74) to retain the white areas.

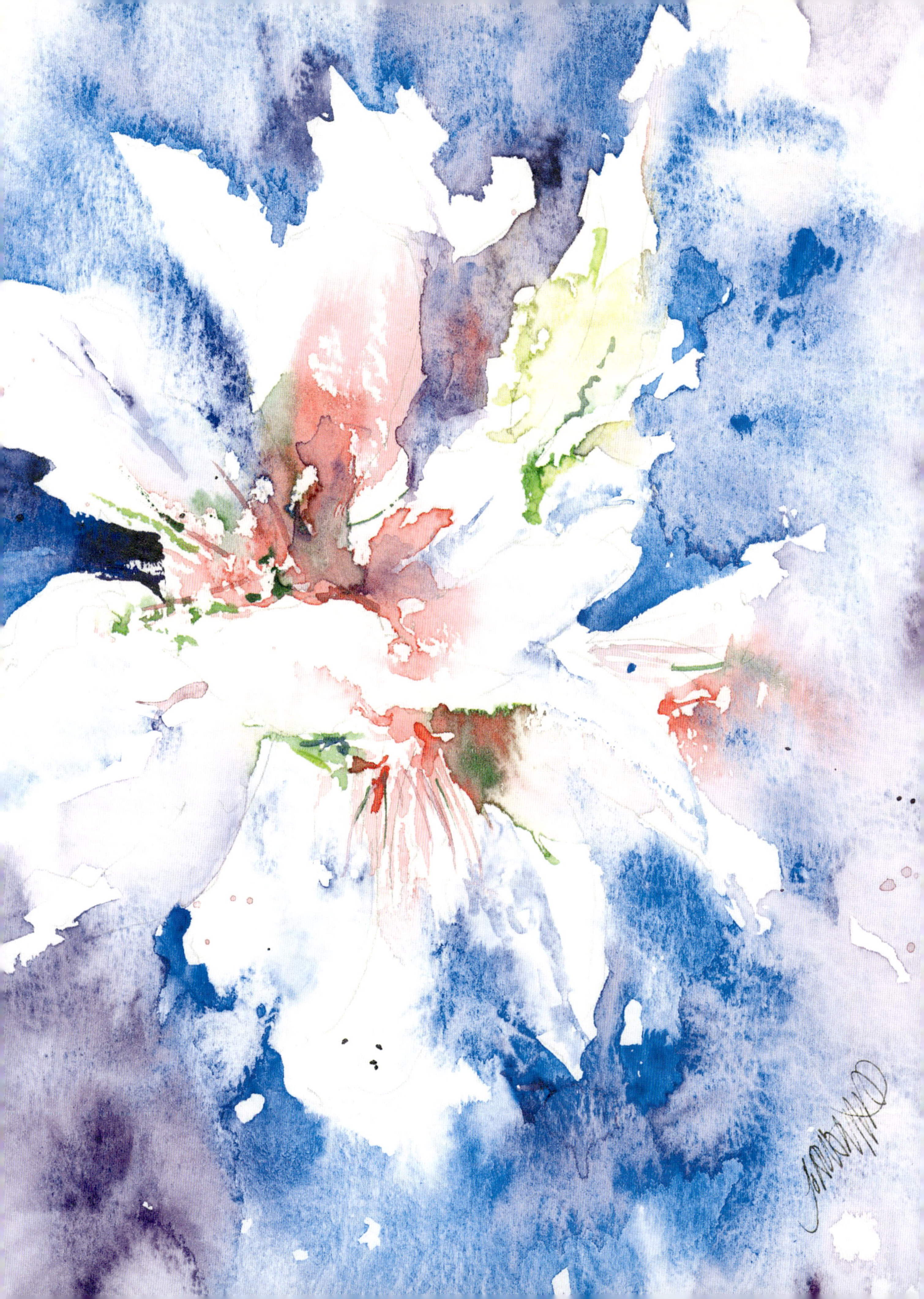

Finding inspiration

Ever since I purchased my very first set of 'real' watercolour paints – a little pocket set from an art shop near to where I once lived – I have always loved painting flowers. I remember being so excited to try out the paints and I painted some flowers from the garden as soon as I arrived home. Perhaps that's another reason why I love flowers: they evoke some great memories for me.

I strongly believe you should always paint a subject that you're passionate about. Inspiration for my paintings comes mostly from the colours of the blooms – the brighter the better. I am drawn to pretty shapes too; I really would not be inspired to paint a flower which I didn't find to be aesthetically pleasing. If I had to paint something unsightly – Rafflesia, the so-called 'corpse lily', for example – I can't imagine it would help with my motivation nor inspiration, and it wouldn't be releasing a rush of endorphins either! However, inspiration strikes in different ways, so when choosing what to paint, look inwards to what you love.

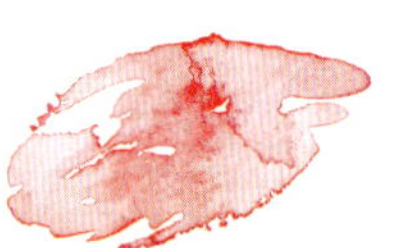

What you paint doesn't have to be flashy or grand. I think my favourite flower has to be the simple daisy, perhaps due to nostalgia: being young and carefree, making daisy chains in the great outdoors with friends. As you can see to the right, even the most humble everyday flowers can make beautiful subjects.

Another favourite of mine is often considered the most beautiful flower in the world: the rose. The vast array of colours, the iconic shape and the scent – I remember picking roses as a child and making my own 'perfume'. I also remember seeing roses where my Nan used to live, and so these bring back so many fond memories of spending time in North Wales visiting her.

There are so many flower varieties to choose from and so it has been very difficult to decide which to include in my book. I hope you enjoy the ones that made the cut.

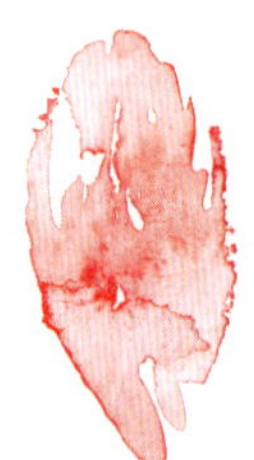

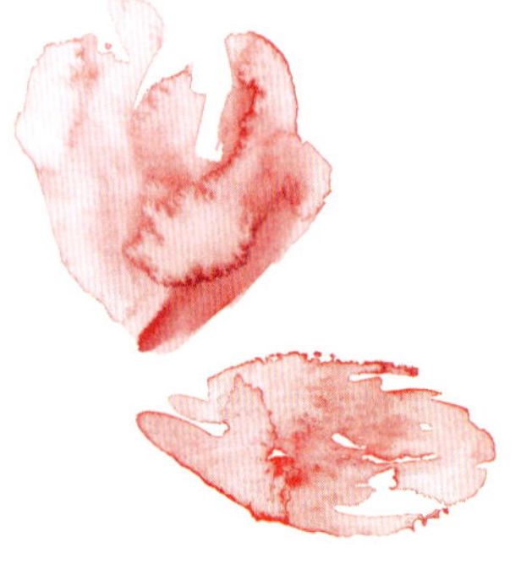

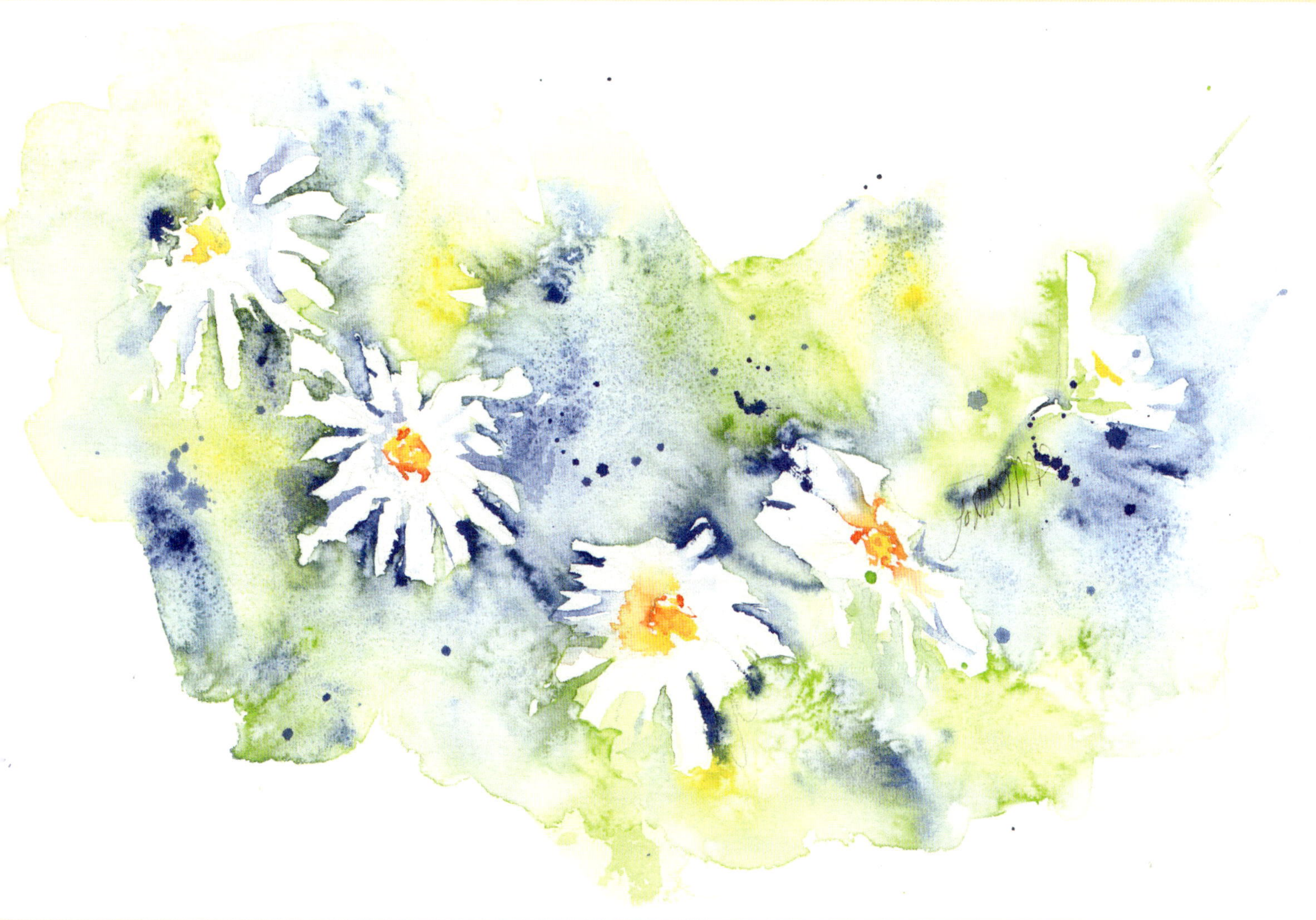

DAISY CHAIN
25.5 x 18cm (10 x 7in)

Another example of negative painting to produce bright,
clean results. Salt was sprinkled into the wet watercolour
as described on page 124 to produce texture.

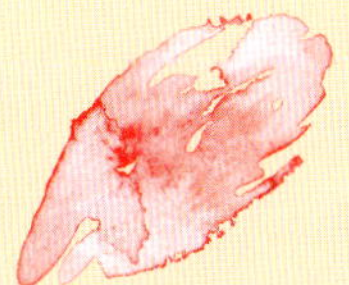

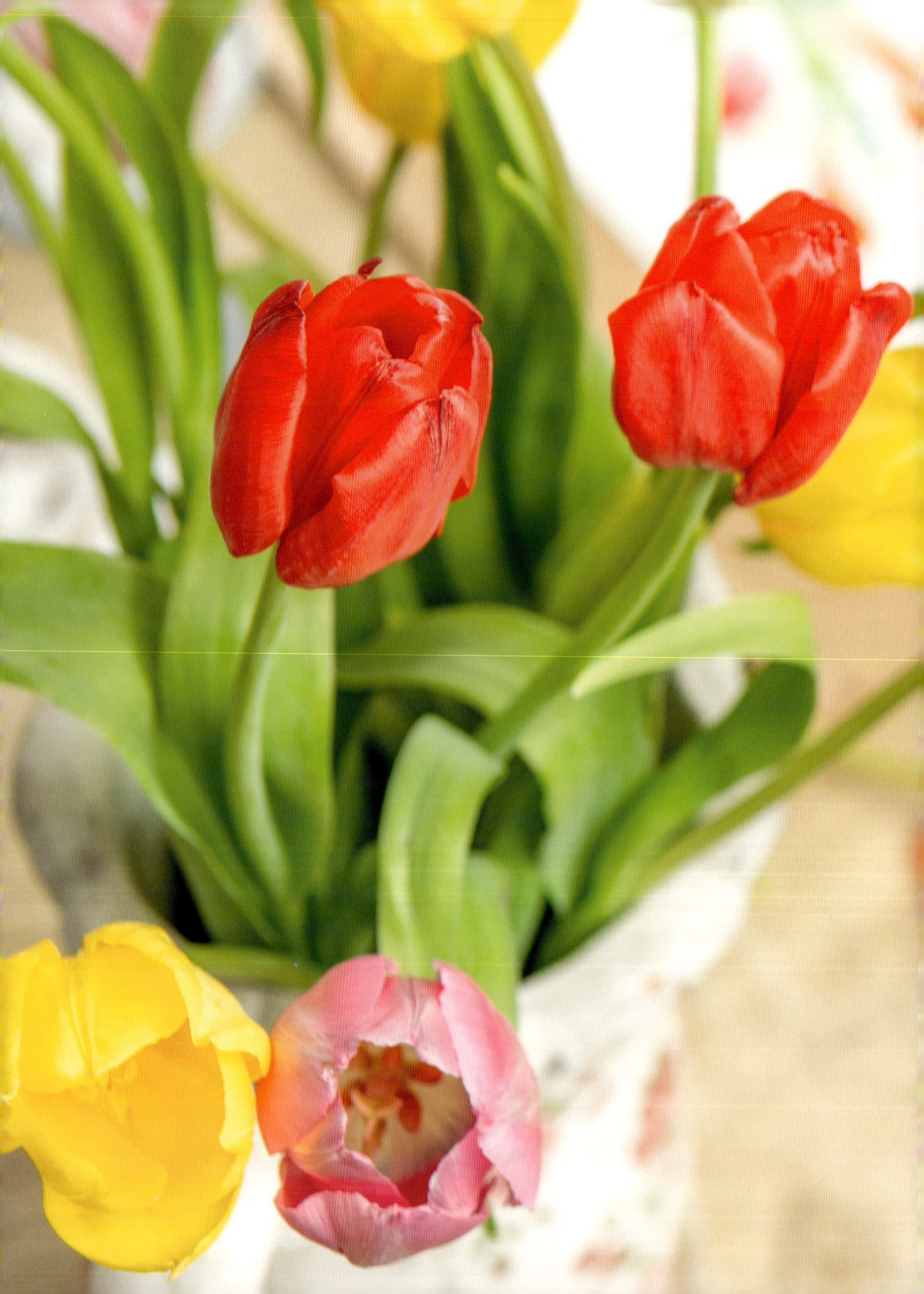

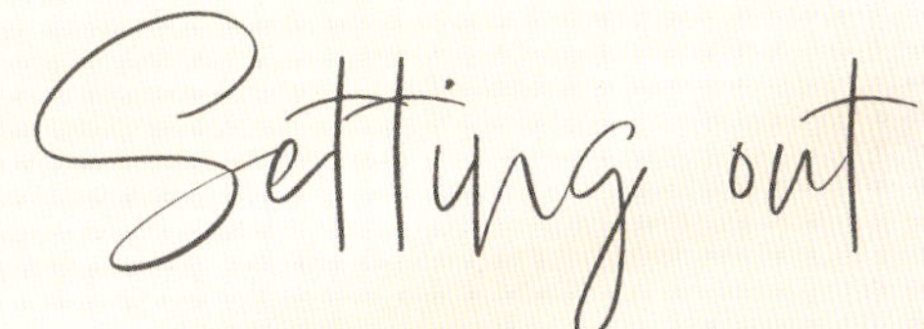

Setting out

Before we start, I'd like to share some advice on how –
and where – to prepare for painting flowers. A little
forward planning will set you up for painting success and
ensure the process is fun, relaxing and enjoyable.

Once you have decided on which flowers to paint, you
will need to go outdoors to find them, or buy a bunch from
which to paint indoors. While you can of course paint
from your imagination, there is no substitute for working
from life. Looking at flowers, whether on a screen, a
photograph or in front of you, will reveal lots of inspiring
(and sometimes surprising) details.

Sometimes you won't be able to paint from life, such as
when you want to paint rare flowers or those that aren't
available where you live. In these cases you will need to
rely upon photographs. I take lots of photographs for my
own reference when walking our dog Alfie and when
visiting different countries, but I am lucky that I also have
photographer contacts and family members who take
some wonderful pictures that they kindly allow me to
paint from.

Pictures of flowers can be sourced online too.
I sometimes use stock image sites to paint from. If you
intend to display or sell your work, make sure that your
reference is copyright-free and/or properly credited.

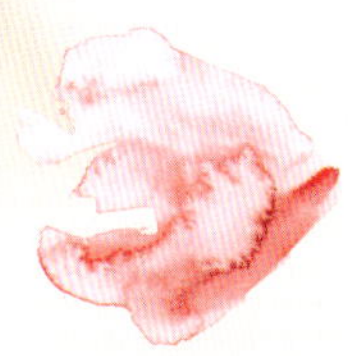

Painting indoors

Find a space where you won't be disturbed, with good lighting and somewhere comfortable to sit. Take a break from painting every now and then – it'll help keep you feeling fresh, and that energy will show in your work.

Working from flower arrangements in front of you will train you to better observe your subject. It's easy to get distracted and move around – so always try and sit in the same relaxed spot as when you first started your painting. This will ensure your drawing and painting perspective remains consistent and correct throughout.

Arranging flowers to paint

Whenever I am gifted bunches or pots of flowers, I arrange and paint them from life while they are fresh. You don't need to be an expert florist to arrange flowers – the key thing to remember is that you need to be able to see the flowerheads that inspired you. Set the flowers in a pot or vase so they sit nicely together and don't obscure one another, as in the example opposite.

Beyond this, you don't need to be too precise. I avoid arranging the flowers I paint too neatly, as I prefer a looser, less contrived result. My points of advice are:

Odd numbers Even numbers of flowers look static and still, so having an odd number can add liveliness to the painting.

Improvise While you can use a decorative vase or pot and incorporate it into your painting, a jam jar or even an old paint pot will do just fine to hold flowers.

Change colours You don't need to paint exactly what's in front of you, so if you think it will give a better painting, feel free to tweak the colours – brightening foliage or even changing petal colours entirely.

Take photographs Your display will inevitably change over the course of a few days as the flowers start to wilt, so whenever you have yourself a gorgeous floral display, take photographs while it's fresh. You can then paint your still life from direct observation, with the photograph as a back-up reference.

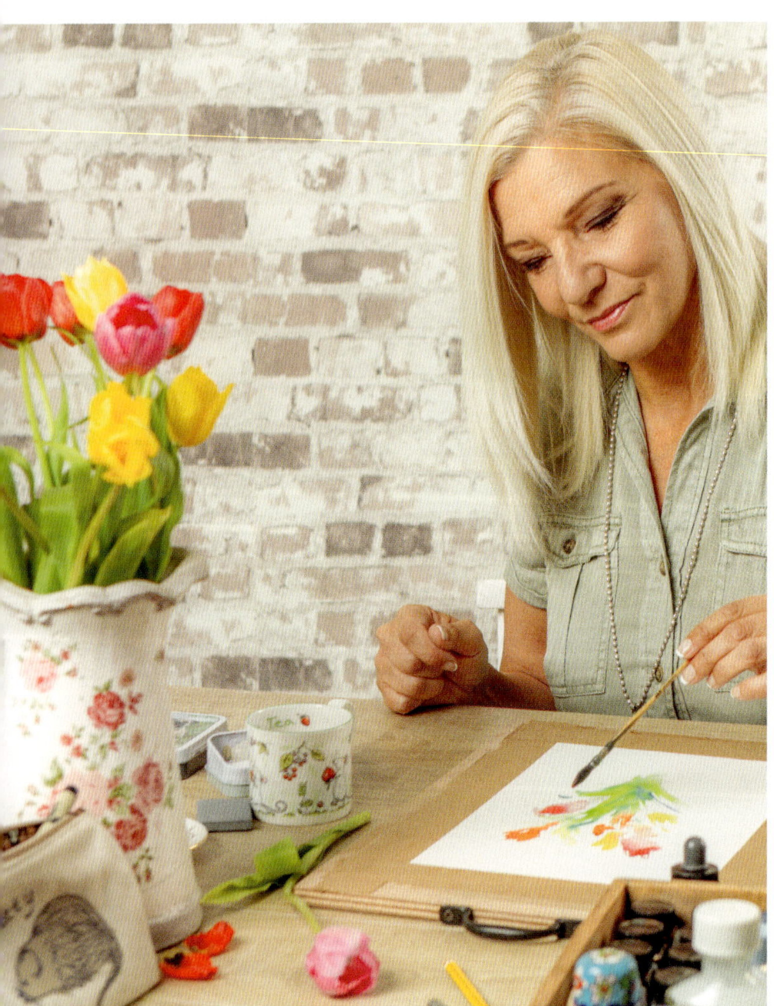

Painting in the studio, with both the flowers and my materials close to hand.

After arranging these roses for the painting opposite, I considered including the watering can pot in my painting, but in the end decided that the flowers themselves were all that was needed.

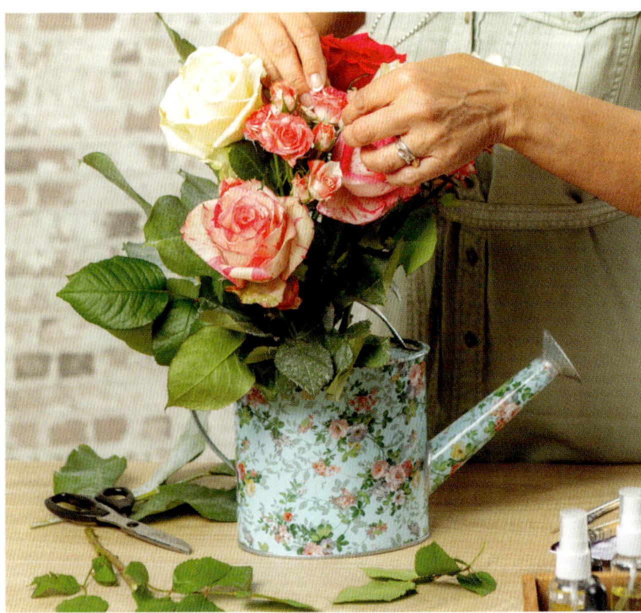

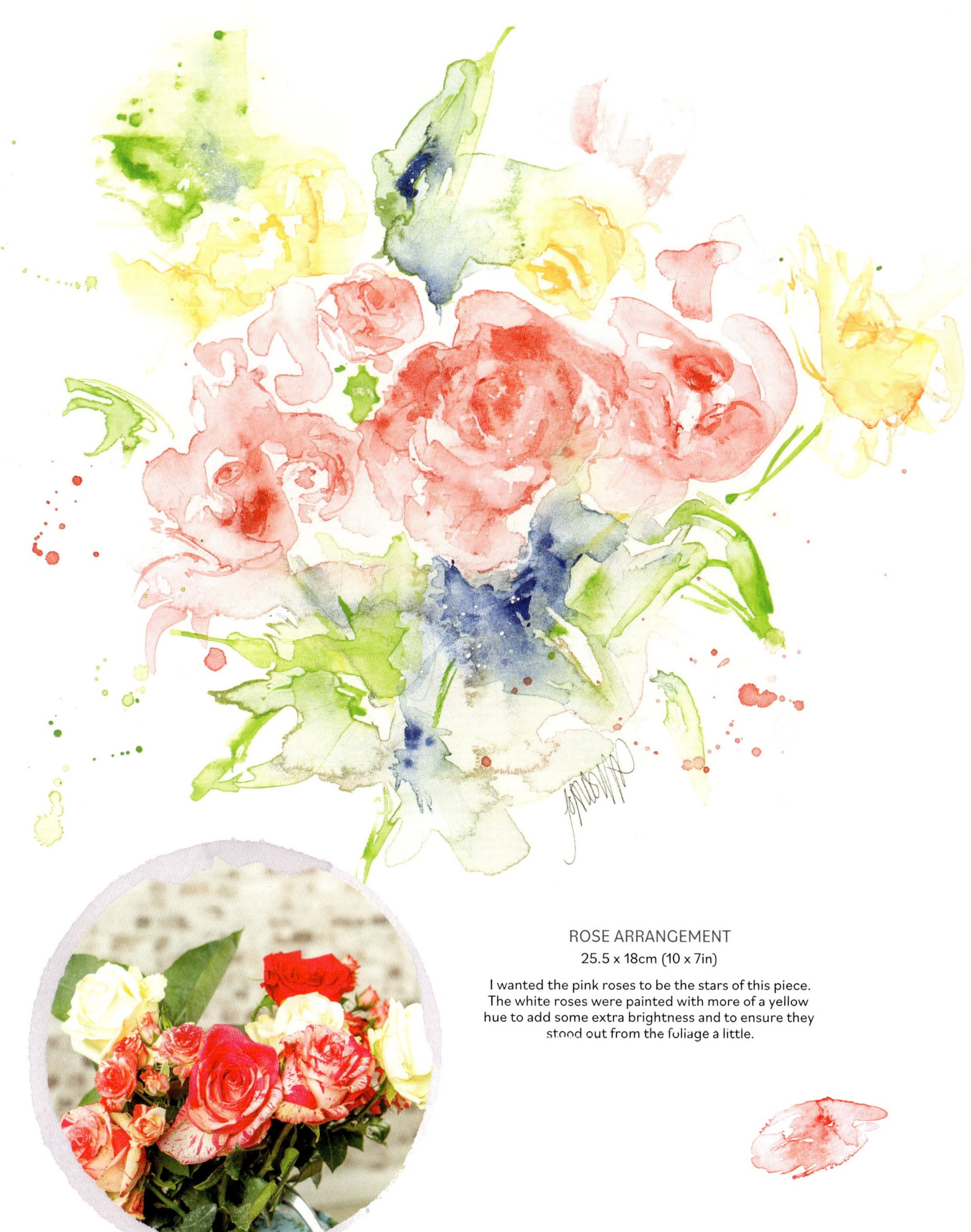

ROSE ARRANGEMENT
25.5 x 18cm (10 x 7in)

I wanted the pink roses to be the stars of this piece.
The white roses were painted with more of a yellow
hue to add some extra brightness and to ensure they
stood out from the foliage a little.

Painting outdoors

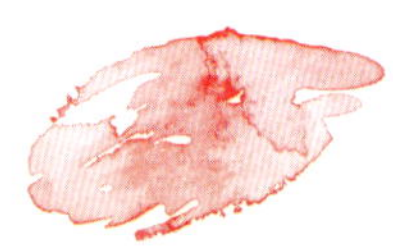

After you have built your confidence working indoors, you might choose to paint outside in a park or garden. It might strike you as more difficult to work outside from real life than from controlled photographs and arrangements indoors, but much of the advice for painting outdoors also applies to working indoors. For example, keeping the same position consistently throughout your painting remains important. Moving position or viewpoints can significantly alter your perspective and proportions. Get yourself comfortable and relaxed for the duration of your painting.

If this is not possible, you could of course take a photograph and work from that, although I encourage you to work from life – it can greatly improve your skills. Persevere working from life outdoors, and I believe that when you go back to working indoors, you will find it so much easier.

What to leave out

When working from scenes outdoors, it can be overwhelming, so bear in mind that there's no need to paint everything – in fact, you'll probably need to omit a lot of information.

To help you work out what to include and what to leave out, ask yourself the following questions:

- Is this an interesting composition? If not, how could we alter this?

- Could we make the painting more visually attractive by placing a flower in front/behind/trail some leaves for example?

- Is the background too busy? Does it detract from our subject?

- Could changing the colours improve the potential painting?

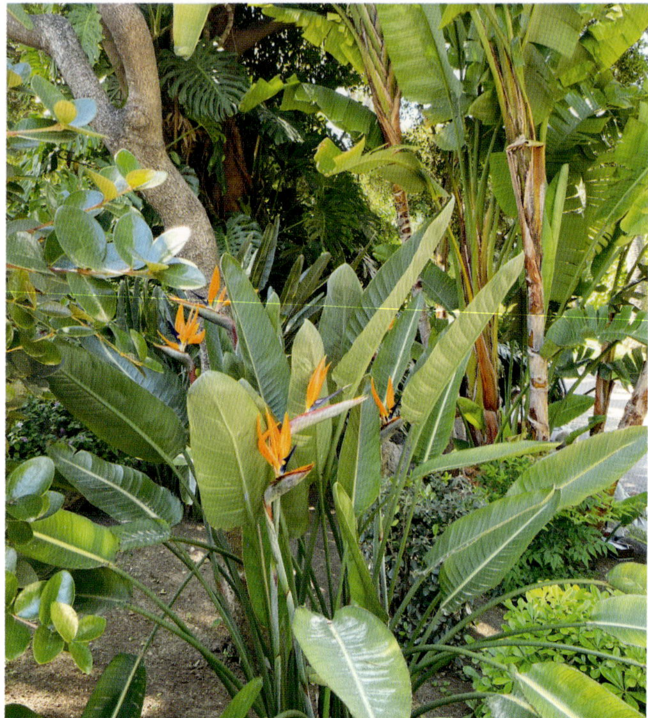

I took this picture of a Bird of Paradise flower in Nice, France. The painting it inspired, opposite, was painted live as a demonstration to my students on the trip.

Supporting photographs

If you find working from flowers in front of you difficult, taking photographs can make things seem more approachable and a lot easier.

Once you have this reference, you can go back to them whenever you want, and try painting the same flowers in various media – pastel, pencils, acrylics – giving you the same flowers in varying styles and colourways.

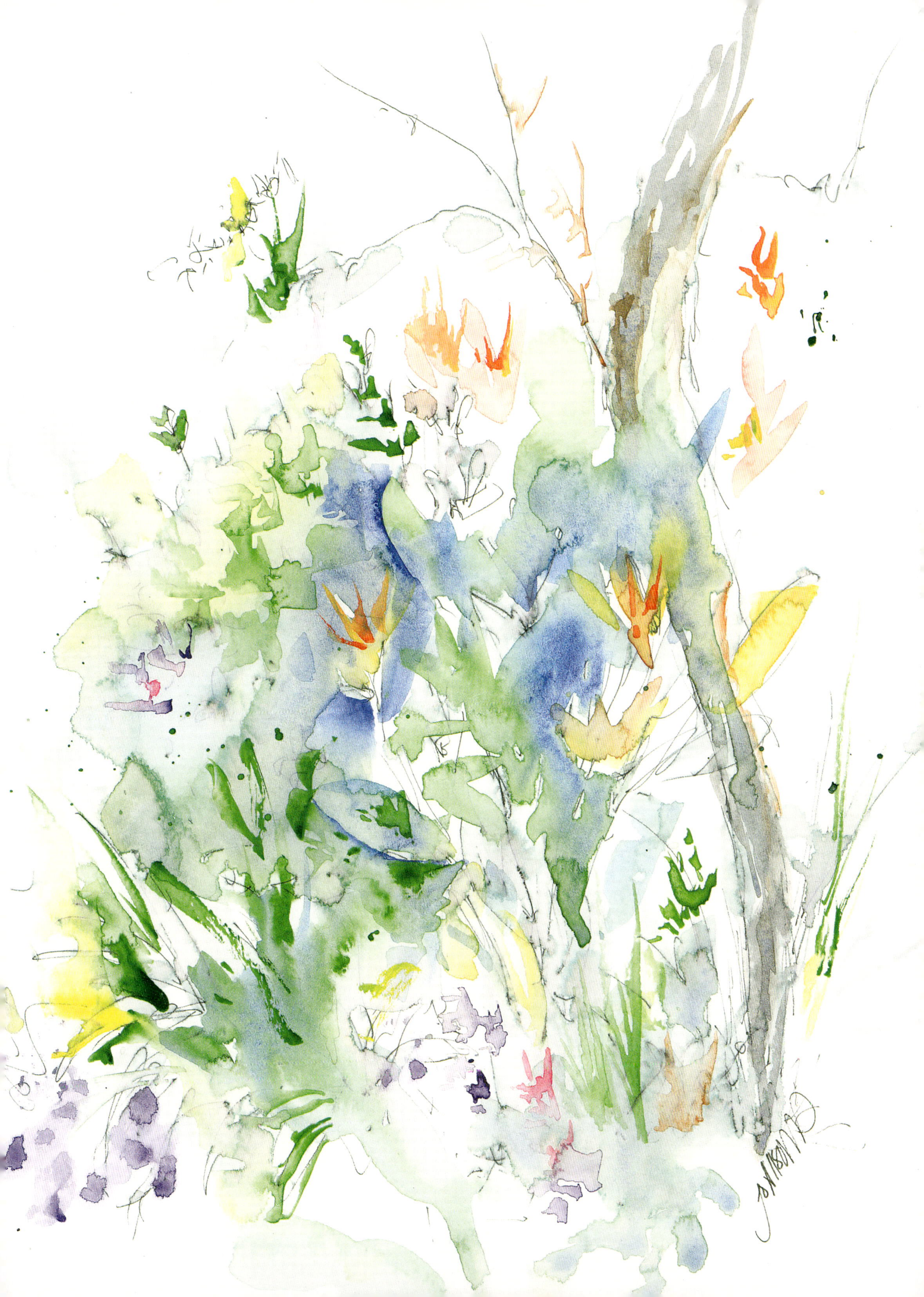

Materials

Try to use the best materials you can – better to use fewer items that give you the results you're after, than buy loads of materials that do not work for you and end up gathering dust. We do not have to own every style of brush and every diluent out there; we just need to take our time and invest only in what we are truly attracted to. For example, sometimes we see an artist perform wonders with a 'special' type of brush or some 'magic potion' only to find that it does not work the same for us. We all make different choices, and colours or tools that another artist loves may not appeal to you. This is fine, and these differences will help you develop a unique style of your own.

Paints

Watercolours are available in soft tubes or hard pans, and a wide range of colours and manufacturers. You can use whatever watercolours you like for the paintings in this book. I have my own signature set of Artists' quality Schmincke watercolours, which contain all my favourite 'go-to' colours:

- Vanadium yellow
- Vermilion
- Rose madder
- Schmincke violet
- French ultramarine
- Helio cerulean
- May green
- Yellow ochre
- Burnt sienna
- Burnt umber

It is important to know what your colours can do as this can assist you in choosing the best colour for a chosen subject. Some paints are staining, some are granulating, and some are transparent while others are opaque. Granulating colours (for example French ultramarine) are great for giving texture without even trying, whereas the opaque colours (such as cadmiums) can be advantageous for depth or to cover an error.

Brushes

Just as with paints, everyone will find their favourite brush or brushes. I have found that squirrel hair brushes really work for me and my style of painting, but it took a lot of experimentation to find these. For most of the paintings in this book you need just these three brushes:

Large Size 3 da Vinci squirrel round

Medium Size 0 da Vinci squirrel round

Small Size 0 rigger

Experiment and find brushes that work for you. The important thing is to have brushes that hold plenty of paint. Try holding your chosen brush or brushes in different ways to feel what works best for you.

For some of the techniques in the later part of the book, a 6mm (¼in) flat synthetic is also useful. I find a stiffer synthetic blend flat works better than a softer natural hair one for lifting out.

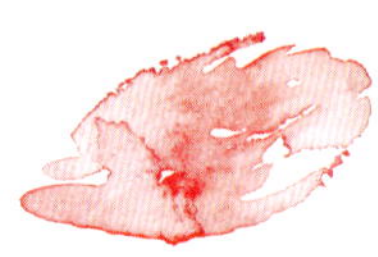

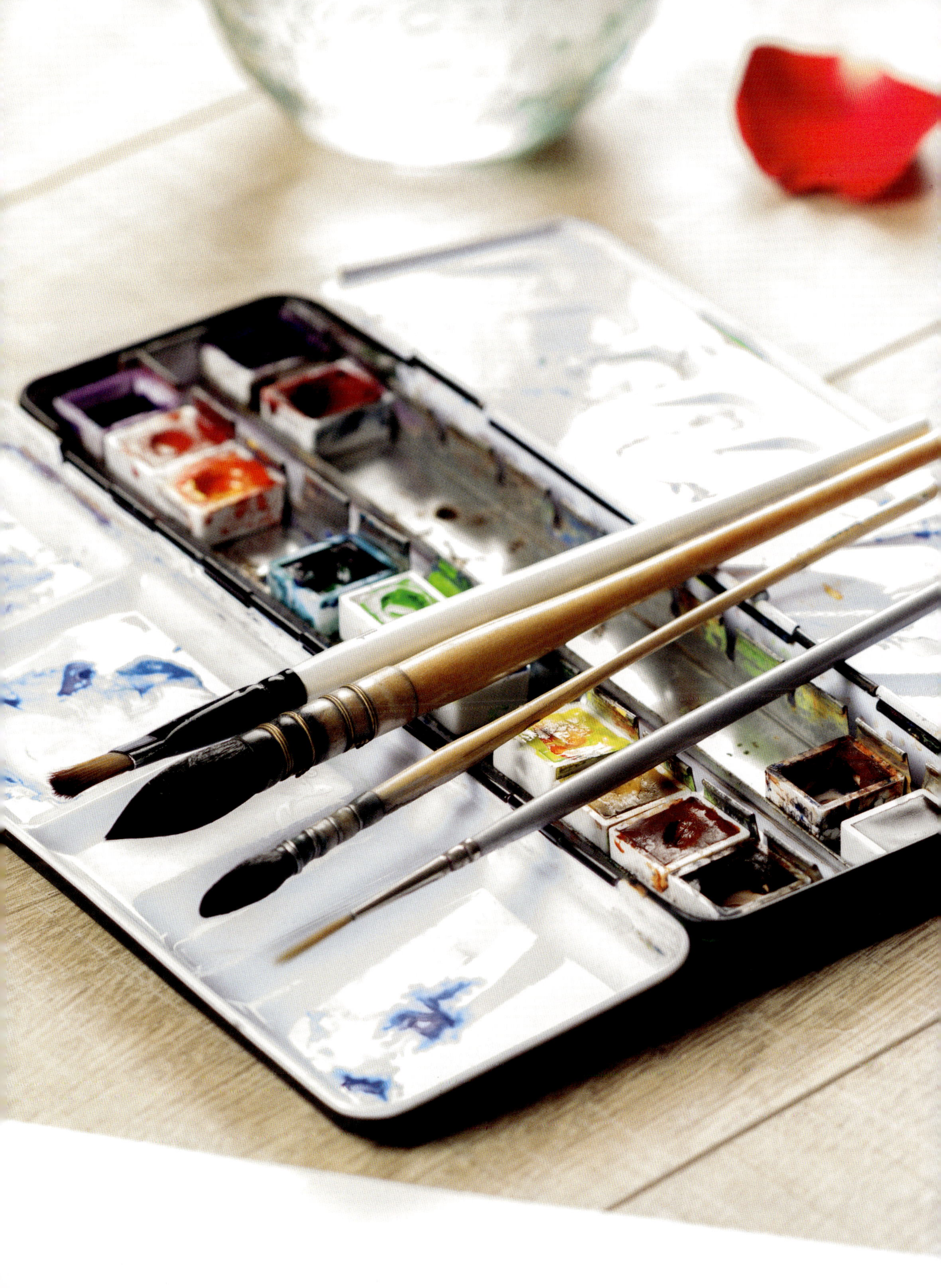

Paper

My favoured watercolour paper is St Cuthberts Mill Bockingford paper, which is available in three different surface textures, shown here. In this book I also use Clairefontaine 100 per cent cotton paper, Arches Aquarelle paper and some handmade papers too – all in different shapes and sizes.

Different papers can contribute to your results as much as the paints and brushes you use, so experiment and find what works for you.

MY FAVOURITE PAPERS

Shown here are sheets of Bockingford paper in all three surfaces detailed here, along with some Clairefontaine 100 per cent cotton papers – and on top, a few handmade papers with flower petal inclusions.

SMOOTH

Light pencil sketches are easy to work on smooth surfaces like this Bockingford HP (short for Hot-pressed). The lack of texture keeps the appearance of petals and leaves looking clean and silky.

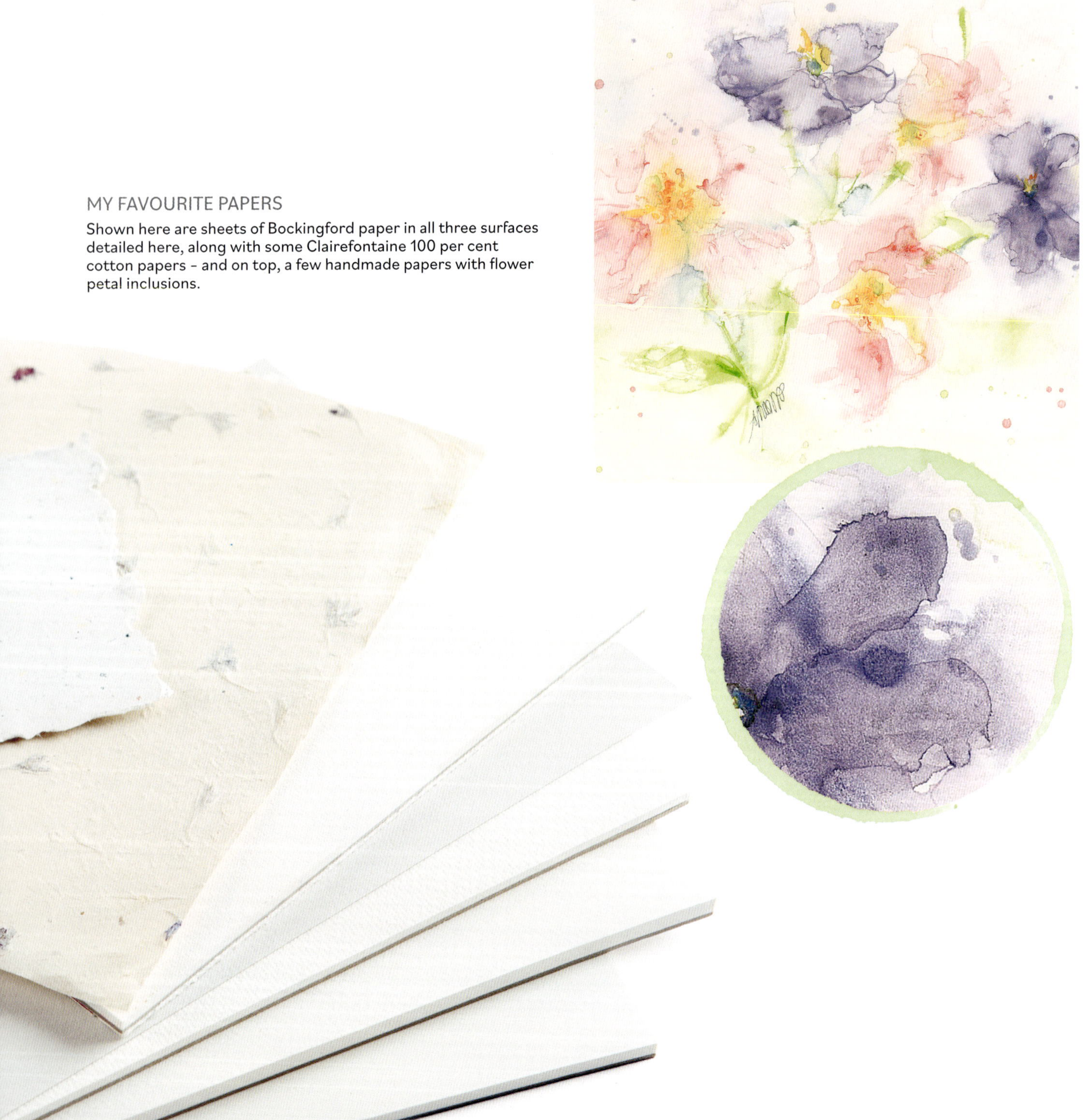

NOT

The piece below was worked on Bockingford Not surface paper, also called Cold-pressed or CP. I've used wax resist here, which works well on the subtle texture of this surface, along with some acrylic ink spatters. Note the slight mottled finish on the pinky-red petals.

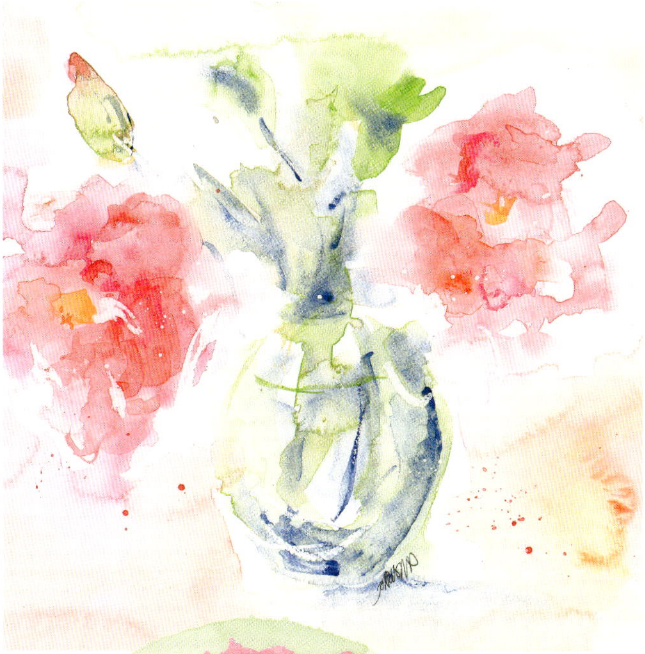

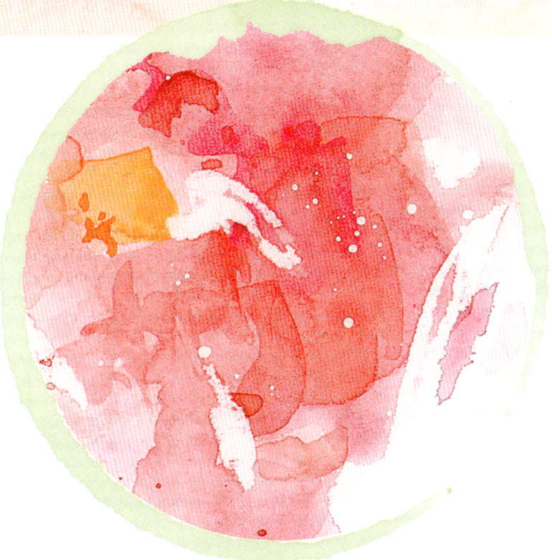

ROUGH

As the pigment settles into the surface texture of this Rough paper, it naturally brings out a sense of light and structure in stems and petals alike. It also sets off the feathers of the hummingbird without the need for fussy detail.

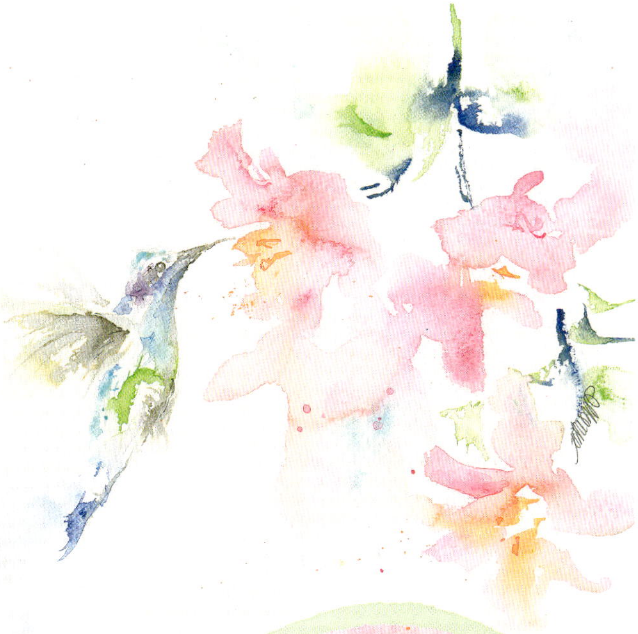

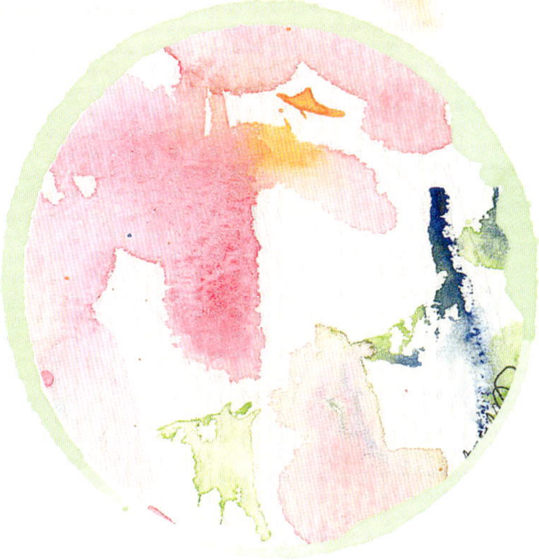

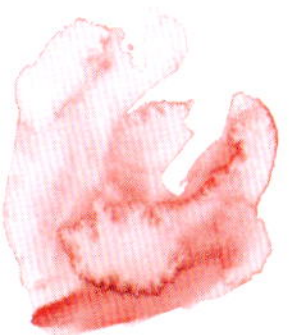

Other tools and materials

We'll look at additional exciting tools, materials and media later in the book, but I wanted to show you that you don't need much at all to get started – just these few simple items.

HB pencil Used for making your initial drawings, an HB pencil will give you nice light marks, easy to erase or cover over.

Kneadable putty eraser Soft and gentle on the paper, this will leave no messy bits. Use this instead of an everyday plastic eraser.

Board You need a lightweight wood or plastic board that can withstand copious amounts of water. Mine was made by my talented husband who cut some marine ply and attached a handle, having sanded it smooth so that I don't get splinters.

Water pots I always have two glass jars: one to clean brushes between washes, the other (which remains very clean) used to apply new washes and keep everything looking fresh. Pick sturdy jars; the last thing you want is to knock one over.

Brown gummed tape This is used to attach paper to the board, as shown below. Once held down firmly, your paper will not cockle (curl up) and become awkward to paint on. Because it is so strong, this tape will not peel away even if run under the tap.

Craft knife Essential to cut away the gummed tape when releasing paper from the board once the painting is finished. This blade is also ideal for scratching out highlights.

Fountain pen While not absolutely essential, I couldn't resist including this here with blue and black Parker ink cartridges, as pen and wash work is just about the most accessible form of mixed media you can try!

Palette (not pictured) While I mostly use pure colours and mix on the paper (see page 27), now and again it's useful to have a palette to mix paints – either with other paints or other media. Any small china dish or saucer is fine. I tend to avoid plastic palettes, as the paint forms beads instead of pools.

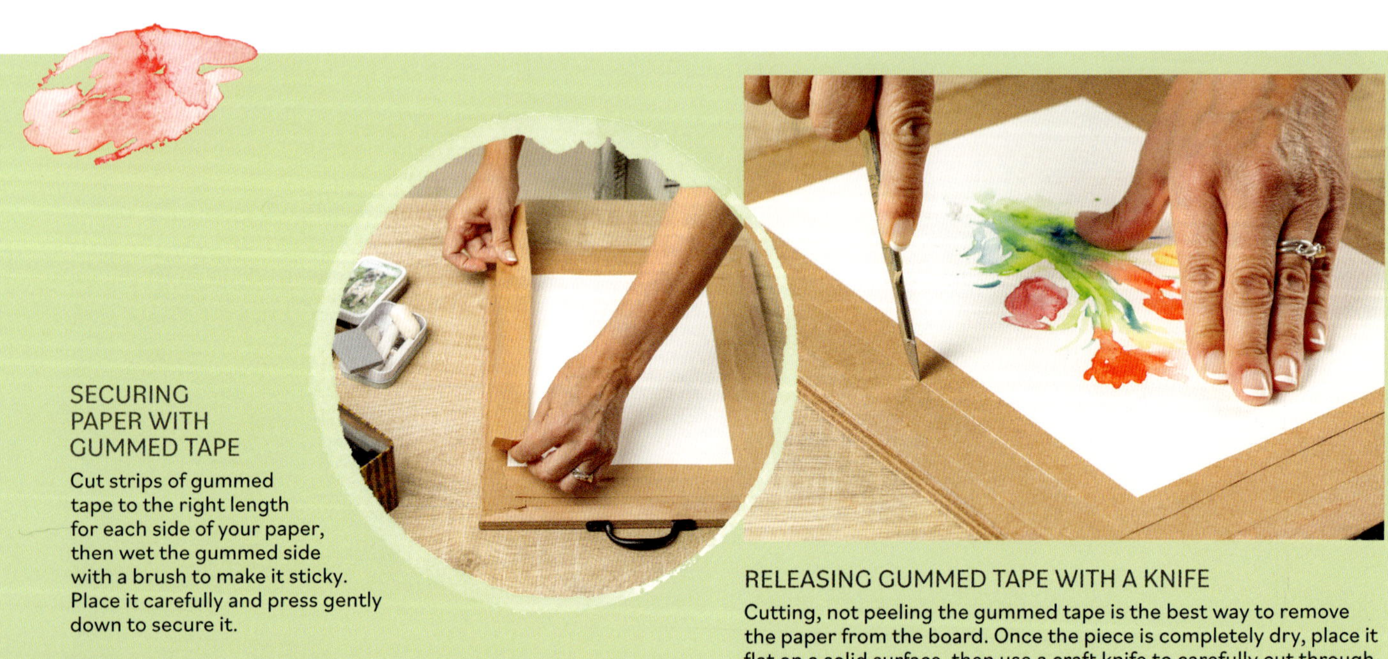

SECURING PAPER WITH GUMMED TAPE

Cut strips of gummed tape to the right length for each side of your paper, then wet the gummed side with a brush to make it sticky. Place it carefully and press gently down to secure it.

RELEASING GUMMED TAPE WITH A KNIFE

Cutting, not peeling the gummed tape is the best way to remove the paper from the board. Once the piece is completely dry, place it flat on a solid surface, then use a craft knife to carefully cut through the gummed tape on each edge of the paper. Look for a slight ridge to find the edge of the paper. Cut away from yourself – just in case you slip – and turn the board for each side, rather than working at awkward angles.

KEEP IT SIMPLE

Besides paints, brushes and paper, these tools and materials are all you need for beautiful pure watercolour flowers.

Wash your brushes regularly in your water pots throughout your painting to keep the colours fresh. You'll find your water will become very dirty in quite a short space of time, but using two pots helps to avoid muddying your painting.

Another great advantage of using two pots is that it saves us from continually having to change them, especially when we're 'in the zone' mid-flow and don't want to lose our spontaneity.

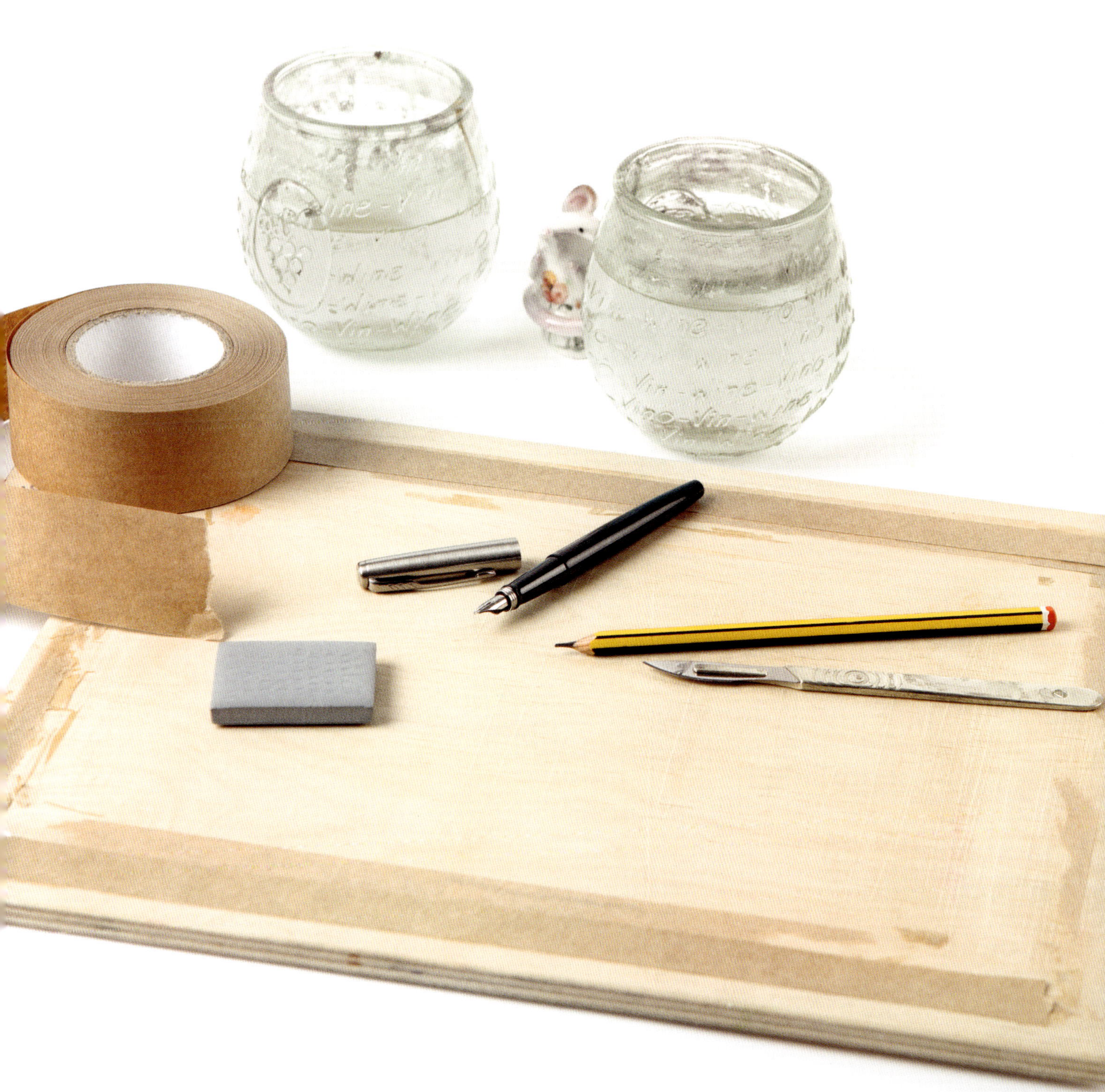

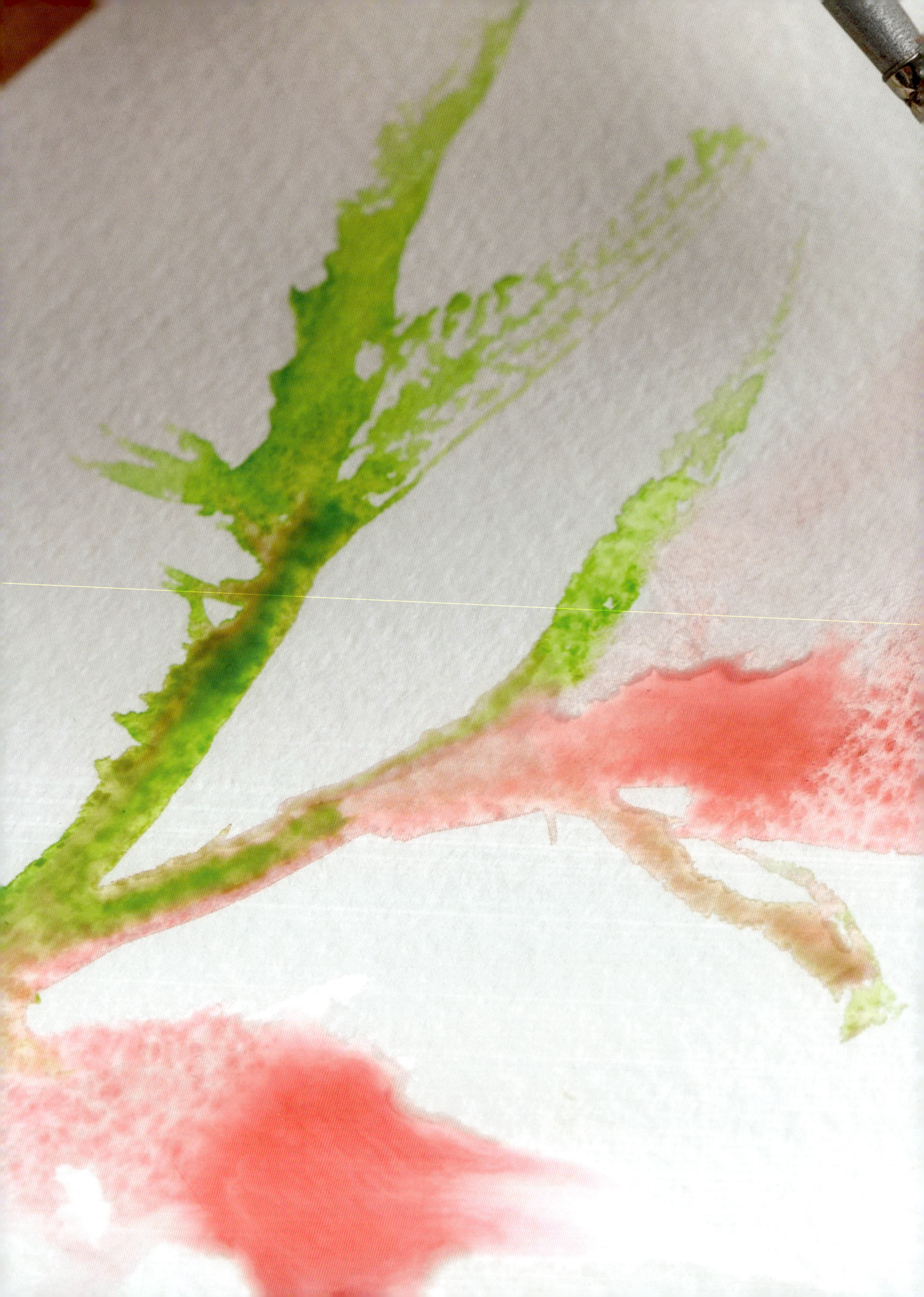

Using watercolour

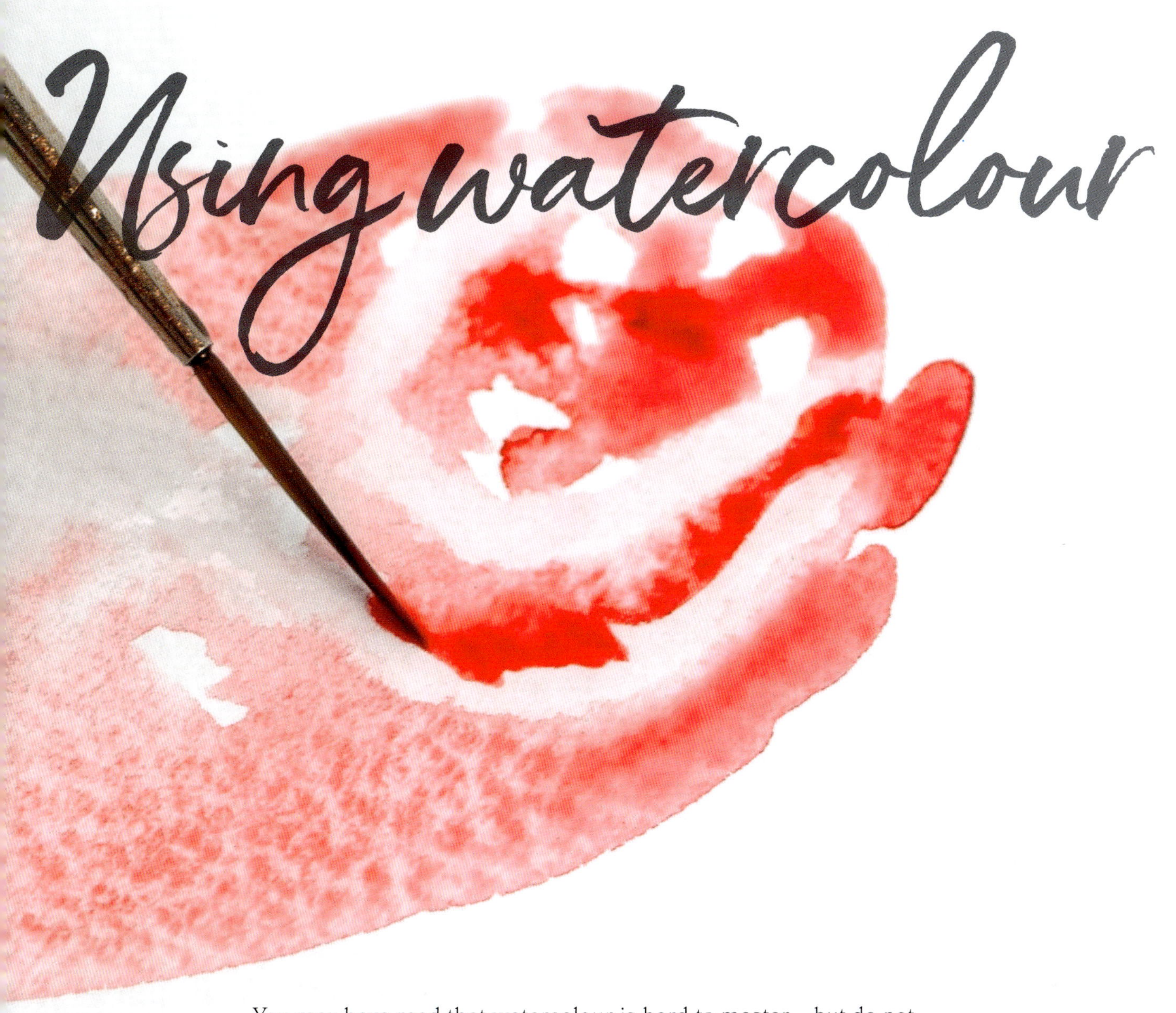

You may have read that watercolour is hard to master – but do not
be deterred by this. Watercolour is both versatile and approachable,
and there's no need to complicate things. Most techniques are just as
they sound: I ask my students 'drybrush – guess what this involves?'
to which the answers are always correct (and I hear them breathe a
huge sigh of relief!). So if I ask you what you think 'wet into wet', or
'scratching out' mean, you'll probably guess these correctly too.

Watercolour might seem scary initially but trust me, once you get
it you will absolutely love it. Let us no longer be watercolour worriers,
and instead aim to be watercolour warriors!

The value of simplicity

My daughters picked some flowers from the garden for me when they were very young, and having just started practising watercolour in earnest, I decided to paint them. The picture below shows the result, and is a good example of how I used to paint – rather tight and opaque in places. The painting opposite was made many years later, using the original as my inspiration. My style has evidently changed quite considerably – and more than that, it shows how the same subject can be transformed by loosening up, letting go of control, and simplifying what is in front of us.

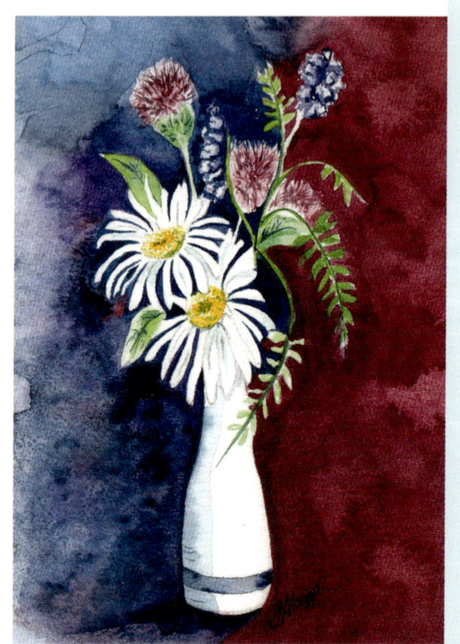

STIFF AND FORMAL (ABOVE)
VERSUS
LOOSE AND LIVELY (OPPOSITE)

Working with watercolour

Trying to depict too much detail in watercolour, and being very literal with the subject oftens leads to results that look heavy, overworked and flat; much like my older piece, on the left. I much prefer the more recent piece shown opposite - it is more fluid, fresher and brighter.

By using more vibrant colour choices and working swiftly and confidently, you'll find your results are much fresher and cleaner. That speed and confidence comes with knowing your materials, so before going any further in the book, take half an hour to play around with your colours, brushes and papers and get to know them.

Keep this idea of simplifying in mind. We don't have to make things difficult for ourselves. We can just go with the flow - quite literally - and have fun.

Opposite:
MIXED FLORALS FROM MY GIRLS
Using more imagination with this interpretation of the same subject, I altered the flower arrangement and changed the vase to glass to ensure that the flowers were the main focus.

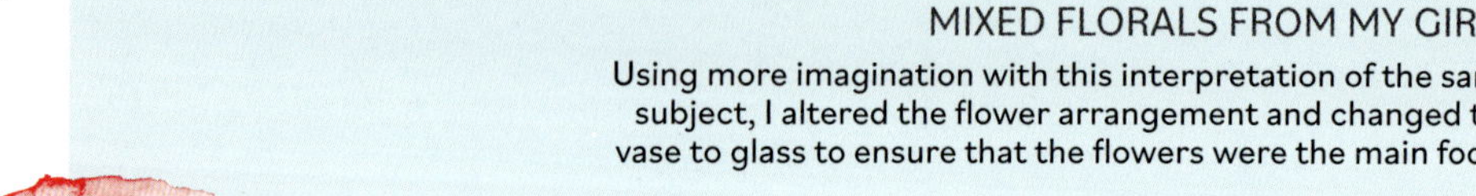
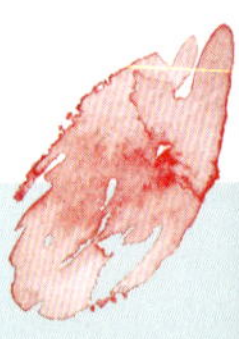

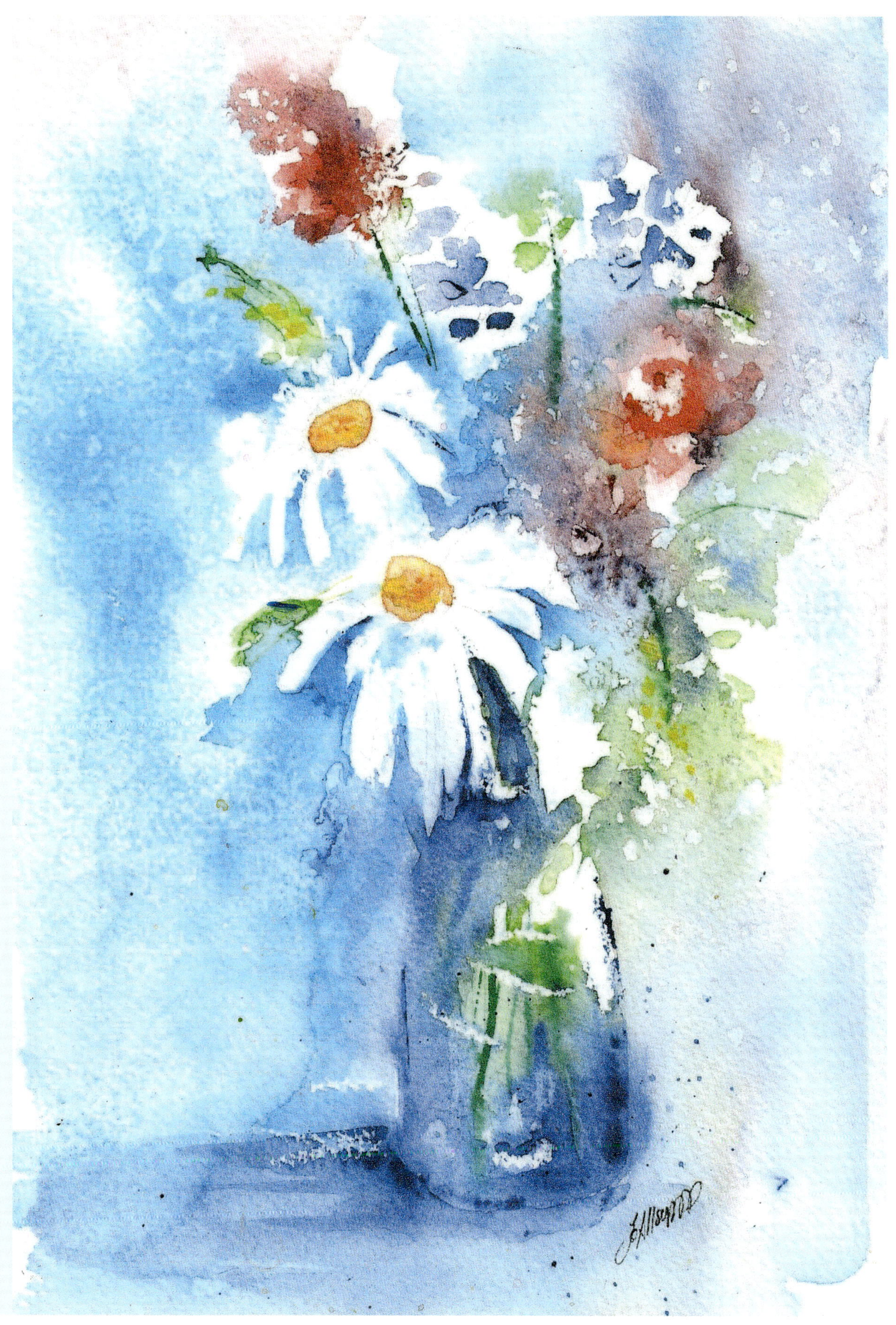

Handling watercolour

Getting to know your paints and brushes will help you achieve success, and playing and practising on a spare sheet of paper will help you to become familiar with your chosen brushes, paints and paper. How much water can your brush hold without dripping all over a piece? Familiarize yourself with how it retains this, and how we can release the colour and so on.

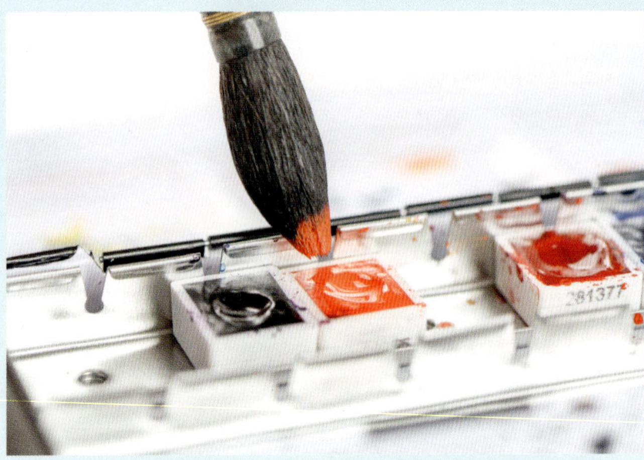

PICKING UP PAINT

Wet your brush in a pot of clean water, give the hairs a gentle squeeze to remove the excess, then use this damp brush to dip into your watercolour pans. Watercolour goes a long way, so you only need a little.

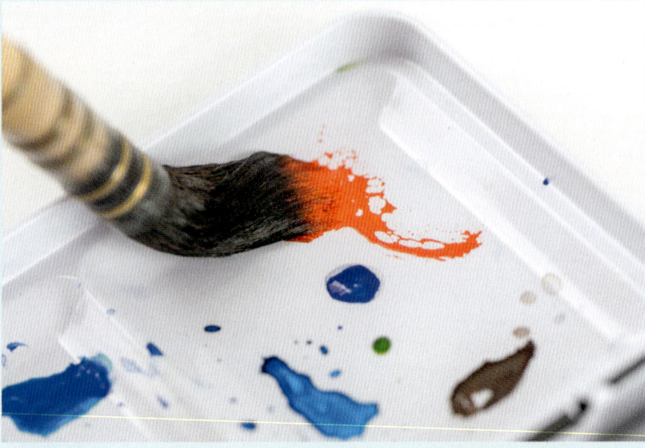

USING THE PALETTE

Gently wipe the brush on a clean area of your palette. This will remove any excess paint, spread it more evenly through the damp hairs, and show you exactly how the colour will appear on your paper.

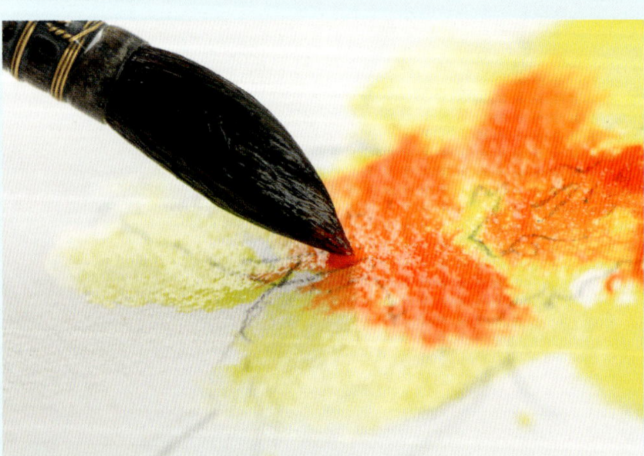

APPLYING PAINT

As soon as the tip of the brush touches the wet paper surface, the paint will flow off the brush and mix with the water or paint already there.

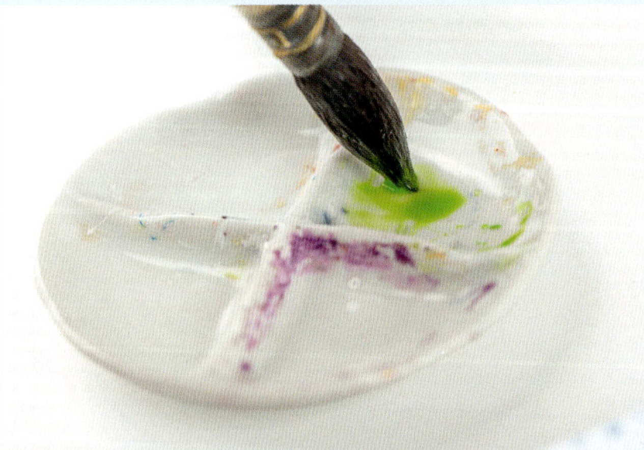

USING A TINTING SAUCER

A tinting saucer can be used to prepare small amounts of mixes away from your palette to avoid muddying your other colours. You can use any small dish or saucer.

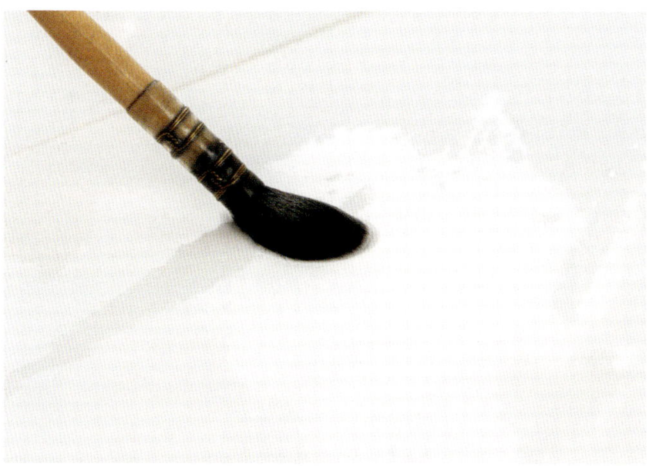

Mixing paints

I seldom physically mix my paints in a palette. Instead, I prefer to allow my paints to mix on the wet paper. For example, I will wet my subject then drop in yellow and red near to each other so that they form an orange where they meet, but keep some evidence of the original red and yellow too... three colours for the price of two! I love how watercolours naturally merge together and create some wonderful patterns.

1 – WET THE SURFACE THOROUGHLY
Load your biggest brush with clean water and wet your paper thoroughly.

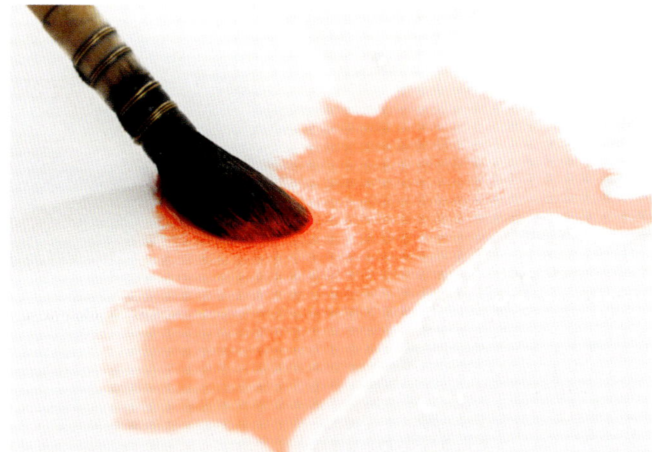

2 – APPLY PLENTY OF YOUR FIRST COLOUR
Drop in some colour, wet into wet. I've used red here, but you can use anything.

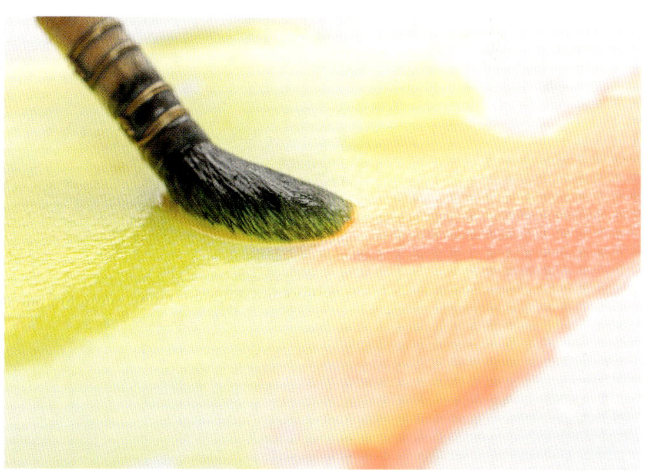

3 – ADD THE SECOND COLOUR AND ALLOW THEM TO BLEND ON THE PAPER
Immediately drop in your second colour to allow both to naturally blend and mix on the paper.

Tip

The only colour I tend to mix in a saucer
is my 'black' which is usually a mixture of
burnt umber and French ultramarine.

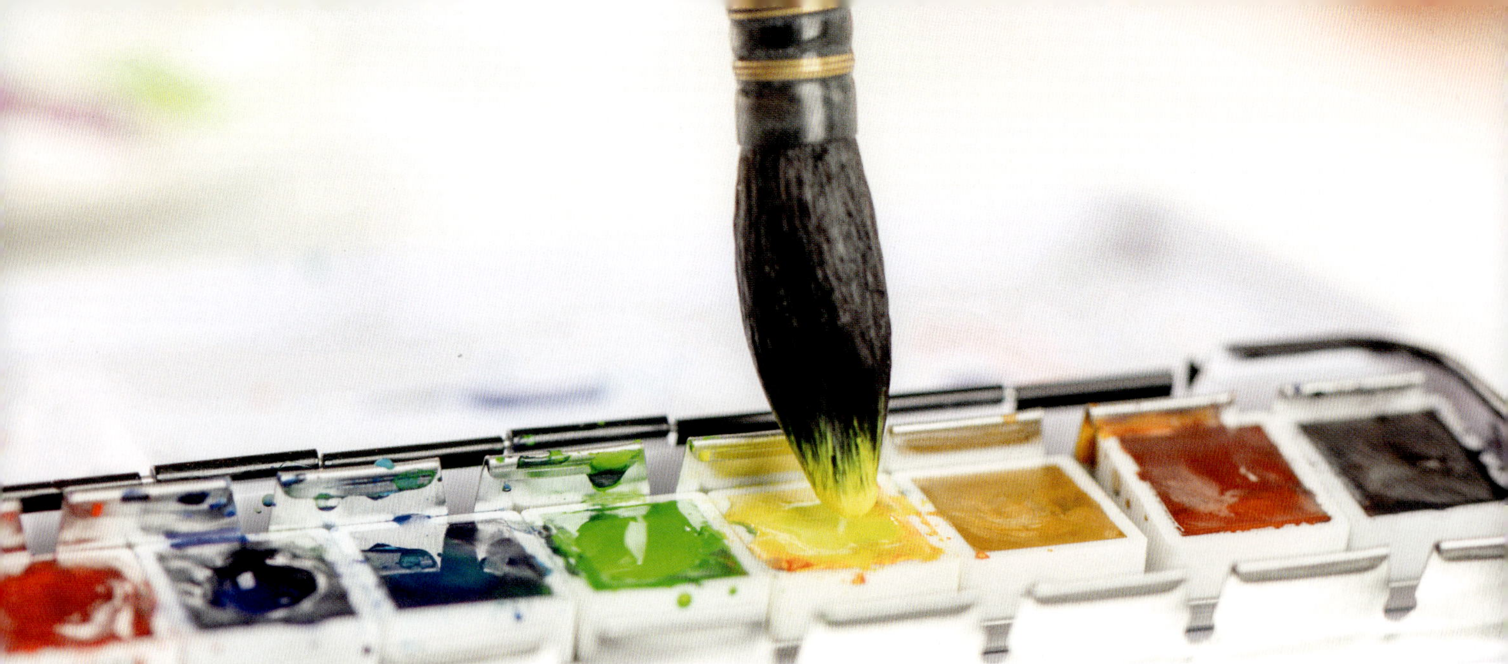

Top ten tips

On the following pages are some practical tips and ideas for working more freely in order to give your paintings more of a loose and lively feel.

Beyond these practical tips, however, I think the best advice is just 'go for it'. Avoid putting pressure on yourself to create a masterpiece and instead tell yourself: 'this is all good practice, and I'm going to do my best, but if I'm not enamoured with the results, I'll try a little mixed media on top to see if any improvements can be made...'

A positive, can-do attitude is going to benefit you far more than negative thinking like; 'I can't do this' or 'I must get this right.' Please do not doubt yourself. Whatever your experience, practice will always lead to improvement – remember to enjoy the process, splash around, and learn to have fun with it.

Simplify

You don't have to include every single detail in a painting. For example, my flowers might be arranged in a vase, with a decorated window behind, on a tablecloth – but there is no need to paint any element other than the flowers should you prefer this approach. Try adding just a suggestion of what is there in the background, or opt to leave such details out completely.

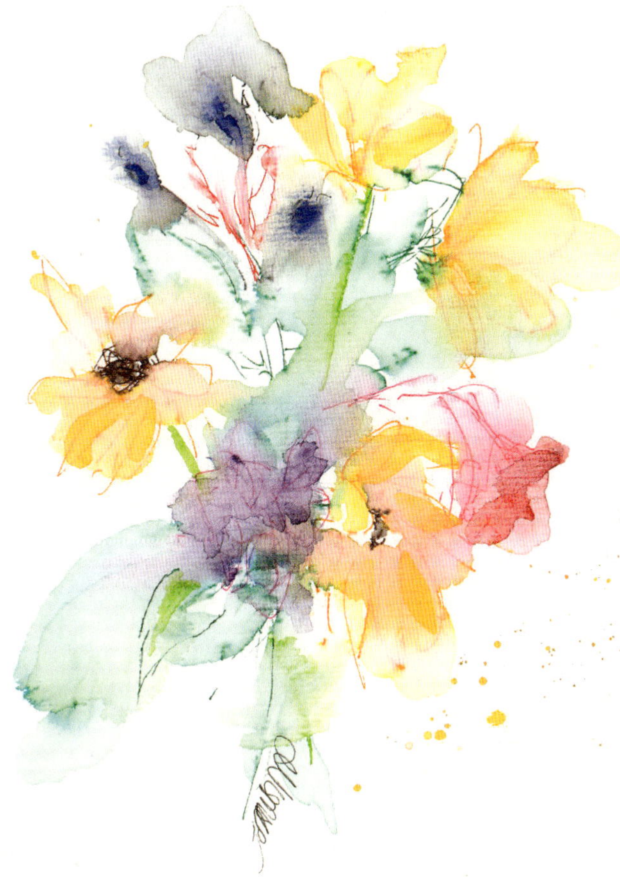

AVERIL'S FLOWERS #2
This was in vase on my desk; I've ignored all the busyness and pulled out just a few flowers from it. The flowers were so pretty, they needed no jug or background to complement them.

Dare to go darker

Change up the colours – make these much brighter. Watercolours dry much lighter and so one of my favourite sayings is: 'dare to go darker.' For example, if there is a flower that appears pale in colour I will sometimes deliberately brighten it up anyway.

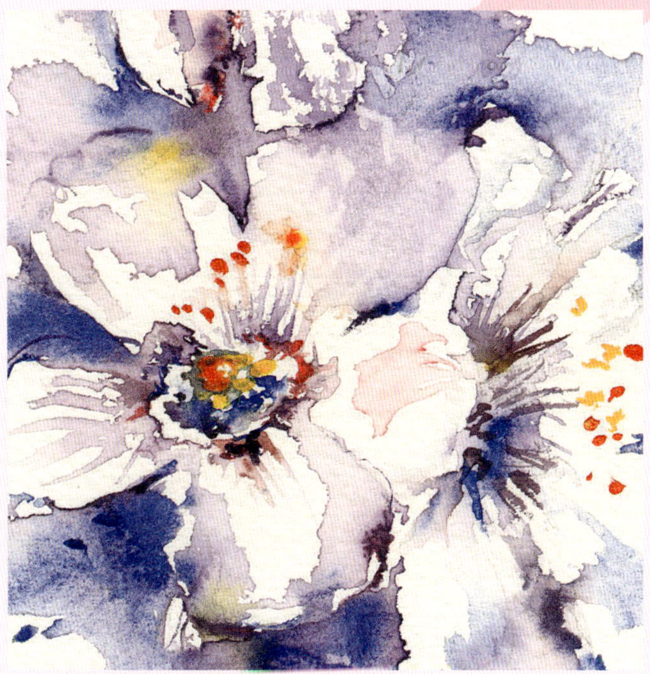

DETAIL FROM *WILD ROSES*
White petals often need some clean paper to look suitably bright, but as you can see, using colour in the shadows on them is what creates contrast and makes those white areas pop!

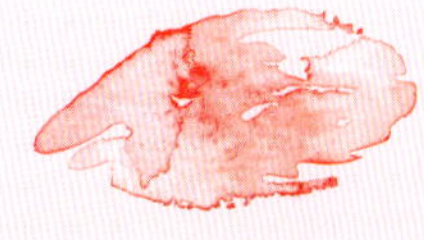

Use new techniques

Experiment with different techniques to liven up your paintings – neither the flower itself nor a photograph of the subject is ever going to show the effects of salt, isopropyl or bleach. This is where we use our artistic licence to say 'This is what I would like to see here on this painting. This is my way of emulating the texture of the background.'

It is your painting – do whatever your heart desires, and whichever techniques you enjoy best. The suggestion of pollen, for example, could be spattered on rather than painted with deliberate strokes. There's more than one route to success.

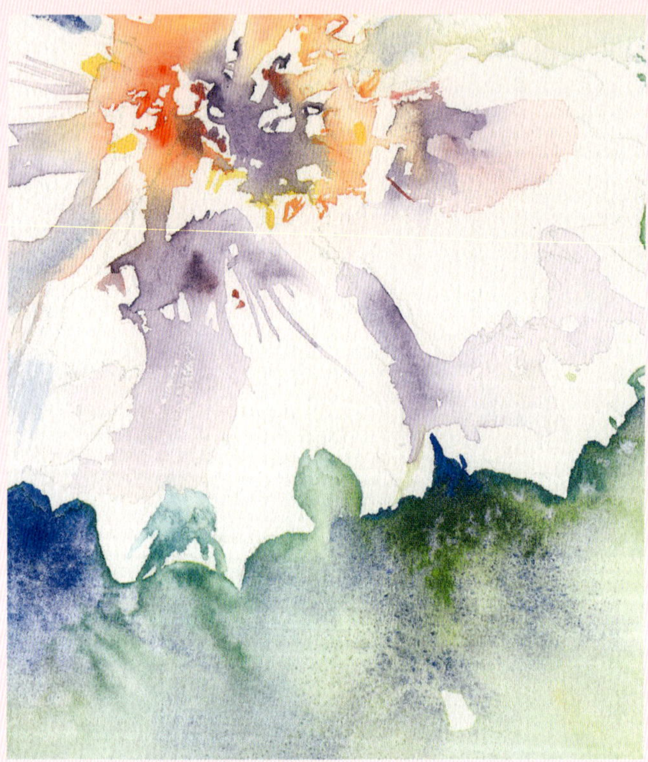

DETAIL FROM *TREE PEONY*
A picture inspired by my friend Sue Russell's photograph. I used negative painting (see page 72) and salt to capture the sense of bright sunlight, but I might just have easily chosen a different approach.

Speed through the sketch

A fast, light sketch will encourage a looser style of painting as a detailed drawing is just going to entice you to apply more detail with the brush. I never paint inside the lines either – something as a child we were encouraged to do, not anymore!

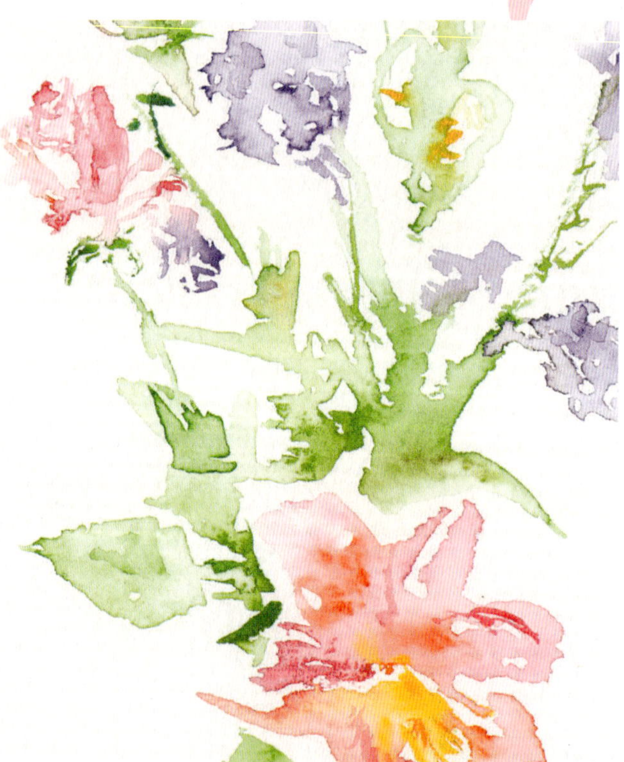

DETAIL FROM *MIXED FLORALS*
You don't have to start from a sketch at all, if you don't want to – this small piece was painted straight onto blank paper.

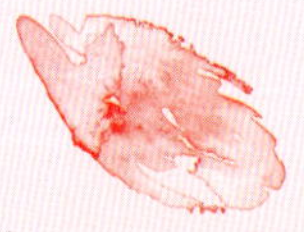

Big brush

A larger brush will encourage looser shapes. With a big brush, we can better achieve more of the bold and expressive marks so I would suggest starting off with a big round. Of course, we can then use some smaller brushes (or other media, like pencils or pens) to add a little more detail, but starting bigger gives us suggestive marks and makes things look much less detailed to begin with.

Embrace backruns

Encourage backruns (sometimes called cauliflowers) by dropping big splodges of clean water into an already drying wash. You will create these gorgeous blooms which often emulate petal shapes. Embrace these and let them add texture to liven up your art.

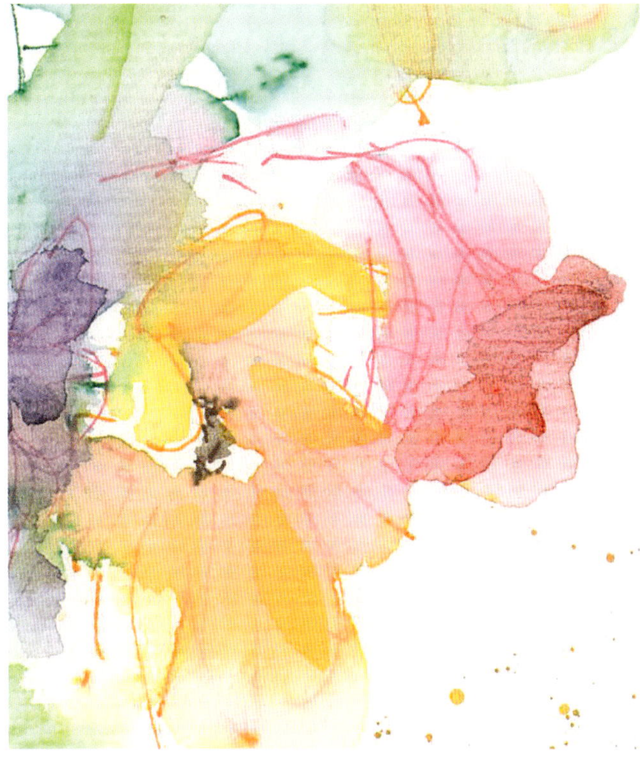

DETAIL FROM *AVERIL'S FLOWERS #2*
I started from a loose drawing made with coloured watersoluble pencils, but aside from that, I only used a single large brush for this piece.

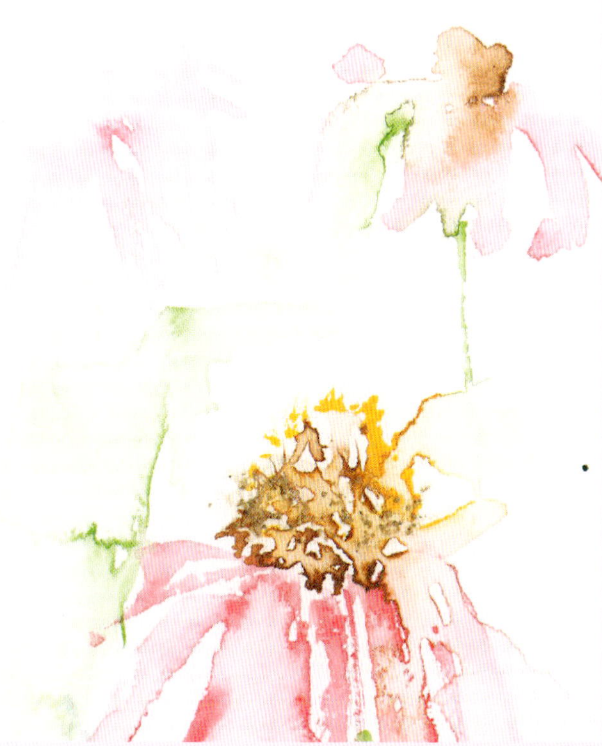

DETAIL OF BACKRUN FROM *CONEFLOWERS*
In this painting, backruns were encouraged to form to help break up the clean lines and shapes of the coneflower.

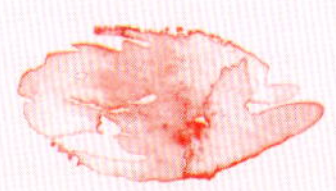
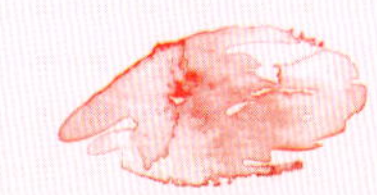

Involve the background

Make your subject bleed and merge into the background. Push clean water up to a wet image so that the colours run back from the subject thus creating some subtle colour to form some of the background. I much prefer to unify a painting this way as opposed to a flat wash. A flat wash has its place but is just that: flat – and we want loose and lively!

Be messy

Use different techniques to intentionally create a little messy area here and there – having everything too neat and controlled can give dull results.

Salt, spatter and isopropyl alcohol are just a few suggestions for hard-to-control techniques that will encourage you to let go of any artistic inhibitions and have fun! Remember, it is just a piece of paper.

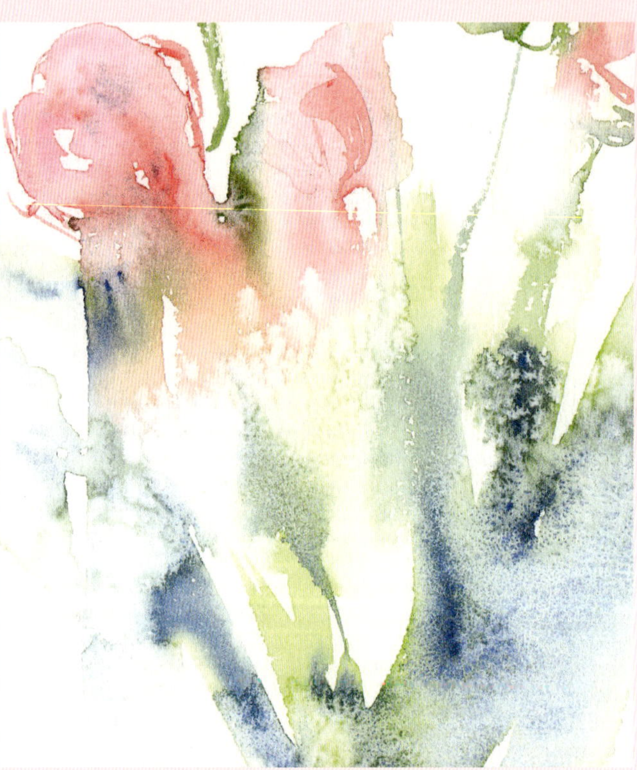

DETAIL FROM *PEONIES*
The background here is formed simply from letting the colours of the subject bleed out – a process encouraged with plenty of water.

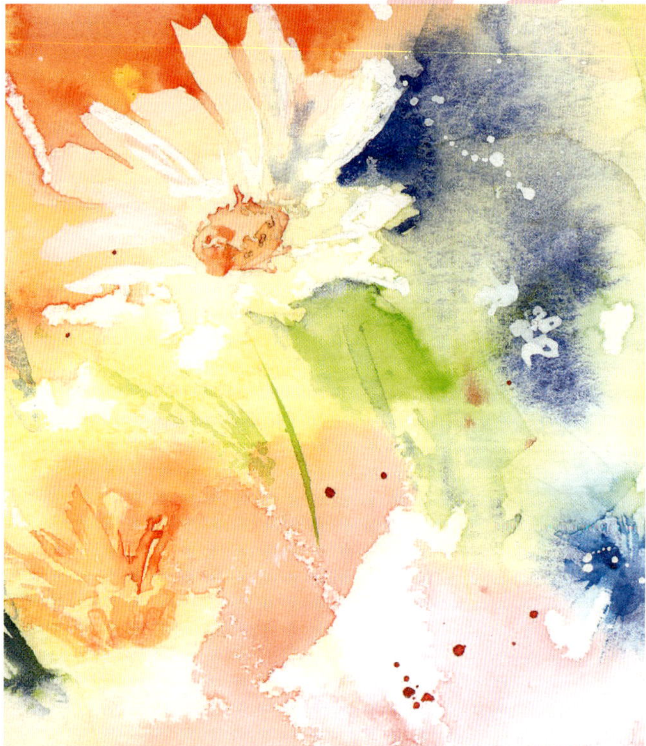

DETAIL FROM *FIELD OF FLOWERS*
White and acrylic ink spatters hint at detail and contrast with the loose, flowing washes.

Pick up the board

Manipulate the board to encourage movement in a painting. Tip the wet paint from side to side until you get some interesting effects as the paint moves. Sometimes I use the hairdryer to assist me with this – you could also blow through a drinking straw to direct the paint.

Splash!

And my favourite tip of all is simple: use plenty of water. I cannot emphasize enough that this is the best way to loosen up any painting. The clue, after all, is in the word 'watercolour'.

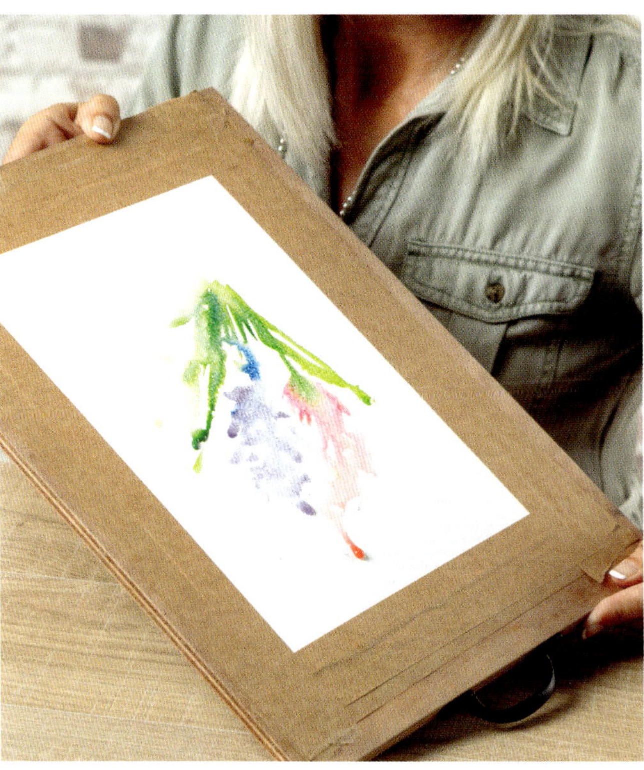

DRIPS AND RUNS
Get used to how water flows and moves on paper as you tip the board – but equally, embrace the sense of freedom, and don't try to impose too much control.

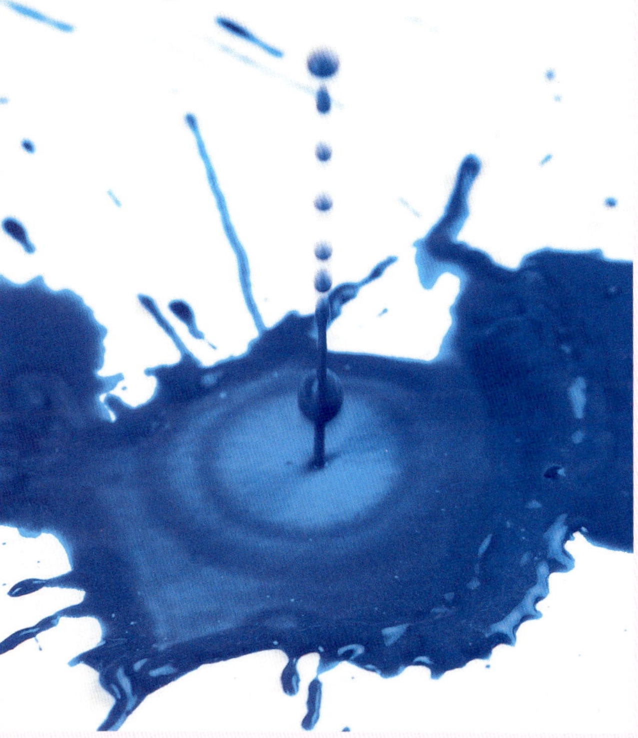

FLUID PAINT MAKES LOOSE RESULTS
You can water down your paints, or add water to your paper before applying it, or apply more water once it's on – whatever you find works best!

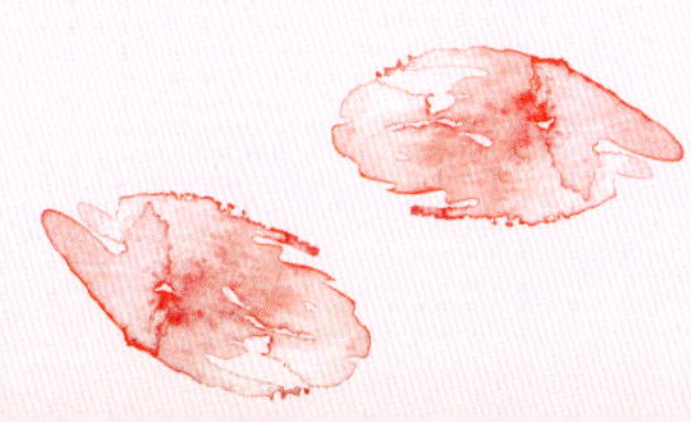

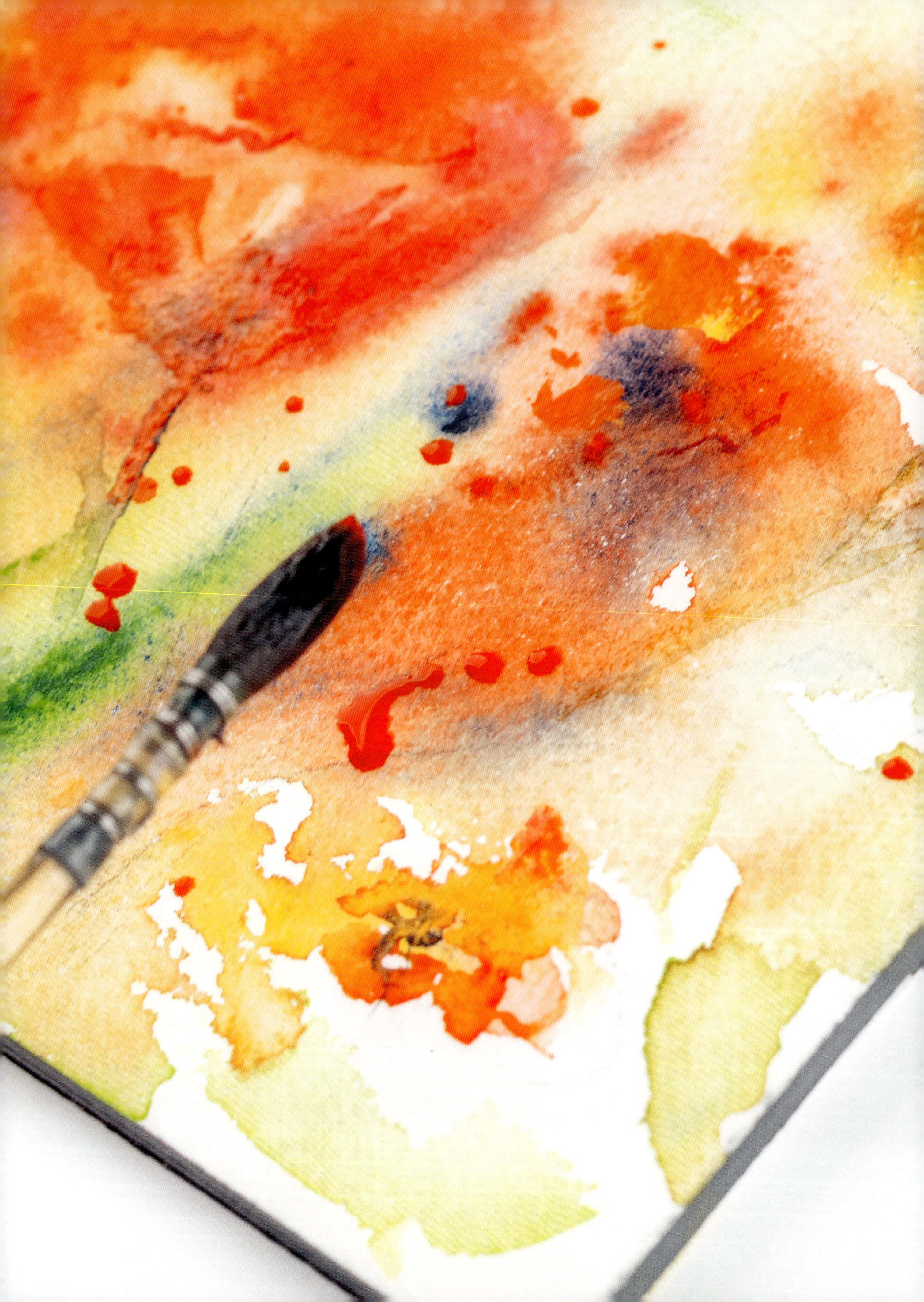

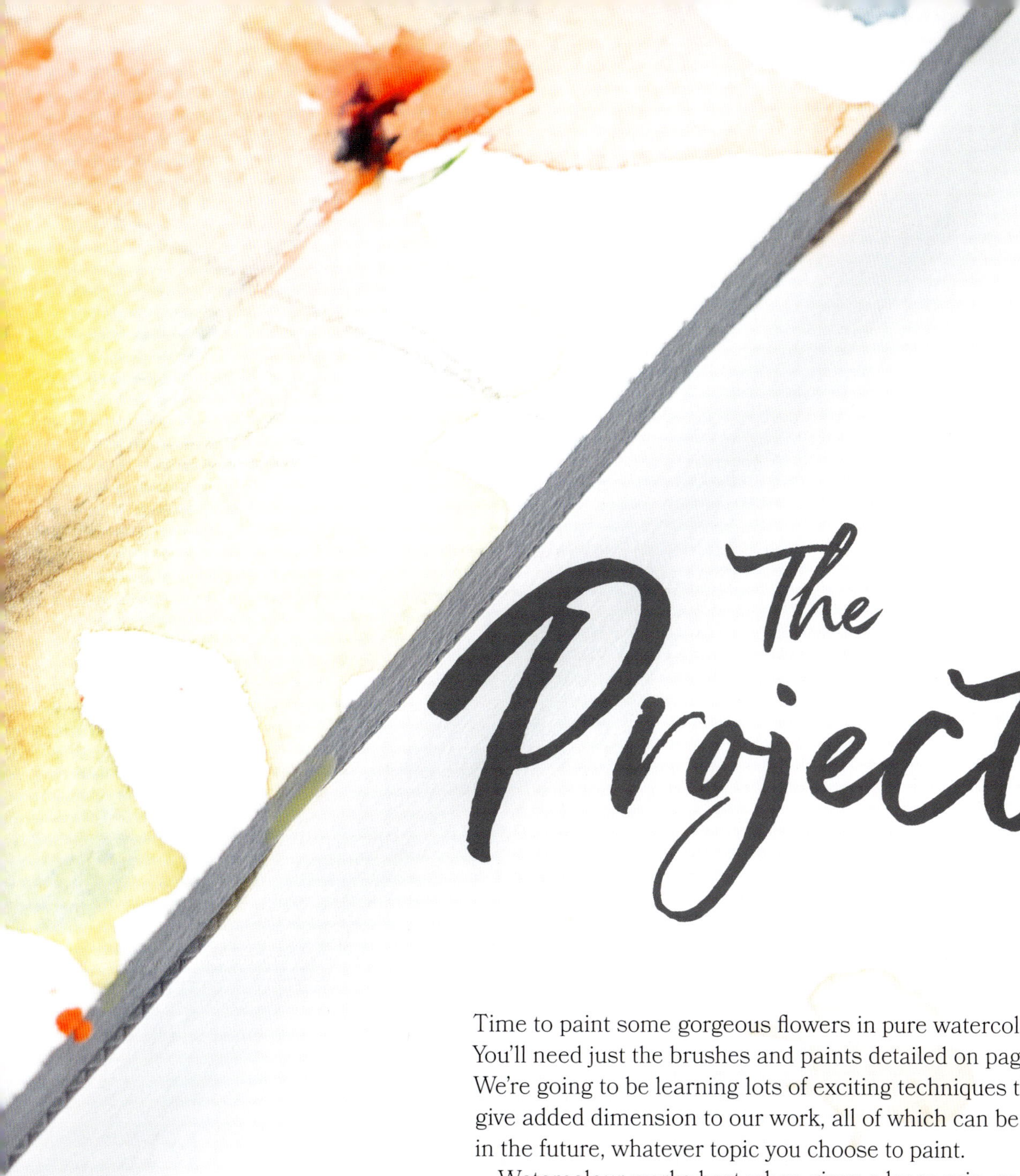

The
Projects

Time to paint some gorgeous flowers in pure watercolour. You'll need just the brushes and paints detailed on page 16. We're going to be learning lots of exciting techniques that will give added dimension to our work, all of which can be utilized in the future, whatever topic you choose to paint.

Watercolour works best when given a loose rein, so don't worry about copying things exactly. In fact, I encourage you to deviate a little – perhaps add a few extra little marks here and there, use alternative colours, or include one of the techniques from in the book.

All rules were made to be broken – this is one of my mantras, and I am sticking with it!

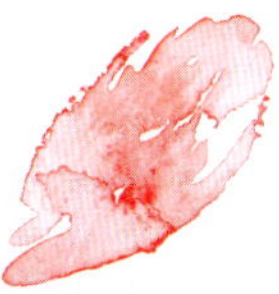

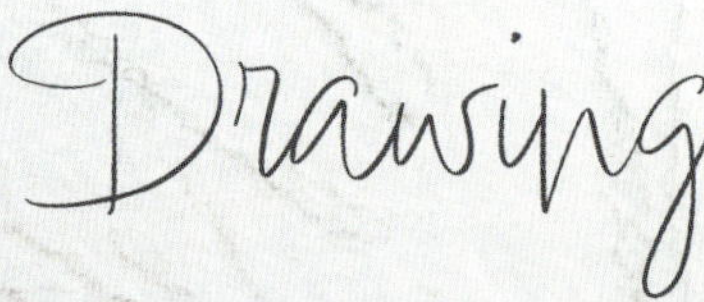

Drawing

Each of the projects includes an initial sketch for you to copy, but I encourage you to try making a sketch yourself from the reference photograph also included at the start of each project. If you'd like some practice before you tackle the projects, give sketching a go with the picture below.

Drawing for loose painting

I like my paintings to be full of movement, colour and life as opposed to formal and more contrived, so I avoid elaborate drawings. Instead, I prefer to do my initial sketch very fast – this ensures that I'm not tempted to apply too much detail.

There is, of course, nothing wrong with detailed drawings or paintings! Botanical art is amazing and takes both great skill and patience – but a looser way of painting gives me so much joy, both in application and again in the viewing. My tips below will give you some starting points for successful sketching.

Keep your eyes on the prize
Keep flicking your eyes back and forth between your subject (whether it's a photograph or from life) and your drawing on the paper.

Start with the bigger picture
Keep your source material close to hand, and work out what you want to include in your painting. Do you want one flowerhead or seven? Do you want to include the stem and leaves, or focus on the flowerhead? Leave out or change anything you don't like.

Leave out intricate backgrounds
Focus on the flower itself – no need for a fussy background, which can detract from the loose feel.

Use the flower head as a unit
You can estimate distances (for length of stem, gaps between flowers and so on) by drawing one flowerhead and using that as your basic unit of distance. For example, the stem might be one and a half flowerheads long.

Use your favourite paper
It doesn't matter what size paper you use, as proportions will always remain constant, so whether you're working within your comfort zone or going bold, focus on having fun.

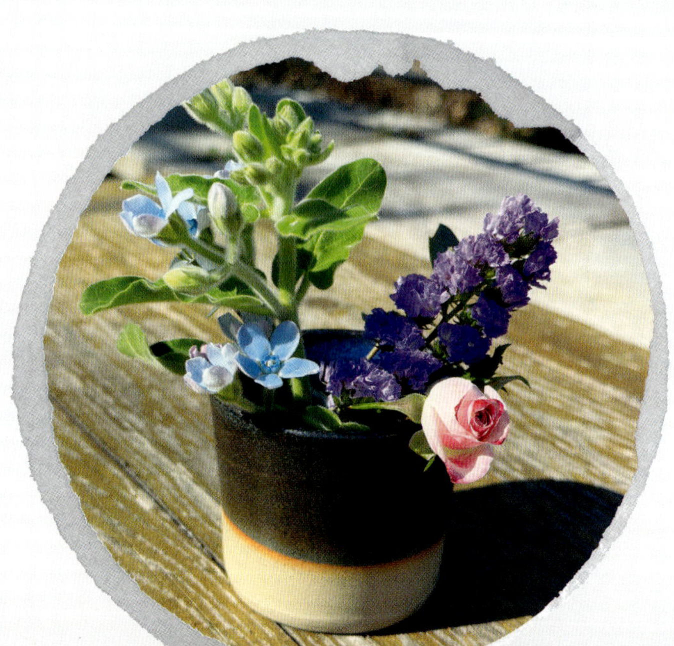

A SIMPLE SUBJECT
Placed into a container, a few well-chosen blooms can make a perfect reference point – look at the two sketches at the top of the opposite page to see how I've drawn it out.

Don't be tight – loosening up

Practise making light sketchy marks using an HB pencil. Hold this loosely, your fingers away from the tip, and simply scribble various shapes onto the paper. Moving your hand, wrist and arm loosely will allow you to make freer strokes. Once you have warmed up, you can start to draw and you will feel more free.

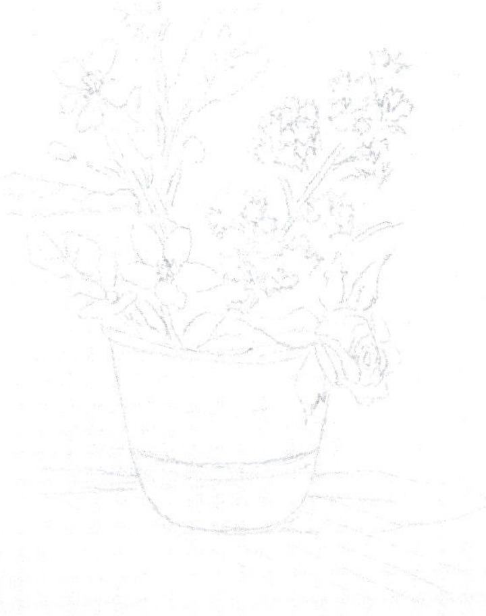

CONTRIVED AND TIGHT　　　　SPONTANEOUS AND LOOSE

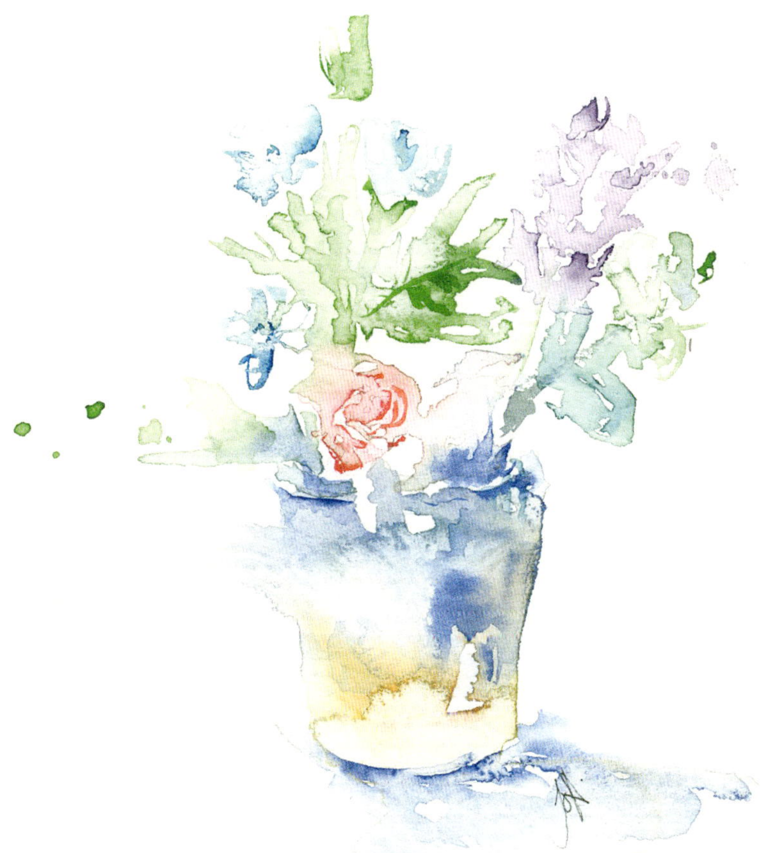

DRAWING A LESSON FROM YOUR SKETCHING

Loosening up your painting starts with loosening up your sketches. For both, my suggestion is to hold your tools, whether brush or pencil, more loosely than you normally would.

Go for that bigger brush for the first washes. This will enable you to be bold and more expressive with your marks – you can begin to add detail in the later stages. Always start loose and with lots of water. Plus, and I cannot stress this enough: 'dare to go darker', as watercolours dry lighter!

Tulips

A simple shape and simply stunning. This project will show you how to start a painting very loosely, as we begin with a big brush and use lots of water. We will work quite fast and messily – and while this may be out of your comfort zone, it will definitely bring liveliness to your painting. Working through the brush sizes, we will start big and bold and then close in for a little detail towards the end. The techniques you will learn are wet into wet, wet on dry, lifting out with a brush and creating patterns with backruns and spattering.

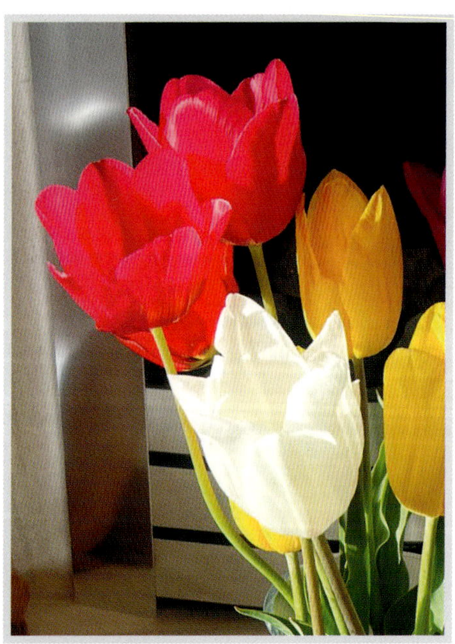

REFERENCE PICTURE

Although tulips are highly associated with the Netherlands – their popularity there was so great that it led to 'Tulip Mania' where some rare varieties cost as much as a house! – the National flower for the Netherlands is actually the daisy.

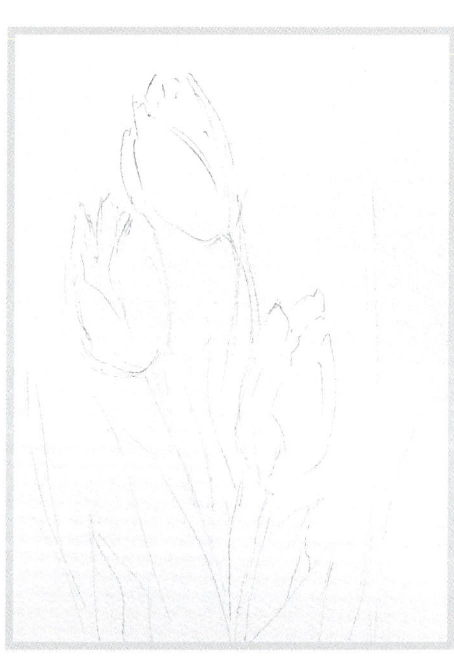

INITIAL SKETCH

Make your initial sketch using an HB pencil, on a 23 x 30.5cm (9 x 12in) piece of Not surface Bockingford watercolour paper.

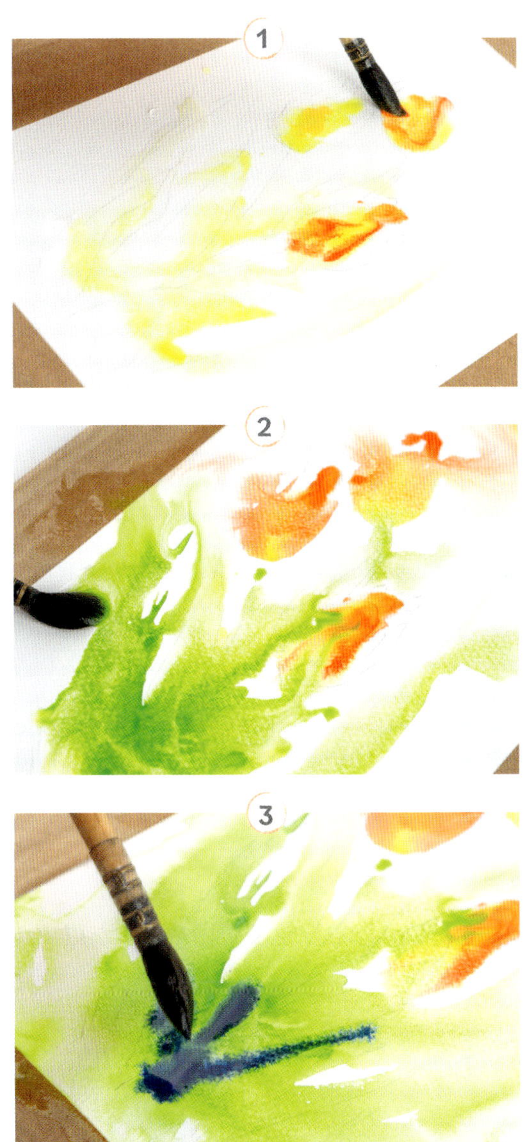

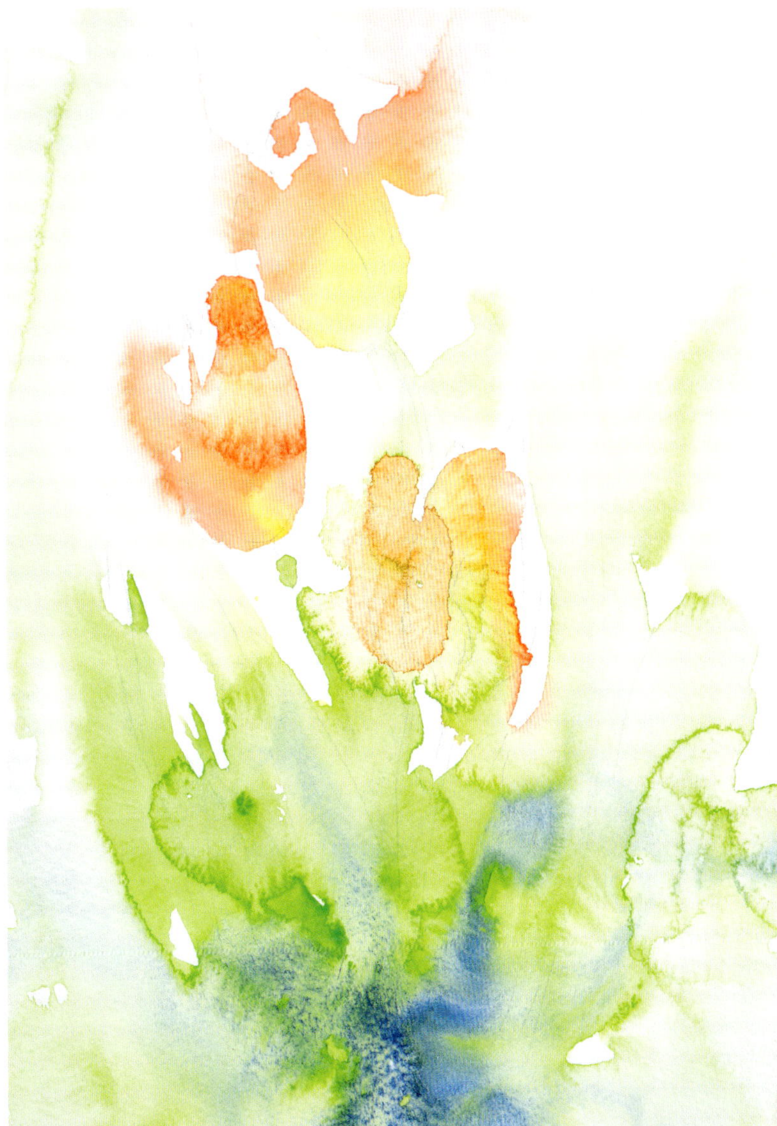

Stage 1 – Large brush and main shapes

In this stage we will use wet into wet techniques to establish the main areas.

It's important to let the painting dry naturally at the end of the stage, as it's only by doing so that the qualities of the colours – the granulation of the blue, for example – will become apparent.

1 Use the large brush to apply clean water to the main subject. Don't worry about keeping within the lines – work quickly and freely. Drop in the lightest colour – vanadium yellow in this example – over the flowers, stems and leaves. Drop in vermilion on the flowerheads only, allowing it to mix on the surface.

2 Wash the brush and pick up May green, dropping it into the leaves and stems. Rinse the brush, and bring clean water in from the edges. Allow it to touch the wet paint here and there, and you will see the colours bloom outwards.

3 As the water starts to dry, but while still a little wet, drop in French ultramarine at the base. Allow to dry completely.

Stage 2 – Re-establishing and refining

Here we'll take stock of how the paint has behaved, and re-establish the shapes before we begin refining.

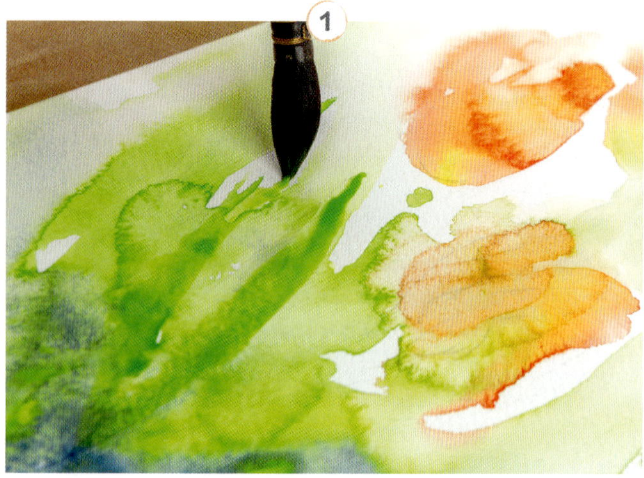

1 Use a putty eraser to remove any pencil marks, then use May green to re-establish the leaves and stems over the top of the green area. Use the same long strokes as before.

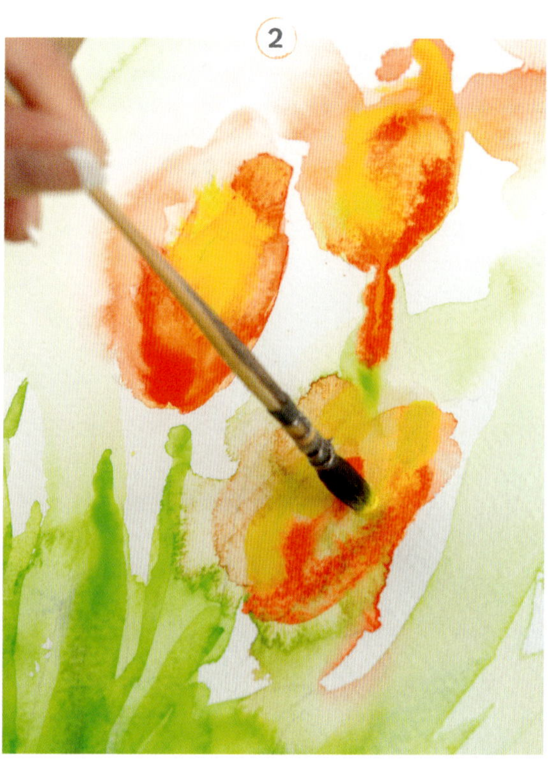

2 For the tulip petals, we want a bit more control, so swap to the medium brush and strengthen the colours of the flower heads with vermilion and vanadium yellow.

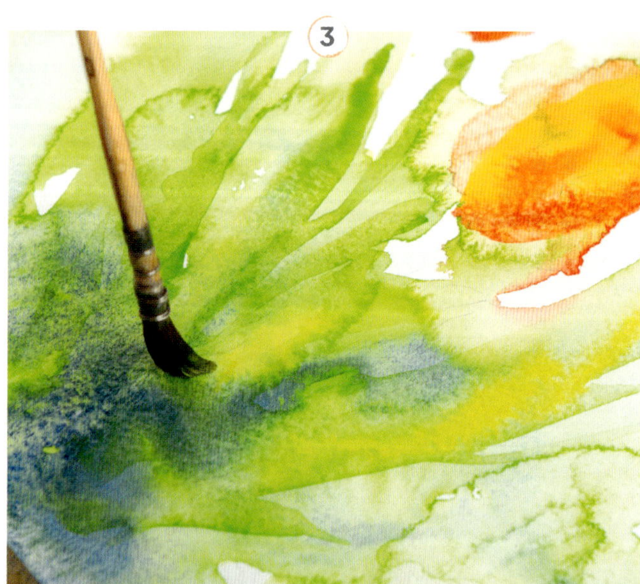

3 If you have any yellow left on the brush, add some sunlight to the leaves. Next, add French ultramarine to the leaves and stem to add some contrasting depth.

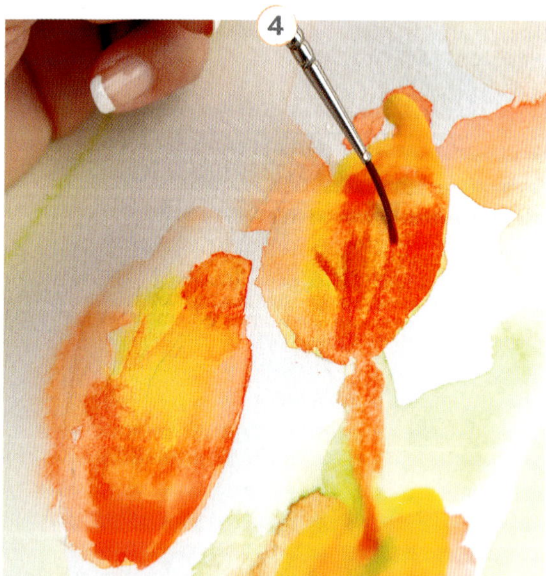

4 Switch to the small brush and add some fine lines to separate the individual petals using rose madder.

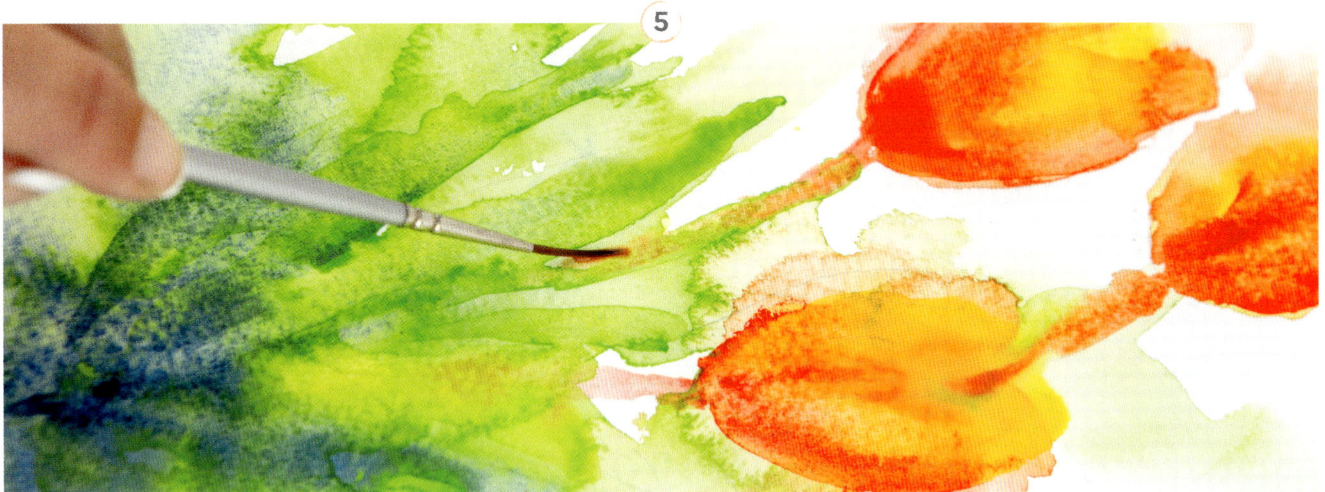

5 To add some warmth to the stems, use the small brush to draw down some of the wet rose madder and vermilion from the flower heads.

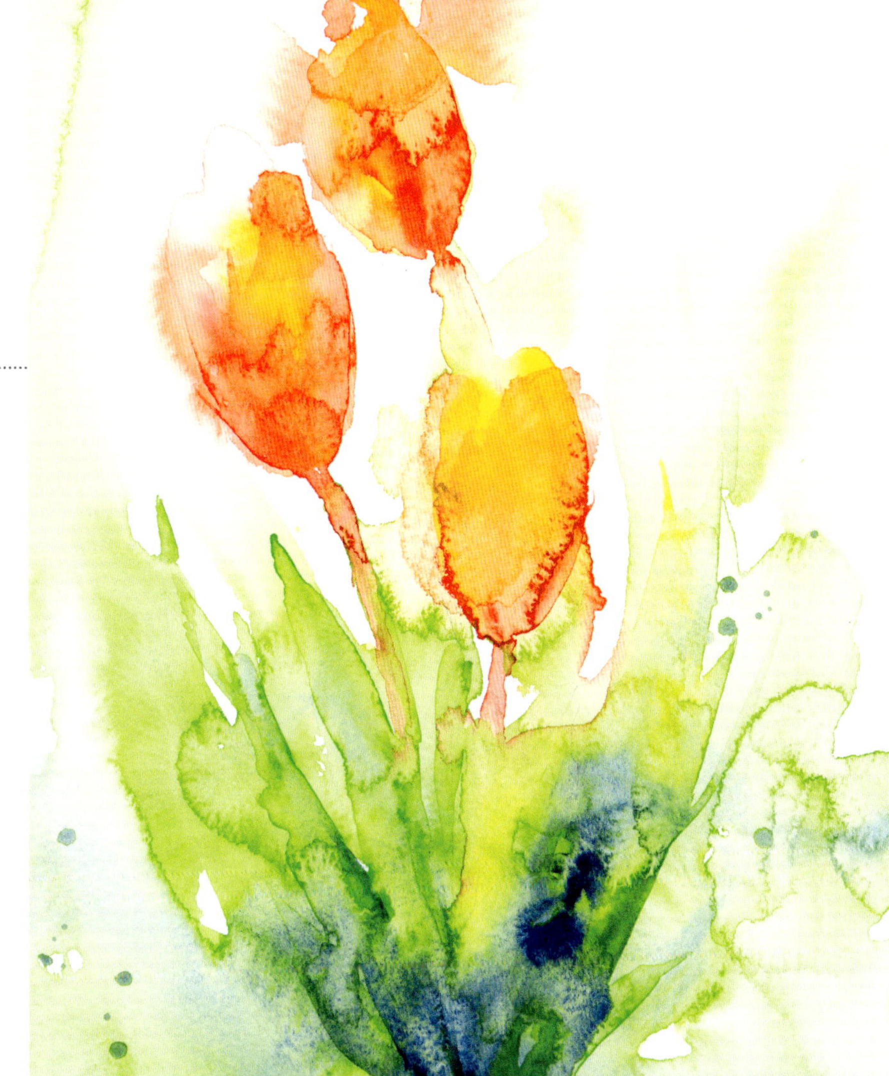

END OF STAGE 2
Again, allow to dry naturally.

Stage 3 – Making it your own

The previous stages will have given you a base to work with. Your painting will be slightly different to mine, but the broader lesson of looking closely to find what you like, and then bringing it out, will always be useful.

We can now look for interesting shapes and patterns that have developed, retain and emphasize those we like, and soften or minimize those we don't.

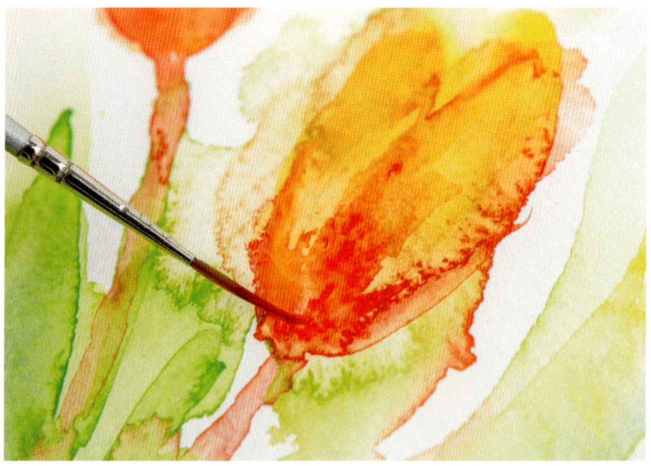

MAKE BACKRUNS YOUR FRIEND

Far from a mistake, backruns add texture and interest, and closely evoke the texture of flower petals. Here, I've used the small brush to add fine lines of rose madder to suggest separation between two petals. I have softened the backrun on the left, but kept it on the right, where it adds depth and interest.

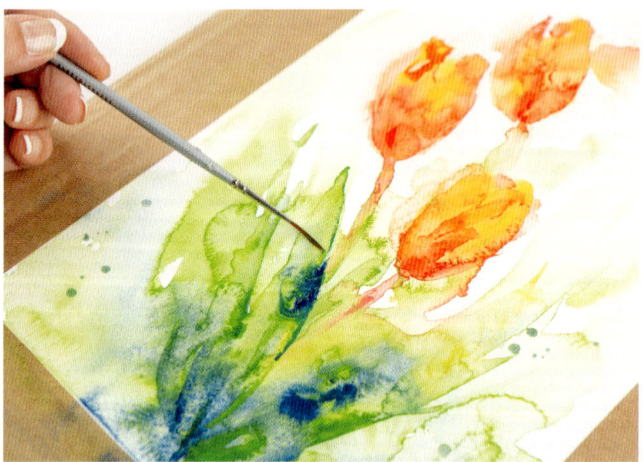

BUILD STRUCTURE – BUT NOT TOO MUCH

In areas like the greenery, you might like to add some fine lines using May green or French ultramarine to create harder edges that make the area easier to read. Be careful not to overdo this – add just what you need, and no more.

If you find a line starts to look contrived, use a wet brush to break it up and soften it once more.

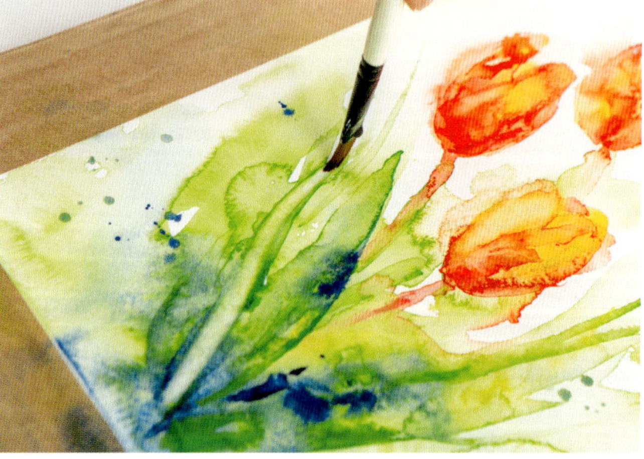

ADD A FLOURISH

Spattering and similar techniques are a great finishing touch to add some dynamism. Lifting out wet paint by drawing a dry brush through it, as shown above, is a good way to bring light into dark areas.

Have a look through *Watercolour & beyond* on pages 70–141 for other ideas on how to add a little extra to your work.

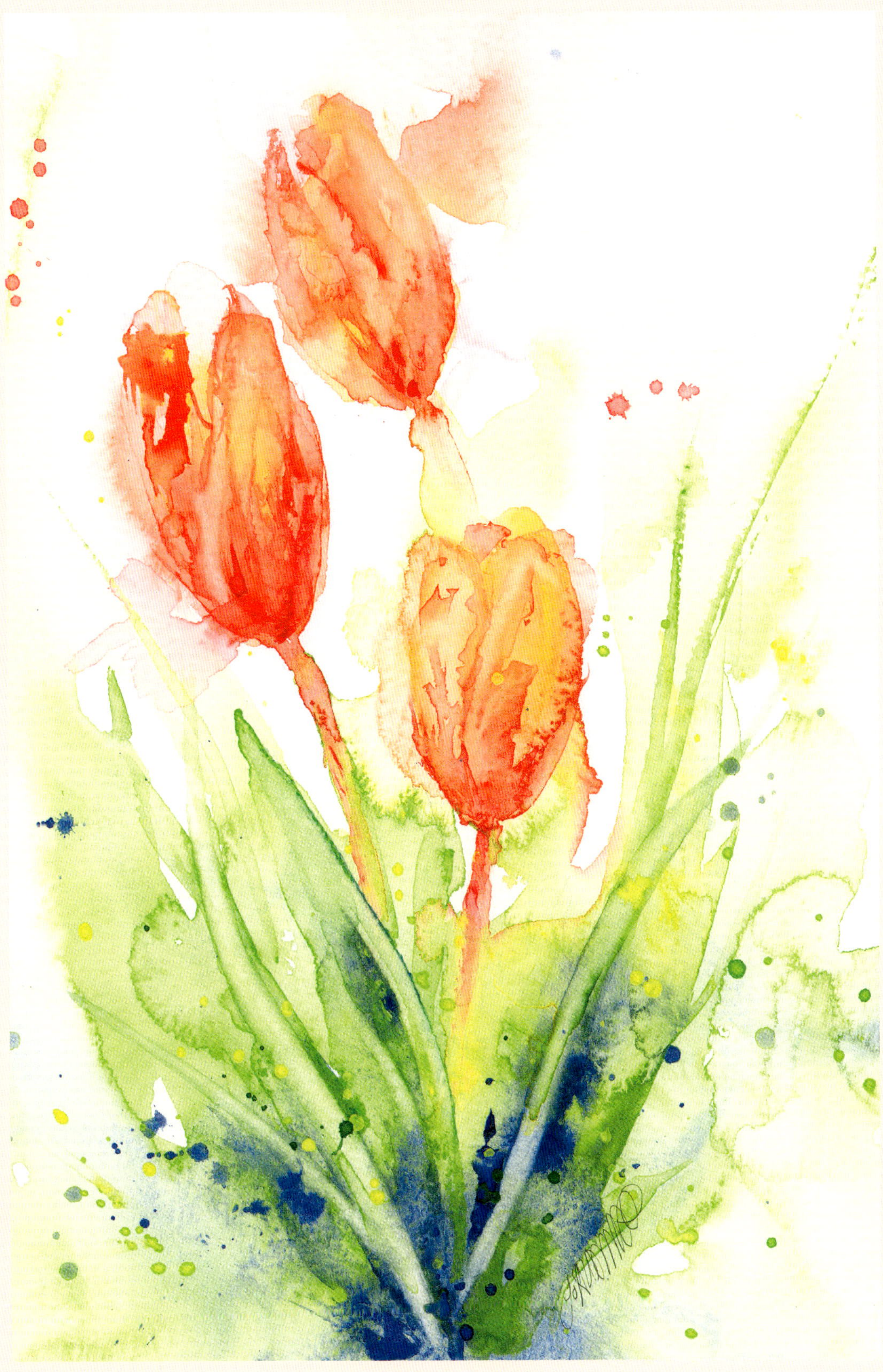

THE FINISHED PAINTING

What next?

We can paint the same flower over and over again and each time we can make it different – not necessarily better, but different. Some people prefer detail, some do not; likewise some are attracted to bright colours while others prefer more delicate hues.

   As the following examples show, we can create so many variations on the same flower using different materials and/or techniques.

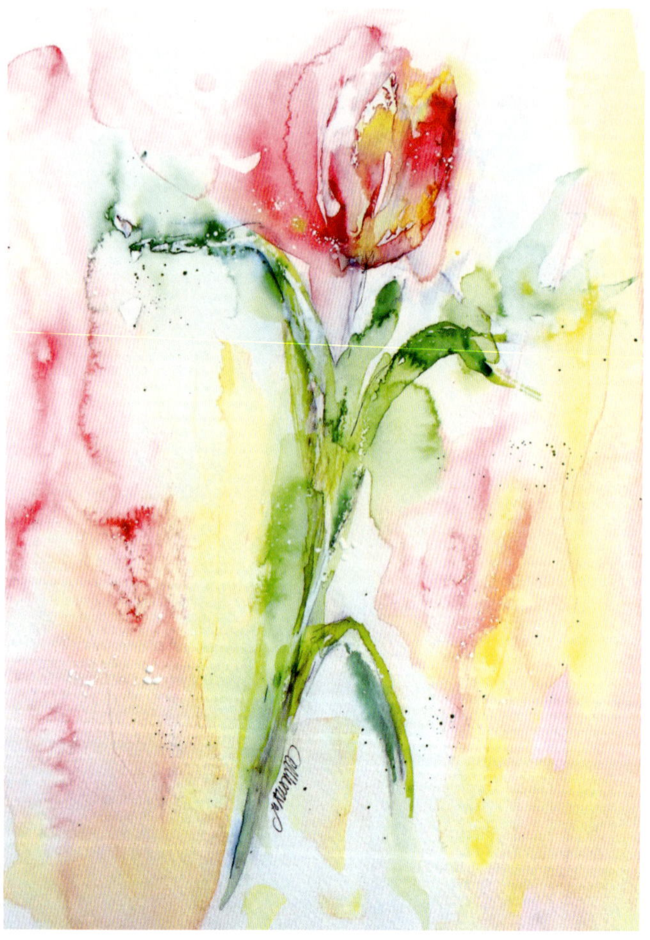
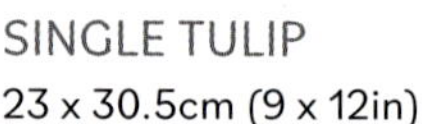

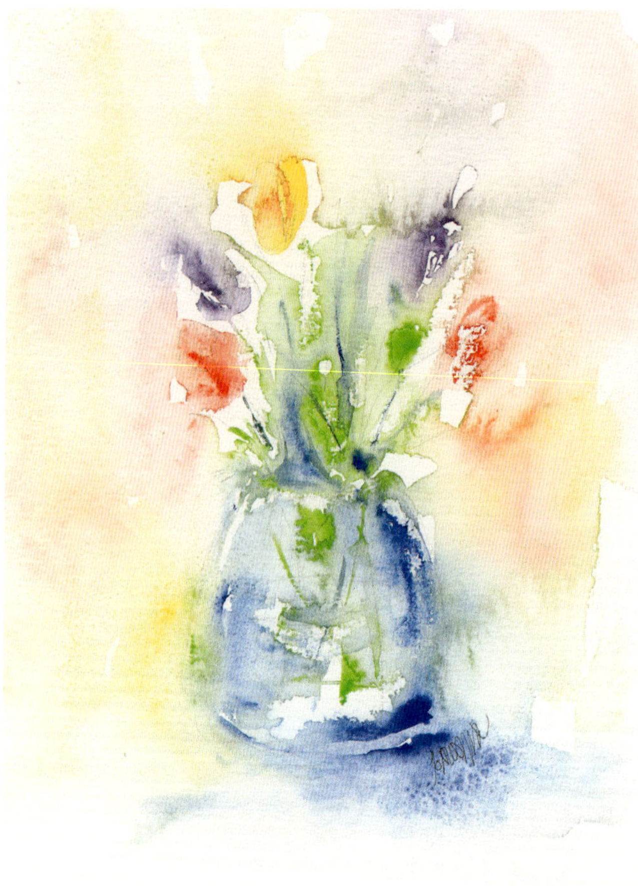

SINGLE TULIP
23 x 30.5cm (9 x 12in)

This single tulip was painted a few years ago and I can never replicate the patterns that occurred on this piece. Watercolour is unpredictable and can often take us by surprise with how it dries.

This one just worked, blooms in the right place, colours sitting for me just right. I love it when this happens.

TULIPS IN GLASS VASE
23 x 30.5cm (9 x 12in)

This was painted really quickly: wax resist was added to a light pencil sketch, then splodges of bold colours were added. These were allowed to interact and create backruns on the surface. Touches of salt were added while the paint was wet – and just look how beautiful the resulting patterns are!

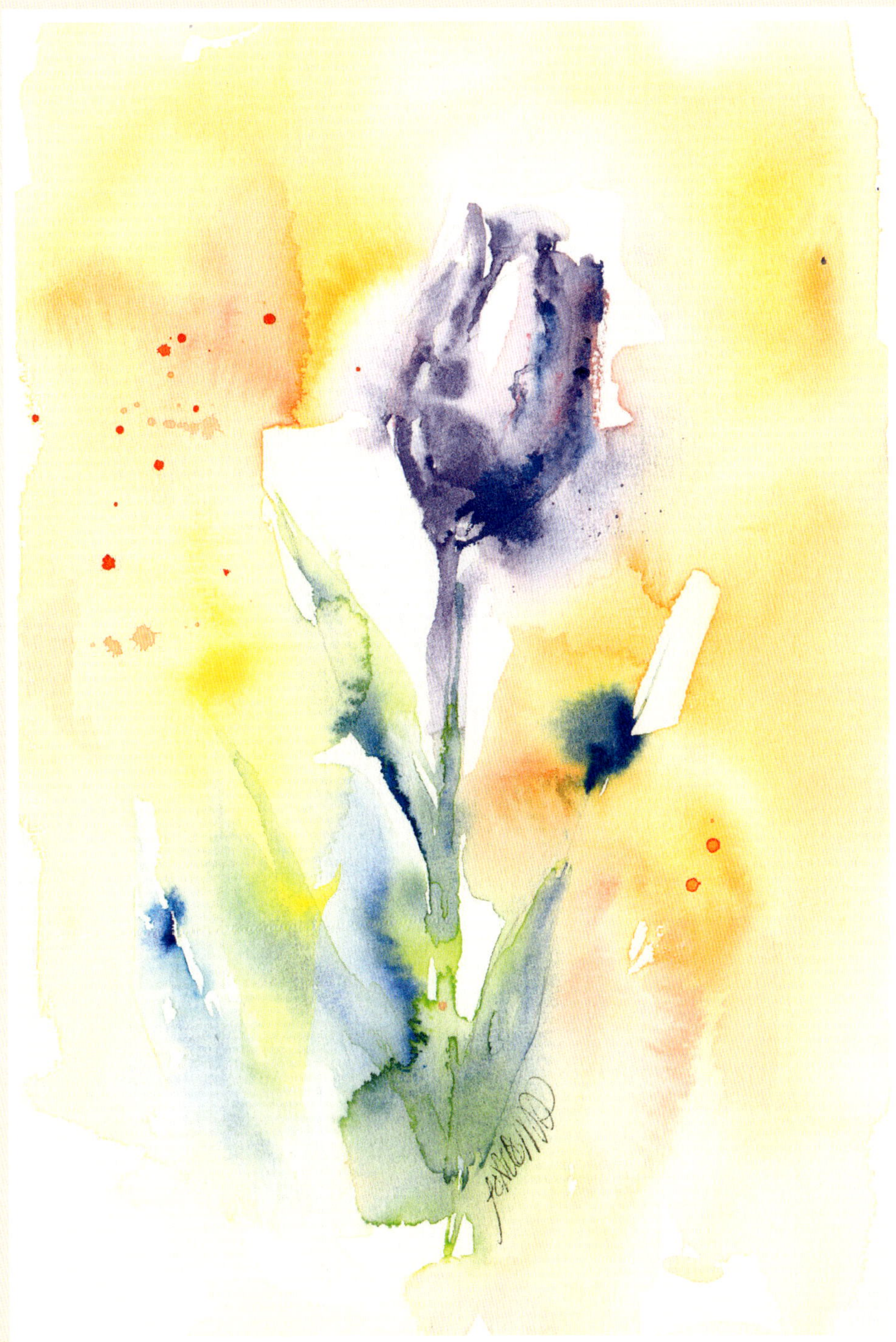

PURPLE TULIP

23 x 30.5cm (9 x 12in)

Here I skipped around the white paper with my brush, leaving big white voids that add unepxected flashes of light and air.

I have often been asked at a demonstration 'Aren't you going to fill those in?' My reply is a simple 'No!'

Daffodils

When painting flowers in a vase or other containers, sometimes it pays to think outside the box. By this I mean that we do not have to paint a vase as transparent if we feel that it is too much of a challenge – we can imagine it plain instead. If there is a complex pattern on the receptacle, we can simplify this or avoid it completely; we are merely using the vase/jug to give a representation of proportions and imagery. Here I decided to paint a blue vase to complement the orange centres of the flowers – this really makes the flowers pop.

As I am actually Welsh, I have a soft spot for these flowers as they are of course the national flower of Wales. These little beauties can pop up as early as February but are more likely to bloom in March. Seeing them always make me think that the brighter months are on their way – my favourite season is Spring and the appearance of these cheerful flowers reminds me that we are almost there.

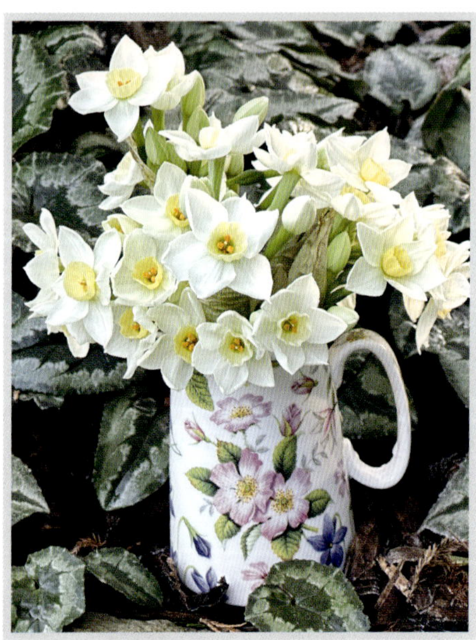

REFERENCE PICTURE

Picked from my own garden, I decided to simplify the jug to bring more focus to the beautiful bright yellow miniature daffodils, or narcissi.

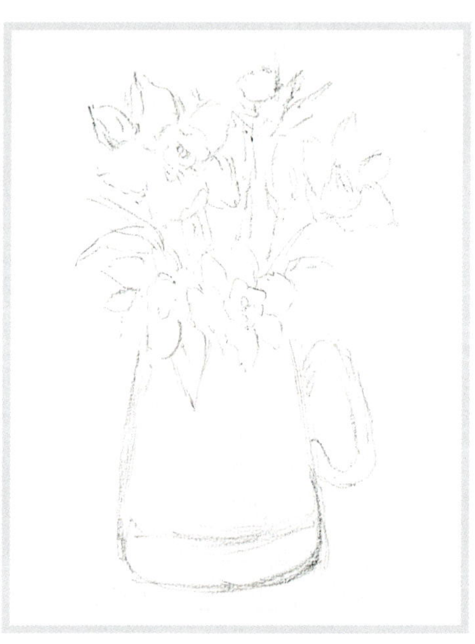

INITIAL SKETCH

Make your initial sketch using an HB pencil. The flowers are the key here, so keep the jug simple. I used an 18 x 26cm (7 x 10¼in) sheet of 300gsm (140lb) Not surface Clairefontaine watercolour paper.

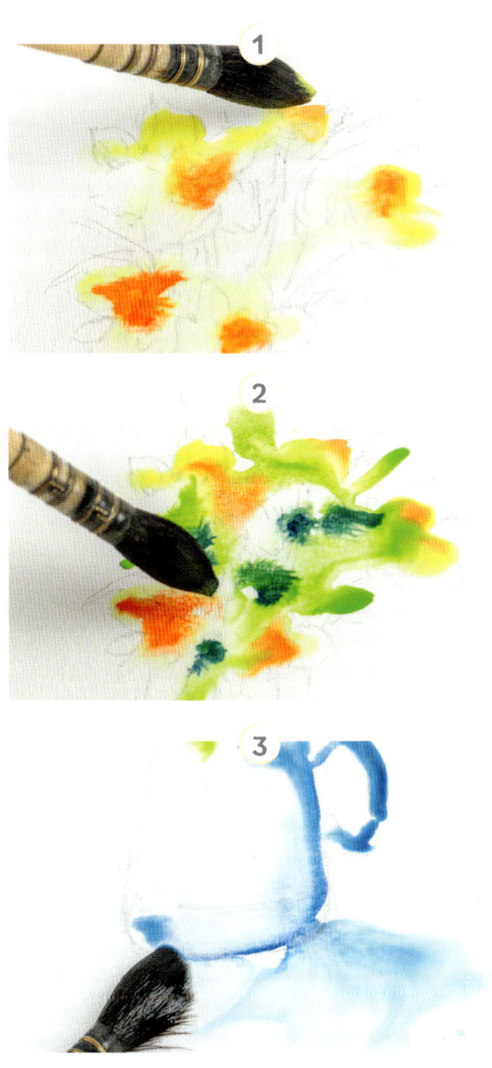

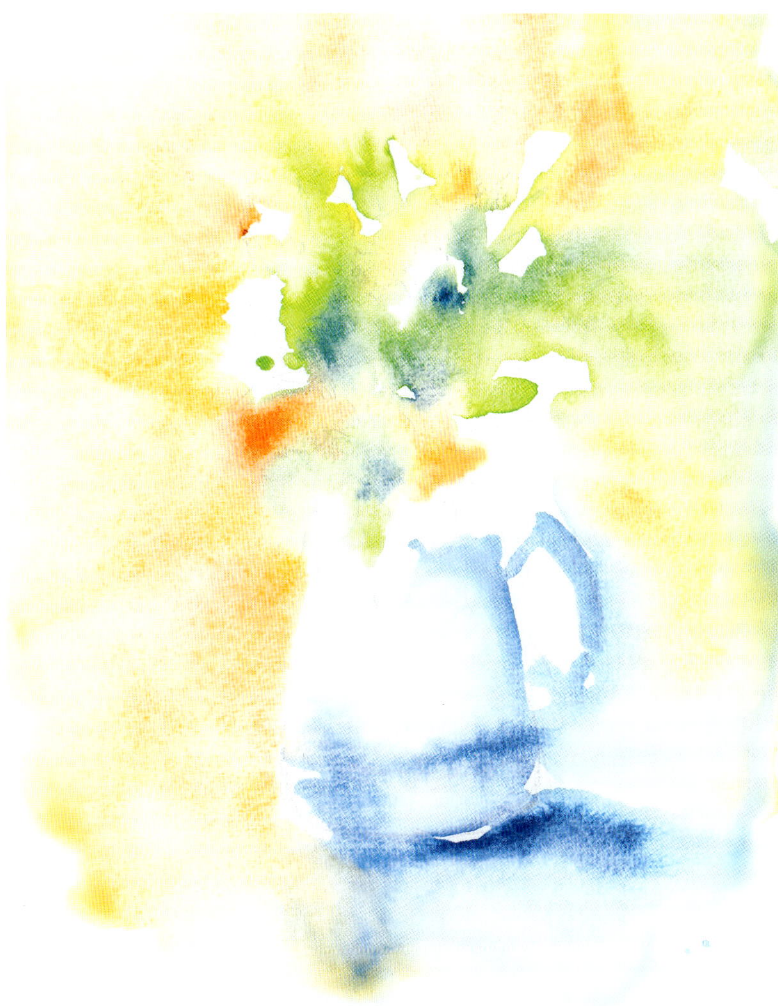

Stage 1 – Make a mess...

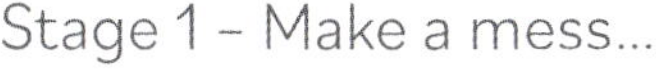

This is a complicated subject, so we want to simplify things. The jug's a perfect example: I like the shape, but trying to include the pattern will draw the eye from the daffodils – so let's leave it blank, and treat it very simply.

We also need to establish some stronger tones in between the flowers at this early stage, as this negative painting is what will make the flowers themselves stand out in the finished painting.

1 Use the large brush to lay down clean water, leaving white spaces. Drop in vanadium yellow around the flower centres. Without rinsing the brush, pick up a little vermilion and strengthen the centres with the resulting orange.

2 Add May green wet into wet; varying the strength of the mix for lighter and darker tones. Add French ultramarine for darker contrasts – again, don't rinse the brush.

3 Extend the blue down into the shadow side of the jug, leaving plenty of white. Rinse the brush and draw clean water in from the background, allowing it to touch the wet paint so it softens and bleeds outwards.

4 Drop in yellow ochre across the background, along with a few touches of burnt sienna and French ultramarine. As it starts to dry, drop in some clean water to encourage the paint to 'bloom', creating intentional backruns. Allow the painting to dry completely.

Stage 2 – ...and tidy up!

We now want to define the shapes of the flowers. Work in small, separate areas to keep things clean and give yourself a little control.

Swap between the medium and small brushes as you need to.

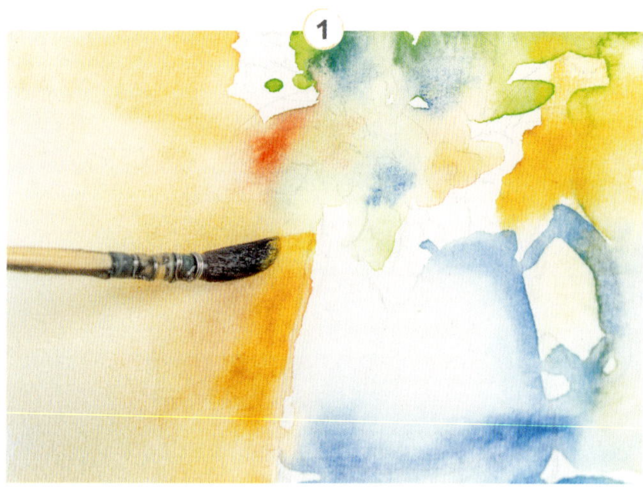

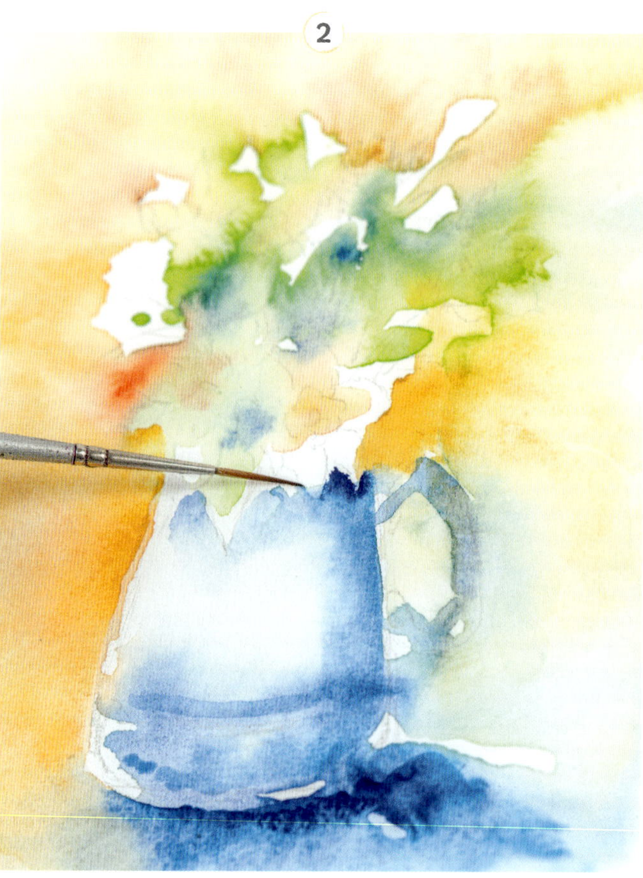

1 Swap to the medium brush. Wet the centres of the lower daffodils and strengthen them with yellow ochre. Rinse the brush and bring in clean water from the background to let it soften away.

2 Develop the shape of the jug with touches of French ultramarine, using quite strong paint for the shadow. Again, blend it away with clean water.

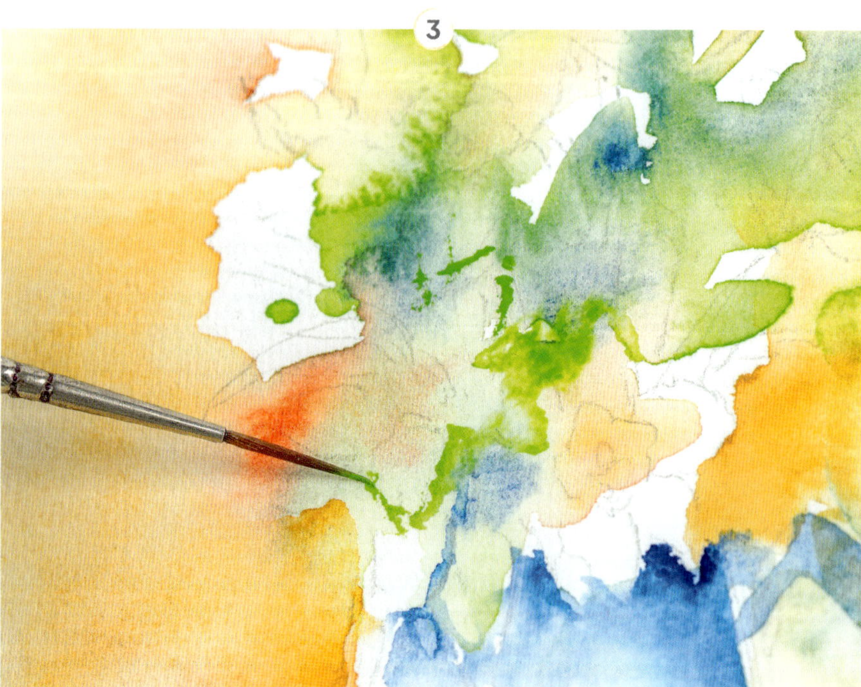

3 Draw out and define some of the daffodil petals by painting the background around them with slightly darker tones of whatever colour is beneath. Use the small brush to pick out the shapes, blending the colour away and revealing the flower – as though in negative. See page 72 for more on negative painting.

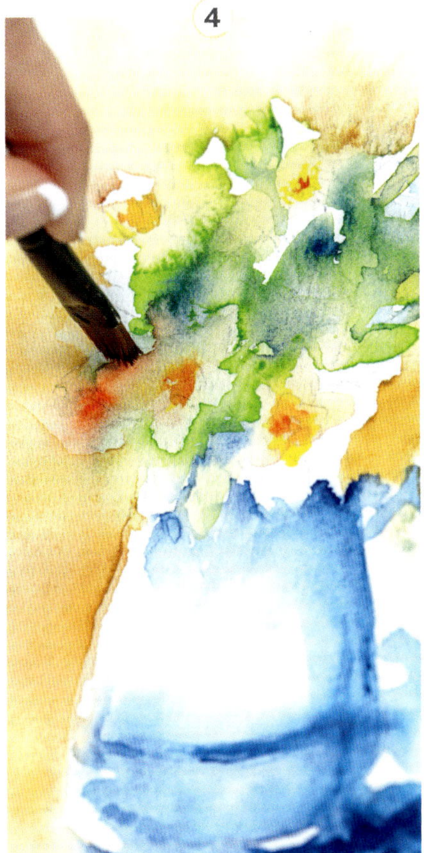

4 Use the large brush to paint the daffodil centres with stronger vanadium yellow, adding vermilion wet into wet. Use the flat brush to lift out any excess.

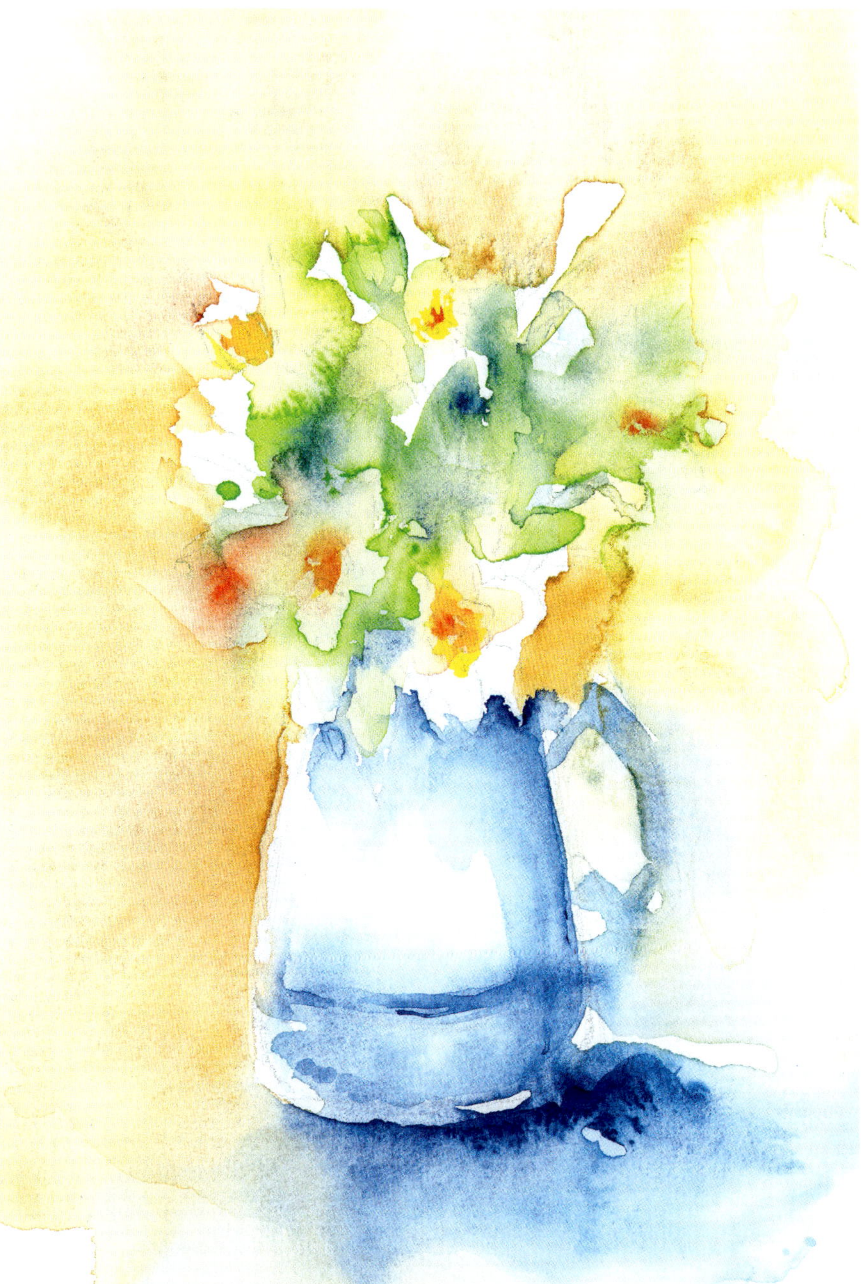

END OF STAGE 2

Allow the painting to dry completely.

Stage 3 – Making it your own

When painting a mass of small flowers like this, it's easy for the early washes to hide their shape and make it difficult to identify them – tricky, particularly if we're working with small marks to pick out the details through negative painting. Fortunately, we can refine things and make sure we're back on track.

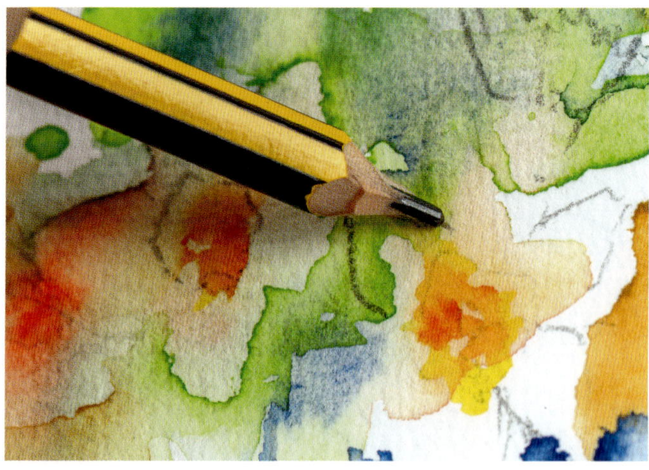

REDEFINE

If you find the petals are getting a bit lost, remove the pencil marks with a putty eraser, then redraw them. They'll help guide you in a potentially complex painting like this.

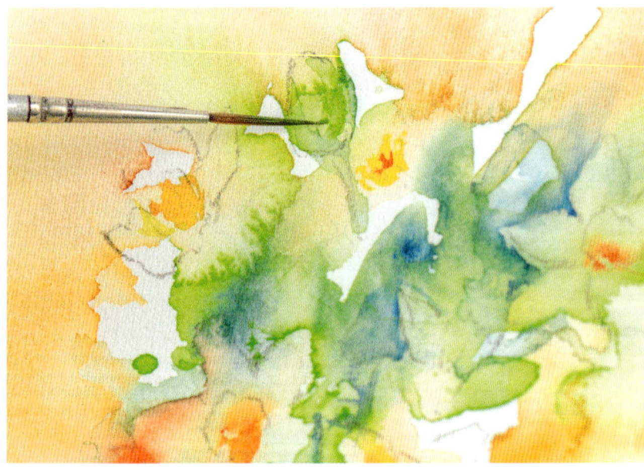

ADD IMPACT THROUGH CONTRAST

A mix of French ultramarine and May green makes a great dark blue-green background against which the flower petals will pop. Apply this with the small brush, then blend it away.

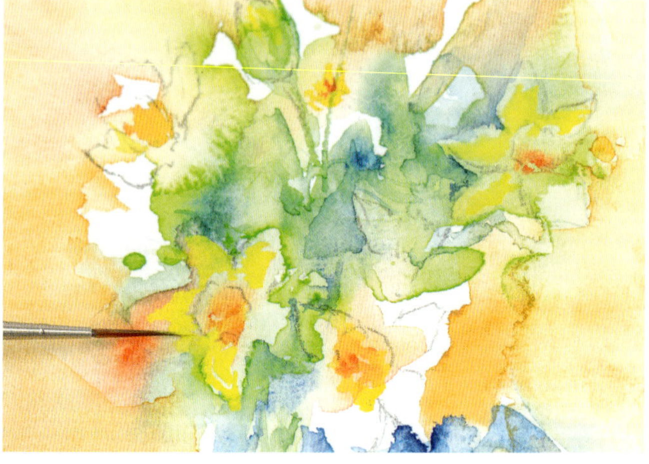

VIBRANCY

Watercolour can appear very vivid while wet, but gets paler as it dries. Generally, this is a good thing, as it helps to give a nice luminosity and brightness to the paler areas. However, you may find that a painting loses some impact – in which case feel free to add a glaze of the right paint to enrich the colour – in this case, vanadium yellow on the petals.

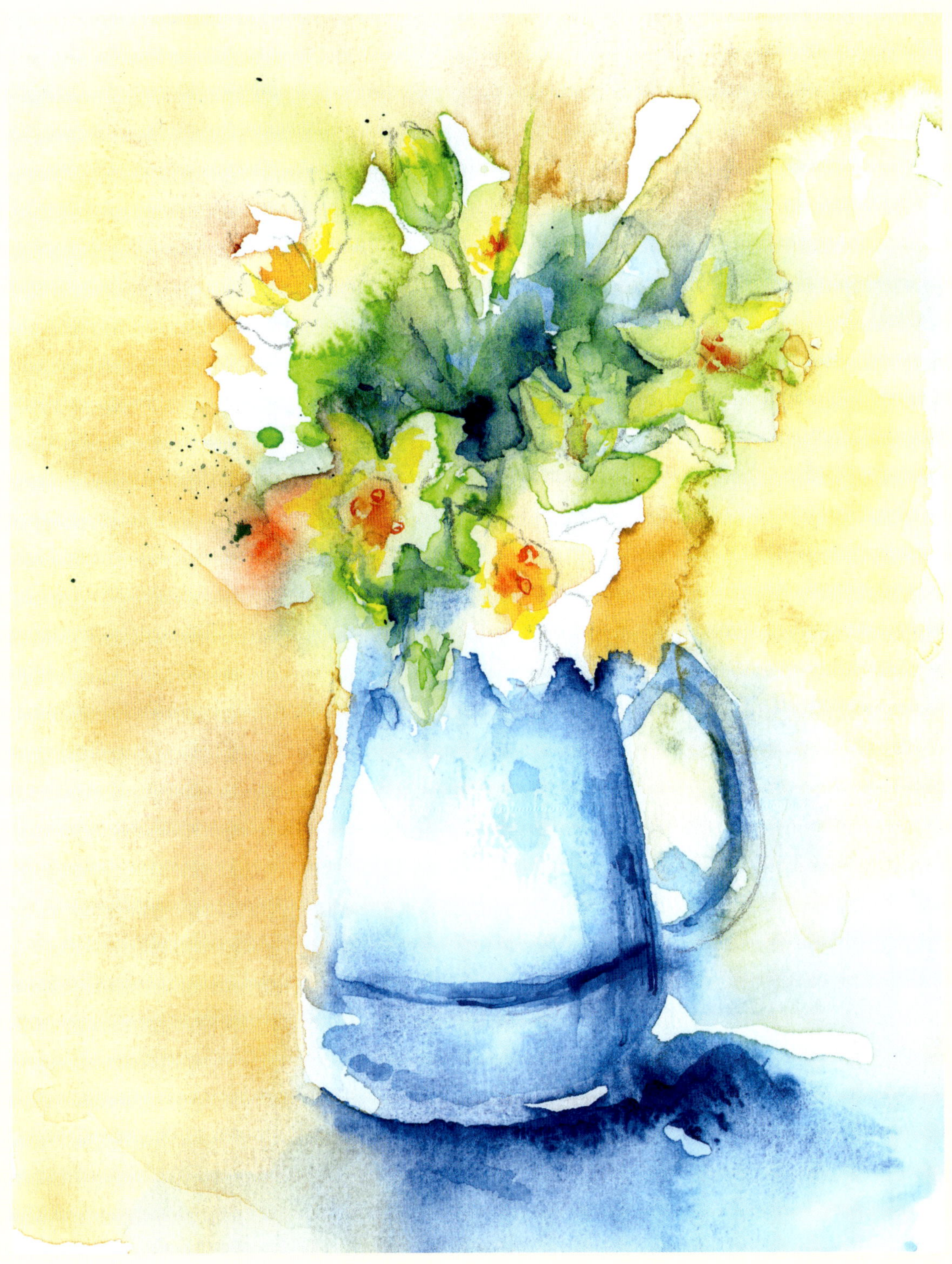

THE FINISHED PAINTING

What next?

Sometimes I will give the vase in a painting pride of place, making it the focal point and the flowers the accent. The mousey jug below is a good example. The jug itself, with its subtle blue flower details, is so very beautiful that I decided it would have a little more detail than the flowers. Of course I also wanted you to look at the colourful, warm, and advancing colours of the flowers, but decided to paint these more loosely so that you would also be led to focus on the unusual jug. The jug was negatively painted: all the white area was painted around, and I definitely dared to go darker to create the unusual shape of the vessel.

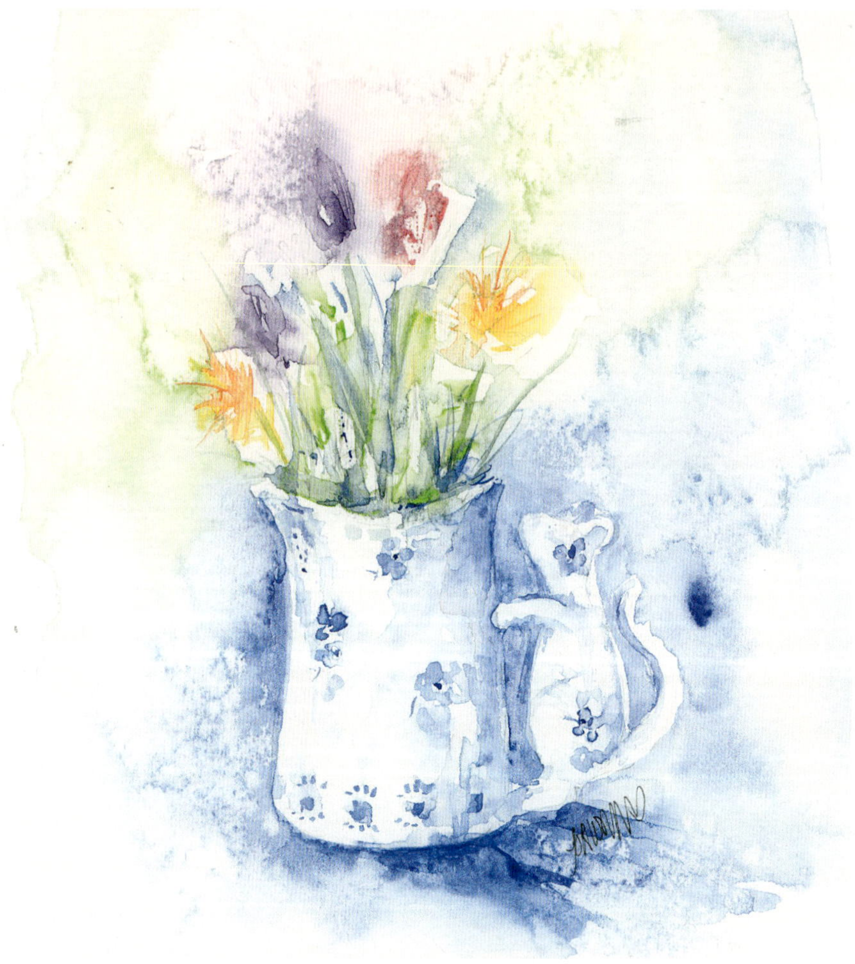

MOUSEY MIX

15 x 20cm (6 x 8in)

Unlike the project, where the flowers are the focus, here the jug is the focus. It was painted using negative painting techniques (see page 72), while the flowers are left loose and allowed to bleed into the background, where salt has been added (see page 124).

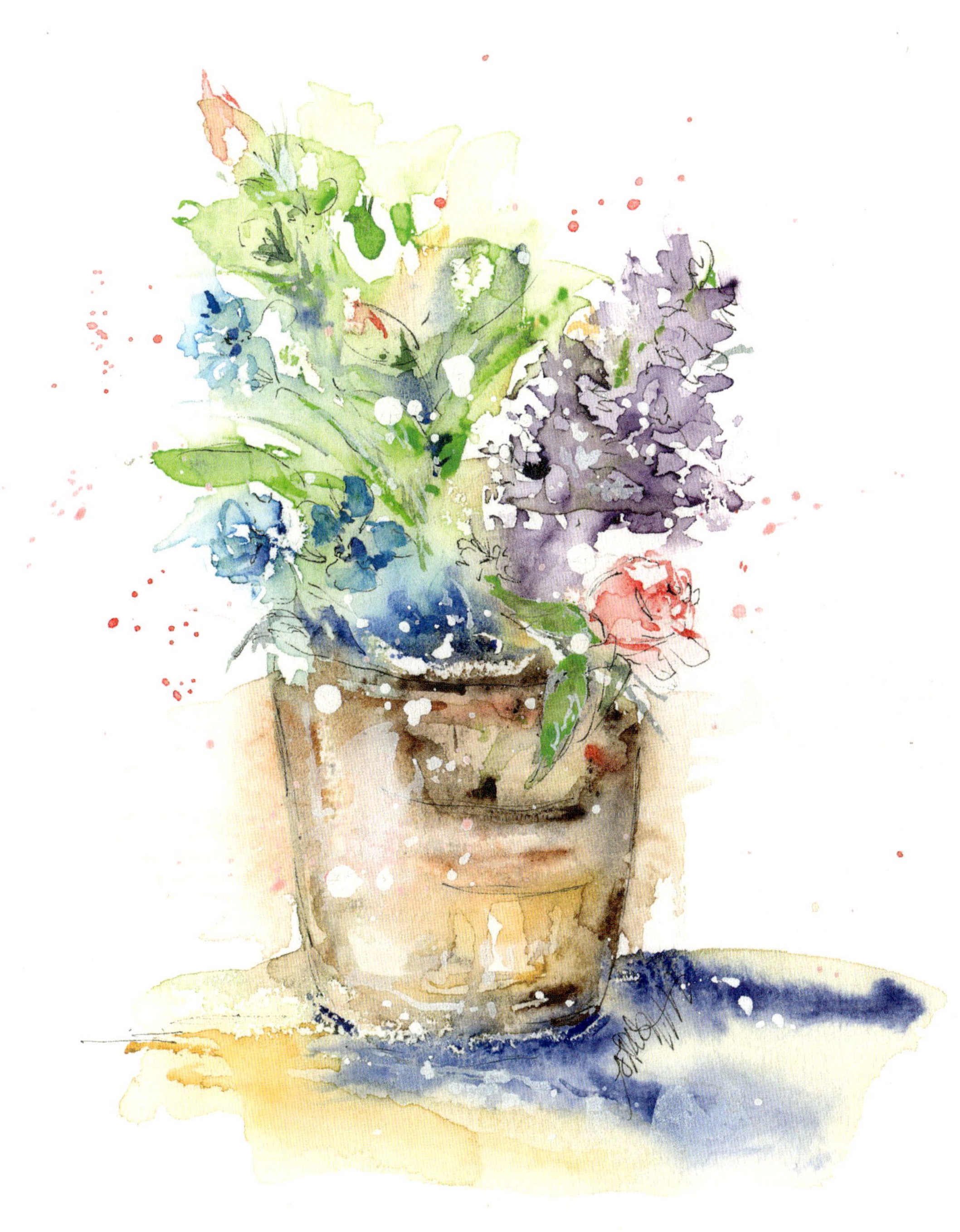

SNOWDONIAN SPRAY
18 x 25.5cm (7 x 10in)

Worked on Clairefontaine paper, this potted flower arrangement was painted with pen and wash (see page 126), and also uses white acrylic paint to give the spattered marks some more strength.

I gave the painting this title, as I had been gifted these flowers just before setting out to climb Snowdon (*Yr Wyddfa* in Welsh). I was feeling a little anxious at the prospect as I had never climbed a mountain before, so I took these flowers to lift my spirits, along with my paints so that I could relax by painting them... I took lots of chocolate and wine too!

Bluebells

Bluebells are another popular flower to paint, and are often depicted in their hundreds as a carpet of blue-purple. As with a lot of wild flowers, bluebells are protected in the UK so it is illegal to intentionally pick these, as they take many years to recover.

Here I have decided to simplify the flower – as they're equally glorious in close-up. To add dynamism, in this project we'll use lots of spattering and backruns. We'll also use a yellow background to help make the blue-purple of the flowers 'pop'.

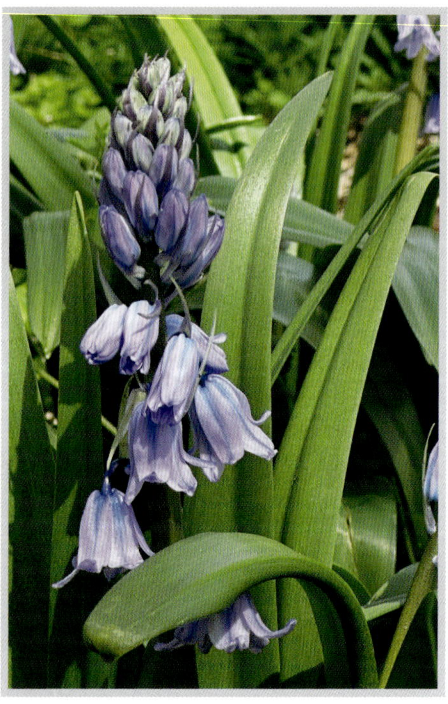

REFERENCE PICTURE

This is a good example of a background best simplified into a semi-abstract wash.

INITIAL SKETCH

Make your initial sketch using an HB pencil on 300gsm (140lb) Not surface Clairefontaine watercolour paper, measuring 18 x 26cm (7 x 10¼in).

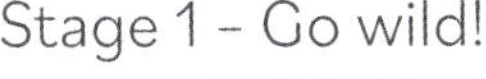

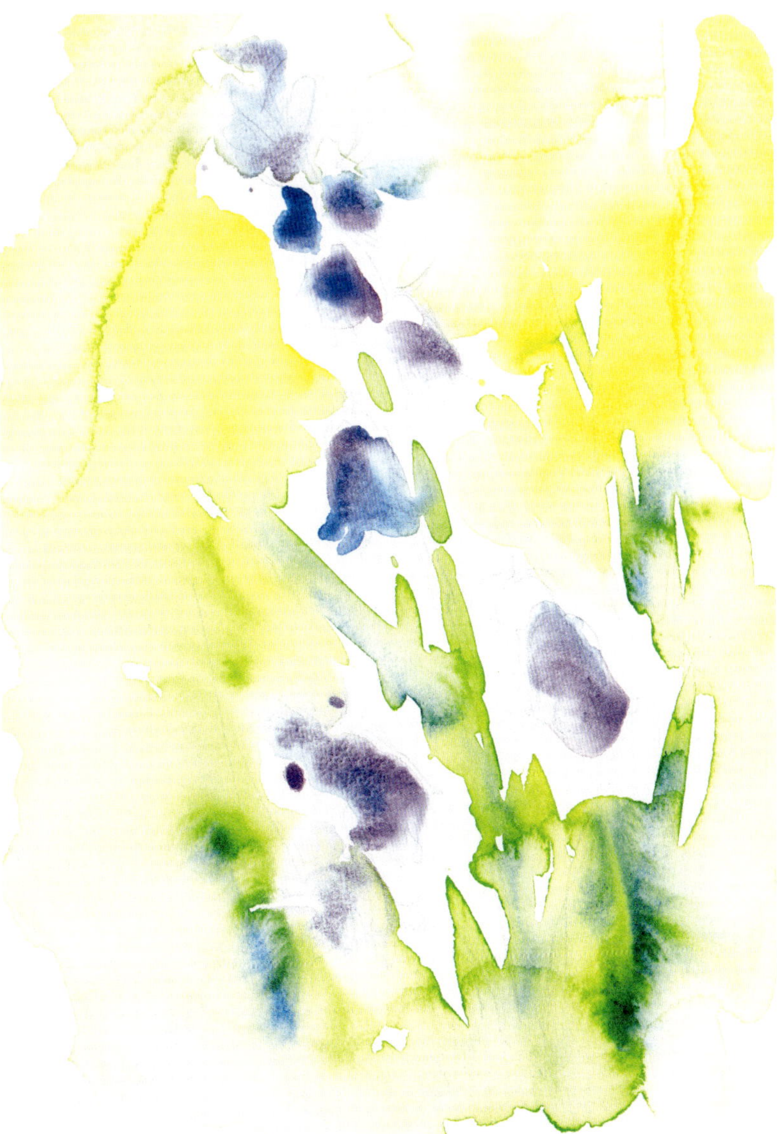

Stage 1 – Go wild!

We want to feel relaxed and enjoy painting, so don't fuss about staying within the lines of the sketch – it adds to the effect if the colours merge and mingle.

When adding the background, leave some areas of clean paper – this is what will give the painting its sparkle and freshness.

1 Use the large brush to apply clean water to the paper. Aim to create interesting semi-random shapes. Drop in Schmincke violet to the bluebell flowerheads. Without washing the large brush, pick up some French ultramarine and touch the tip of the brush into the wet paint here and there to vary the hue.

2 Rinse the brush and add the stems and leaves using long strokes of May green. Avoid the flowerheads, adding the green into the spaces around them. Vary the hue with vanadium yellow.

3 Rinse the brush, then add clean water in from the edges, bringing it in to just touch the areas of paint on the surface. The paint will bleed outwards. As the painting begins to dry, drop in some clean water to encourage backruns or 'blooms'. You can touch in some reinforcing marks to strengthen colours using the same colours, too. Leave it to dry before moving on to the next stage.

Stage 2 – Refining detail

We'll swap down to the medium and small brushes for this stage as we dive into bringing out some detail. We'll 'find' some flowers by strengthening them, and leave others 'lost' and airy.

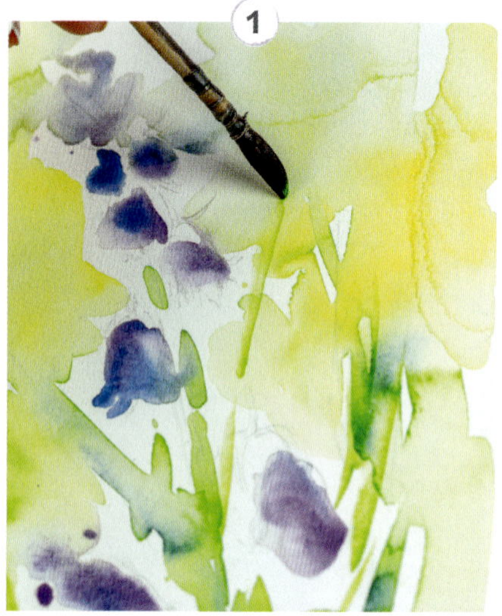

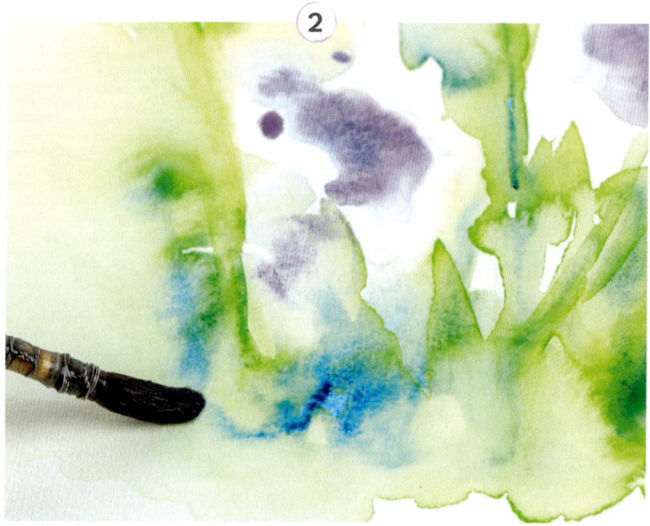

1 With the medium brush and May green, use light, flicking strokes up from the bottom to add grasses.

2 Strengthen some of the grasses by adding French ultramarine wet into wet. Wet the base of the flowers and grasses and add the same colour to help ground them.

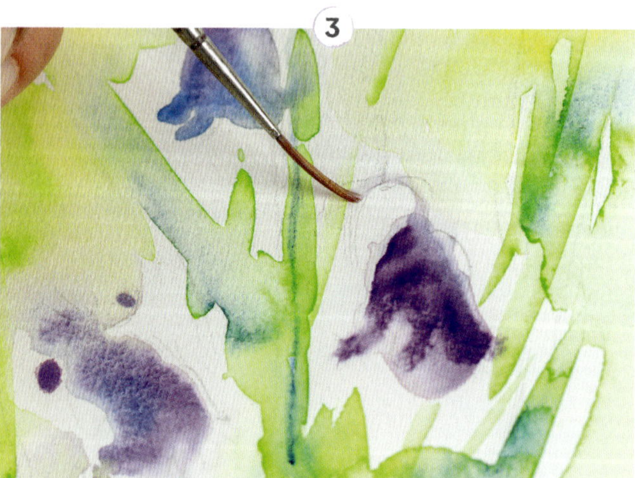

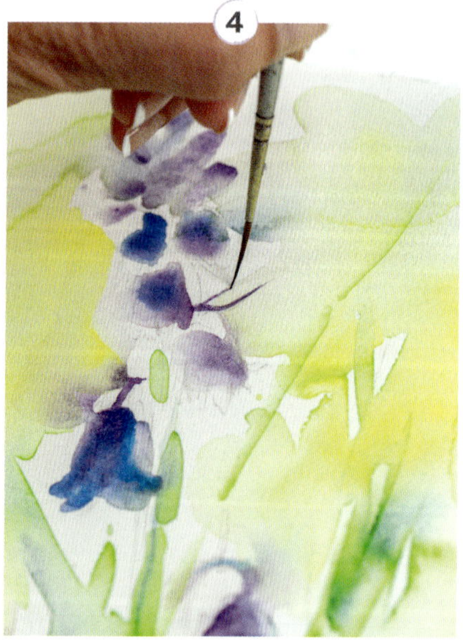

3 Re-establish the shape of the bluebell flowerheads using the middle-sized brush and clean water, drawing in the shape on the sketch. Swap to the small brush to drop in Schmincke violet, and refine the shape slightly.

4 While the flowers remain wet, add some helio cerulean to create bright touches.

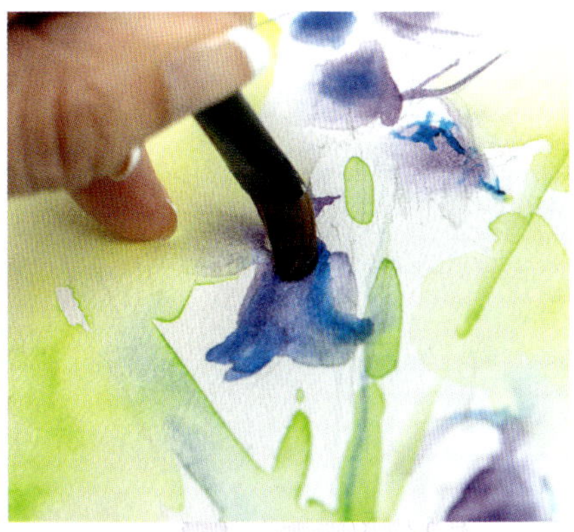

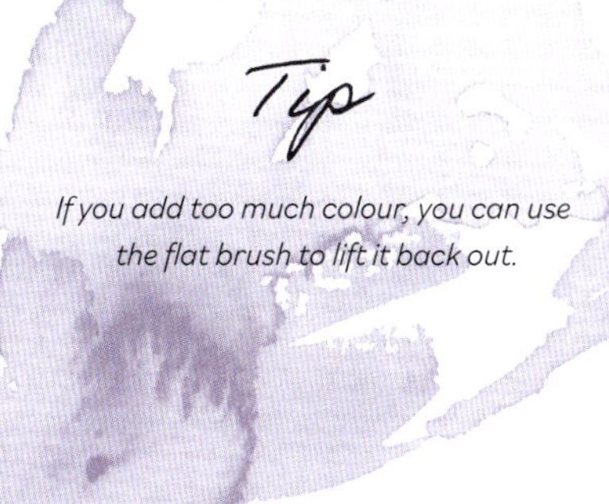

Tip

If you add too much colour, you can use the flat brush to lift it back out.

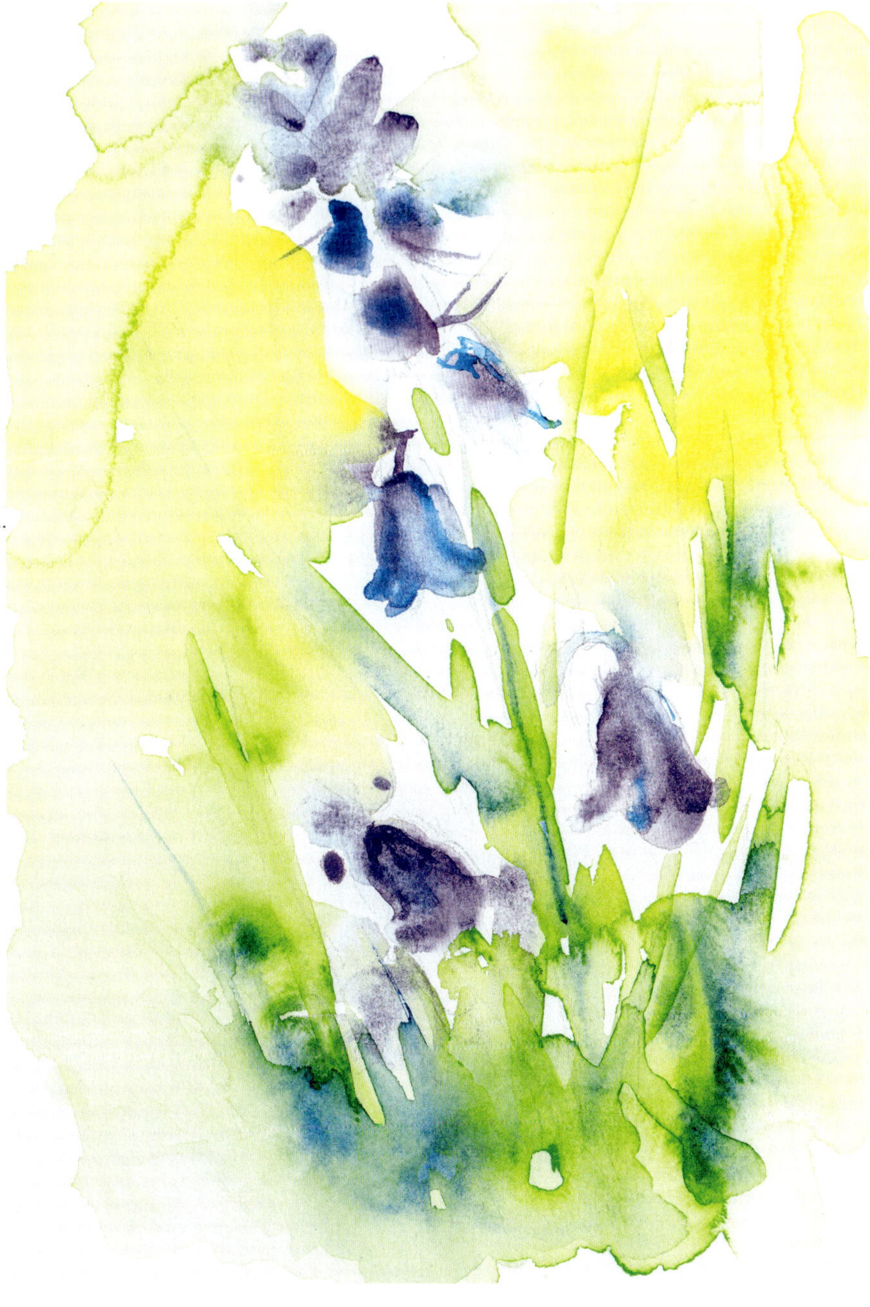

END OF STAGE 2

You can continue to adjust, but remember not to overwork things. Once you are content, leave it to dry.

Stage 3 - Finishing touches

Once the painting is dry, sit back and assess. You'll probably spot areas that you want to improve or make more interesting, or you might like to draw the eye elsewhere.

Of course, if you're happy with it as-is, then there's no need to fiddle! Be careful, when adding finishing touches, not to lose the freshness and sense of life.

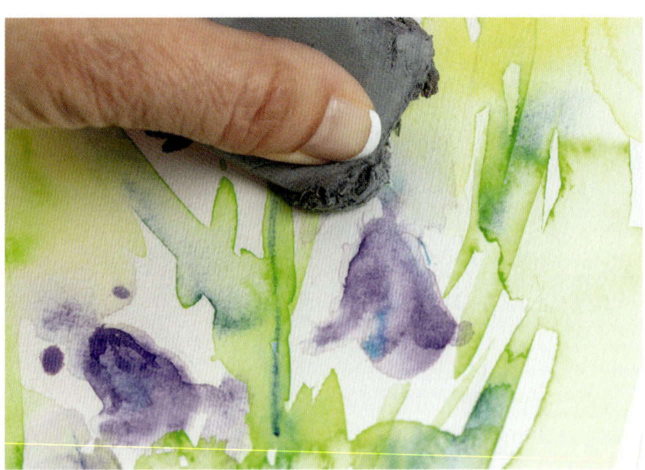

REMOVE AND RECREATE STRUCTURE

Now the painting is completely dry, we can remove any visible marks from the original sketch using a putty eraser. Always work in one direction, rather than scrubbing back and forth. This helps to avoid damaging the surface.

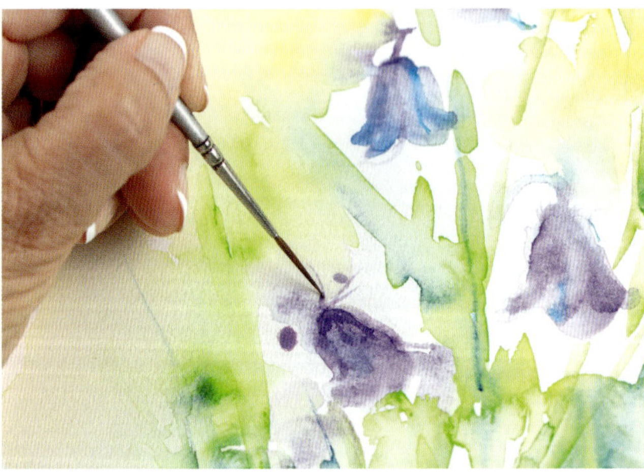

BRINGING BALANCE

With the pencil marks removed, you can now use the small brush to pick out small, darker details. You can layer existing areas to sharpen them up, or add fine marks wherever you like.

Only do this to some of the flowerheads - if you strengthen them all, you'll lose all contrast and balance, and things will look flat.

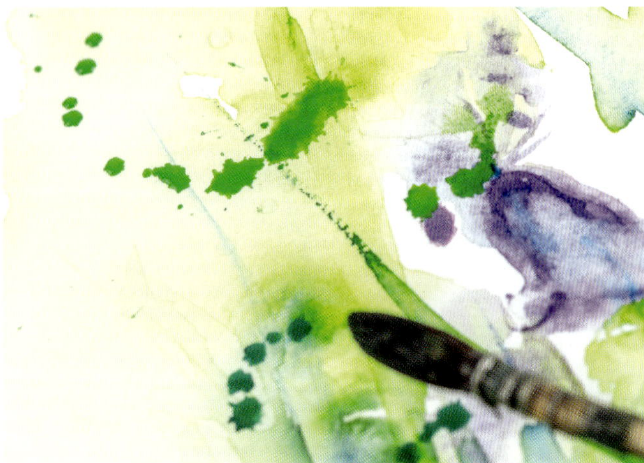

IMPROVIZE

What isn't seen in the source photograph are the yellow-orange stamens I have seen on some bluebells - and this sort of detail is exactly what we can add to make the painting our own. I've used vanadium yellow and vermilion to add these.

I've also added some spatters by flicking paint onto the paper - see page 116 for more on spattering.

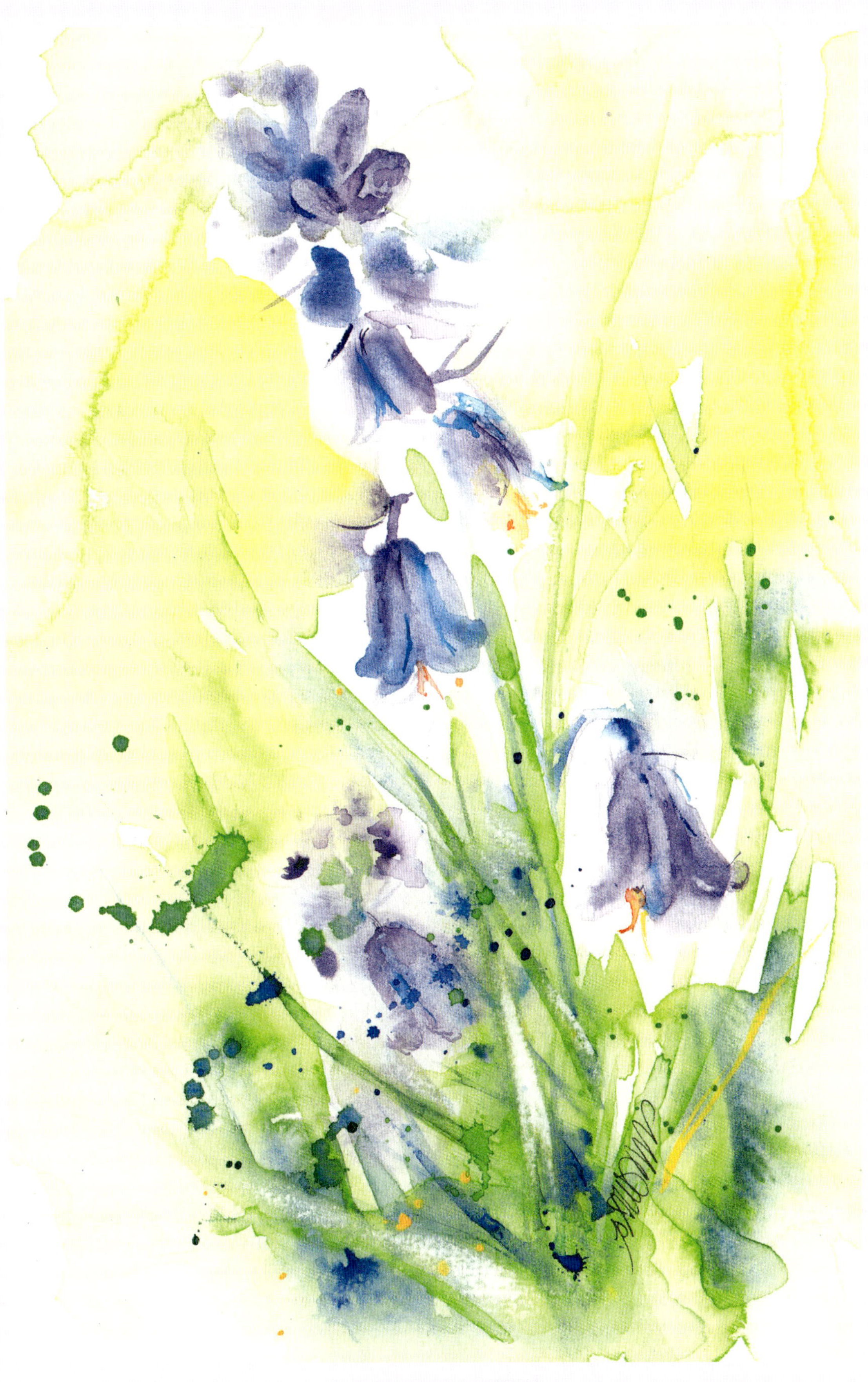

THE FINISHED PAINTING
18 x 26cm (7 x 10¼in)

What next?

Bluebells thrive in woodlands – and happily these beautiful flowers are protected so you'll find yourself getting a hefty fine should you dig them up. Much better to paint them from photographs or from life, so you and everyone else can continue to enjoy them.

For these variations, I have used similar techniques to those in the project – you'll spot lots of spattering and deliberately created backruns. However, you can also see that instead of leaving light areas, I have opted to skip around the white paper in areas to keep some highlights; along with some subtle touches of white acrylic ink (see page 78).

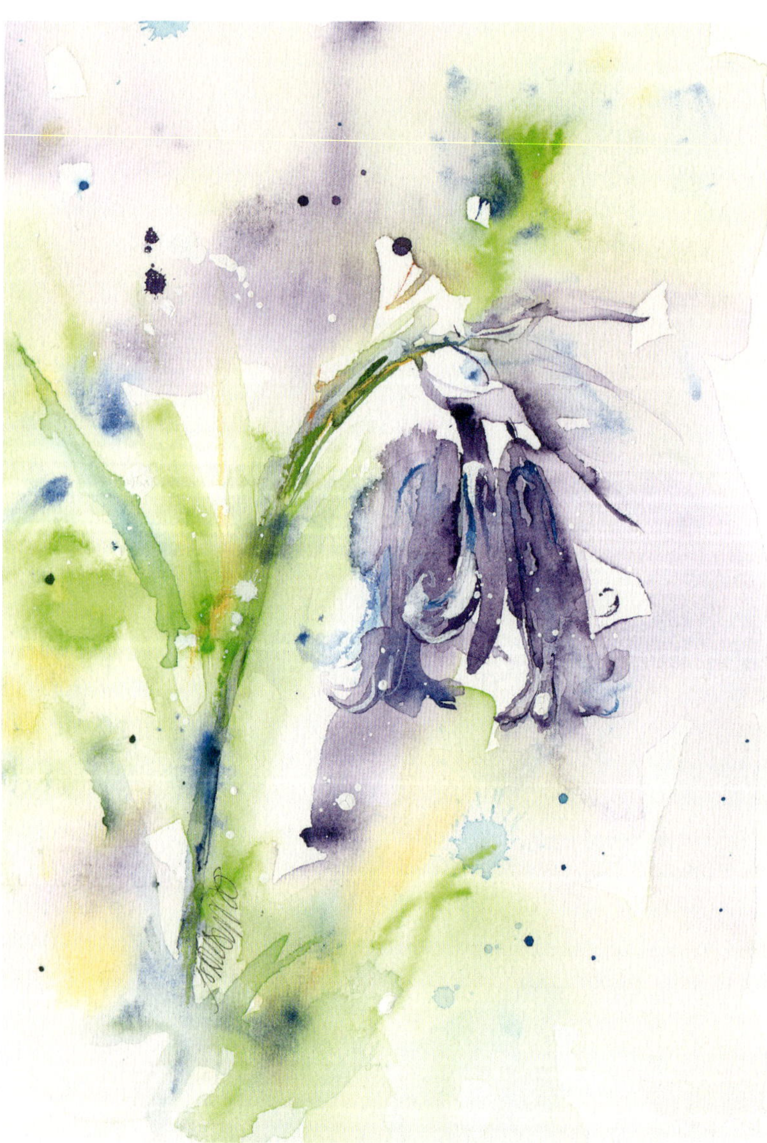

BLUEBELLS

18 x 25.5cm (7 x 10in)

A simpler take on a lone bluebell, here I have added spots of the same blue-purple into the background wet into wet, to suggest more bluebells surrounding the subject.

Within my paintings, I often set off the petals by using complementary colours. In the preceding project, for example, I used yellow touches in the background, as it's the complementary colour to purple.

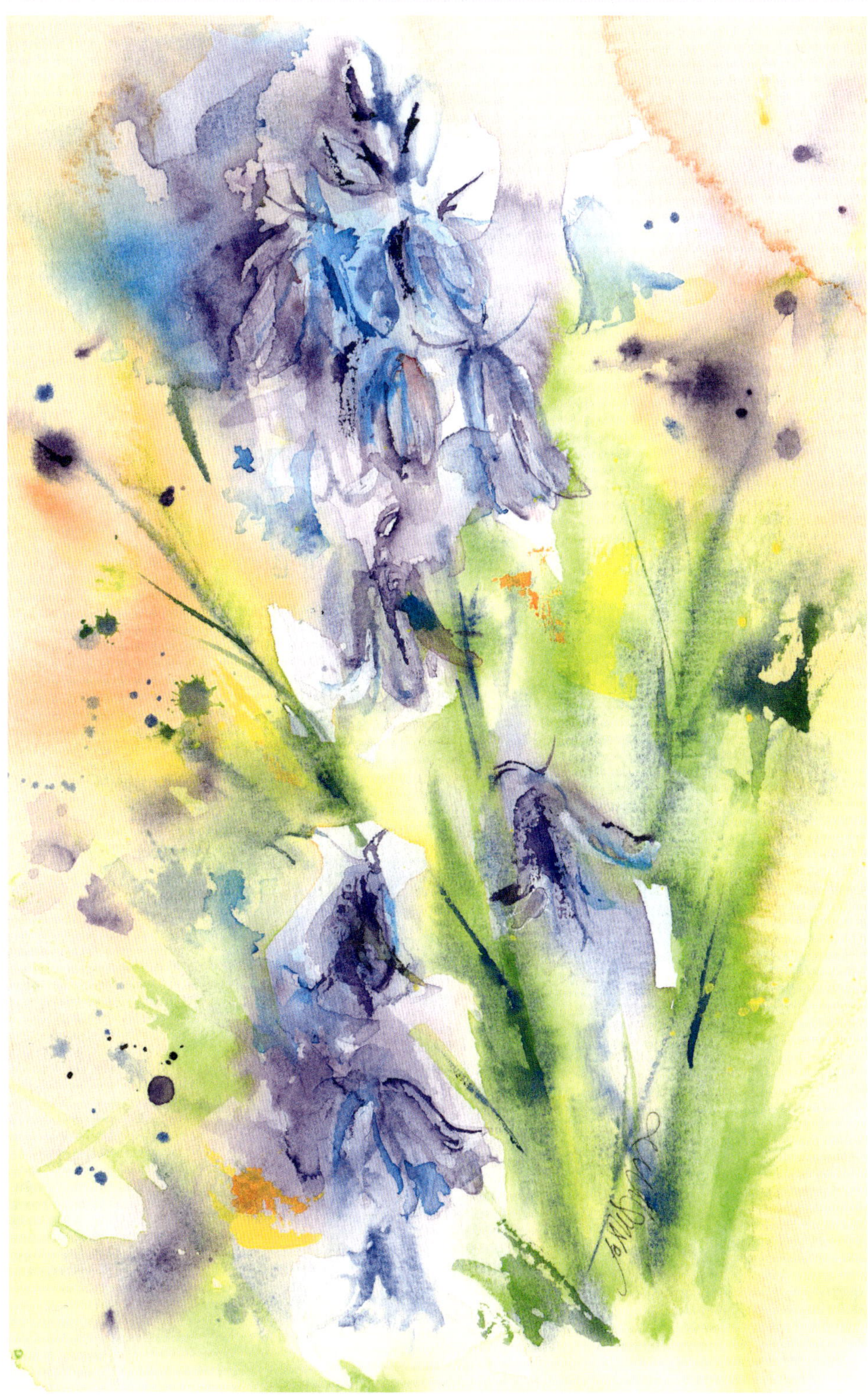

BLUEBELLS
18 x 25.5cm (7 x 10in)

Very similar in composition to the project, here I've taken the detail
just a little further, and used a slightly deeper, warmer background
for added contrast.

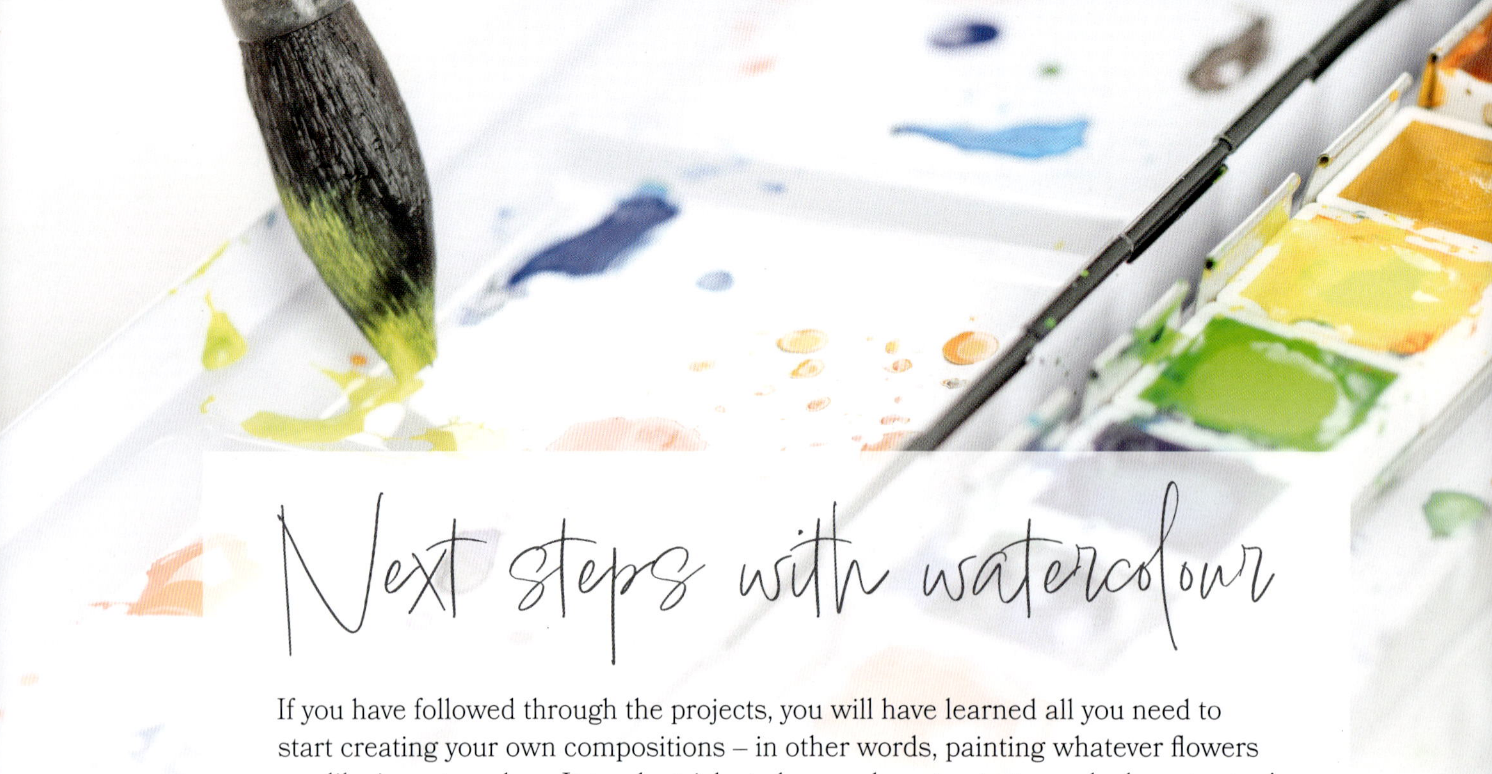

Next steps with watercolour

If you have followed through the projects, you will have learned all you need to start creating your own compositions – in other words, painting whatever flowers you like in watercolour. It can be tricky to know where to start – and where to stop!

The following pages collect together some hints and advice for pure watercolour work, look at some examples of finished pieces, and give you some ideas for where to go and what to try before we carry on into mixed-media work.

Make your painting for you

It is entirely up to you to take out or put into your painting anything you wish. This is the artist in you coming out. What is in front of you does not have to be definitive; this is your piece so improve, enhance, and experiment as you see fit. This is how we can progress.

Yes, it is true that we can learn from other artists, but one size does not fit all, and it would become monotonous should we all be the same. I usually prefer a simple background and lots of bright colours, these constitute my happy painting place – you should paint what makes you happy, too.

Colours and imagination

As mentioned earlier, I often change the colours in front of me if I think it will better suit my painting. Sometimes I will use contrasting pairs – those paints that sit opposite on the colour wheel - to help a painting to pop. When painting a purple flower, for example, a yellow background will help the purple stand out, even if in real life the background is deep black shadow. Other complementary pairs are red and green; and blue and orange.

Sometimes, however, I will deviate from the natural colours and add a pop of red to bring the area forward: hot colours appear to advance, while cool colours recede.

Tip

If you like your painting and are enjoying the process, this is really what matters. If others like it too, treat that as an added bonus.

Where and when to stop

A question I am frequently asked is 'how do I know when my painting is finished? This is a difficult question for artists, because we are probably all guilty of overworking a painting at some point, fiddling away when it was at its best some hours before! The truth is, we are seldom happy with our own results but one thing I have learned for sure is that other people will be fonder of our results than we will ever be, because we humans are just so self-critical.

If you find you often overwork your paintings, try taking photographs of the painting throughout the process and then look back through them to see if an earlier one was where you should have stopped. Once you've done this a few times, you will get better at knowing when to stop. If it is any consolation, even the experts overdo paintings. They might not admit it, but rest assured, you are not alone!

Below, from left to right:

UNDERWORKED

Not enough detail has been captured at this stage.

END STATE

This stage strikes a good balance between showing the detail of the flower while keeping the painting feeling spontaneous. It's a good place to stop.

OVERWORKED

In adding more detail, the piece has lost some of its freshness, and the stronger tones make it seem too bold and brash.

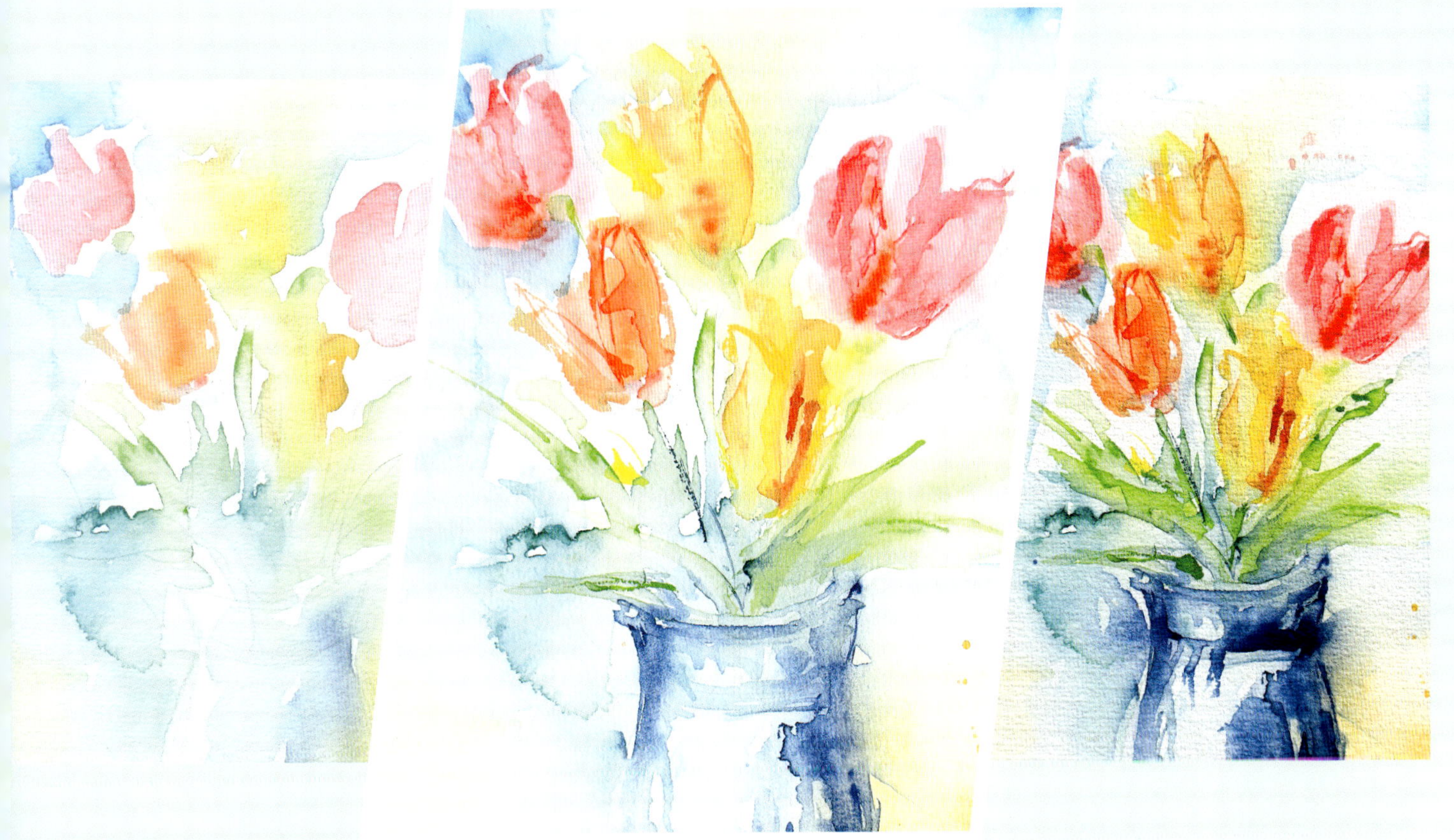

First aid for flowers

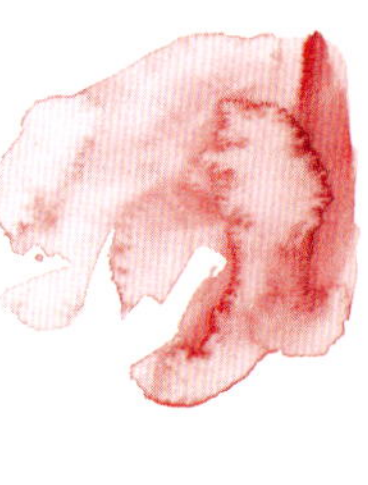

So, I hold my hands up – I've got paintings so very wrong and on so many occasions. In my defence, your honour, I am only human.

When painting, we will inevitably make mistakes and misjudge things; we take steps backwards then suddenly leap ahead, and then go backwards yet again – and while this can be very frustrating, it is also completely normal. I liken it to driving, some days I can parallel park to perfection, other days are not so good. Things happen: we get tired, stressed, hungry… and all of these things can contribute to how we perform.

What to do

Please don't be disheartened if a painting isn't going how you want it to. There is no need to finish any painting in one sitting. If you feel frustrated, walk away and come back to it another day, well-rested and in a better frame of mind. Fresh eyes and a clear head will help you to assess things.

Some paintings can be improved using some of the techniques later in the book (see pages 70–142). There have been countless times where I have managed to rescue a painting with the application of another medium – I have added ink, acrylic paint, charcoal, pen, pencil, collage, pastels, watercolour pencils… the list goes on.

Focus on the lesson, not the mistake

More important than being able to 'save' a painting is the fact that each time we try to remedy a problem, we concentrate on learning how to improve upon the mistake and avoid it next time.

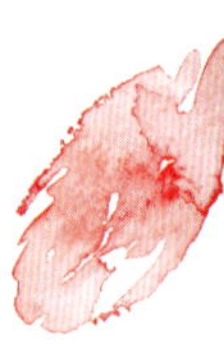

By stopping, taking some time to consider, and returning with experiment and learning in mind, you will build skills to use in the future – whether or not you can fix the perceived error in this particular painting.

None of us is perfect, and this is absolutely fine. I still get things wrong even after twenty-five years of practising. Shown opposite is a 'perfect' example of a painting which I felt I had ruined, and which I later managed to rescue. Only small adaptations were made, but even so, I felt one hundred per cent happier.

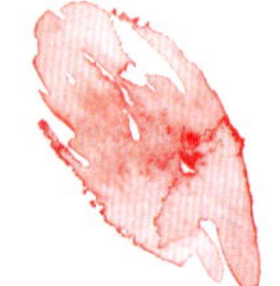
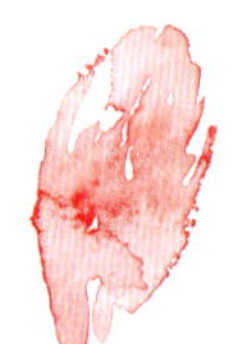
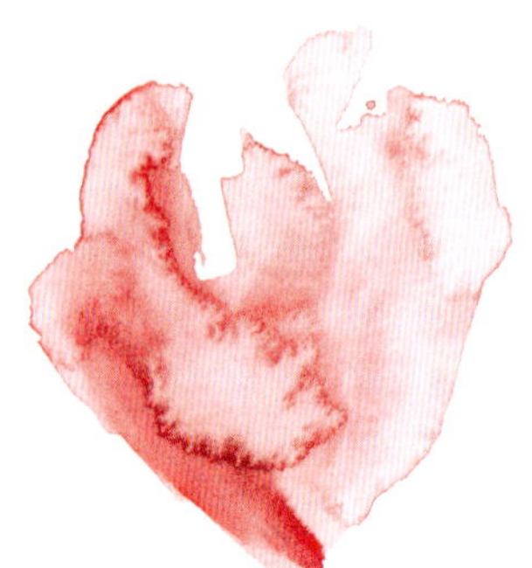
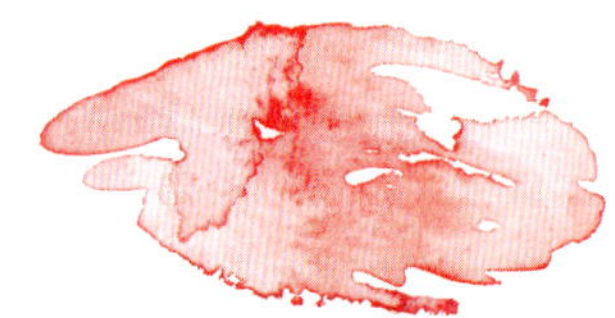

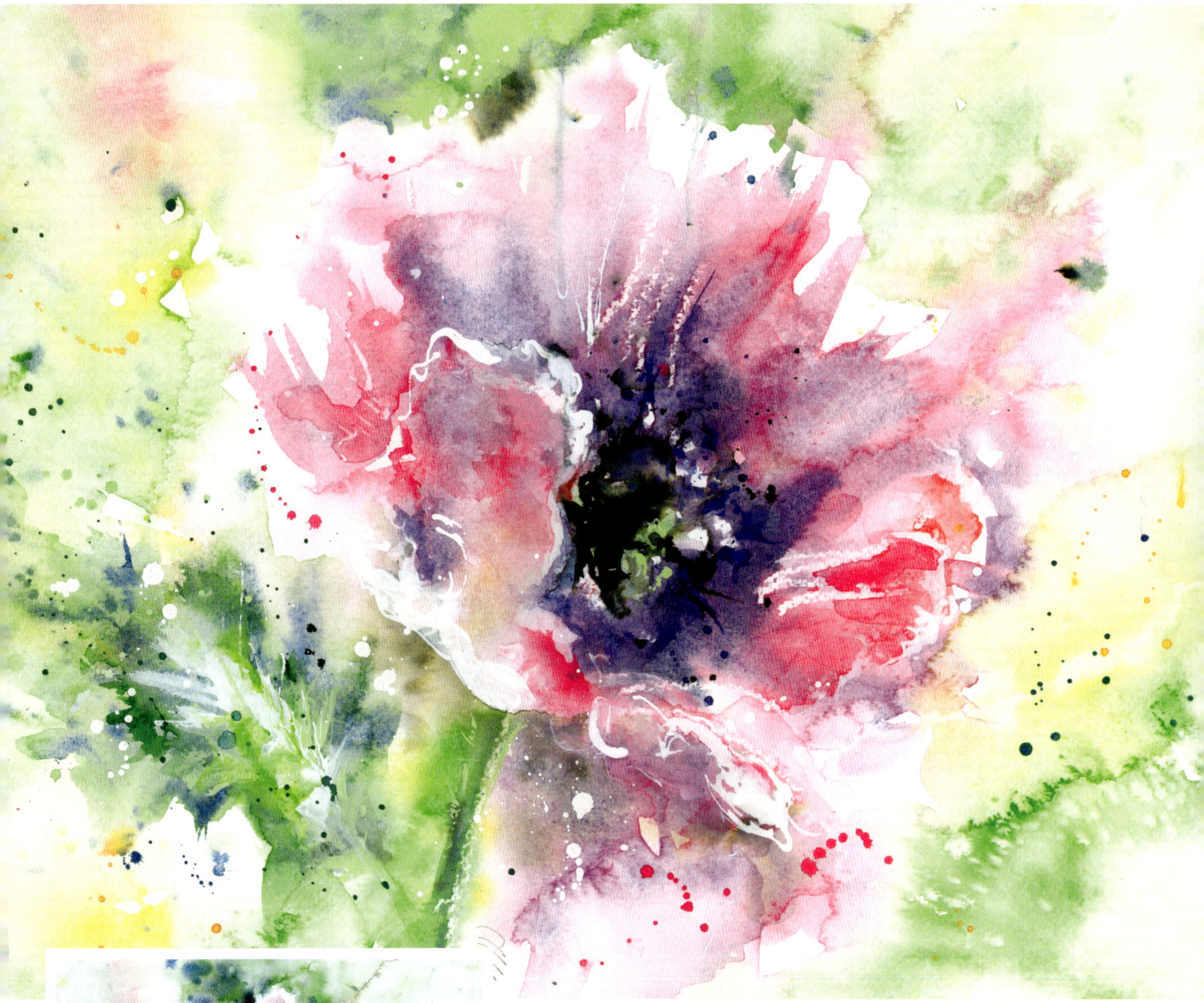

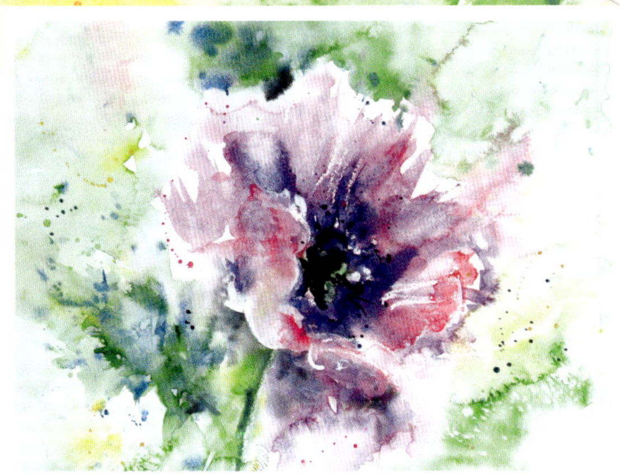

ORIENTAL POPPY
40.5 x 30.5cm (16 x 12in)

Made with watercolour, ink and wax resist plus salt, the finished piece (see left) was okay – but just okay. Even though I framed it, I kept looking at it and thinking it was a little dark in places. Eventually, some twelve months later, I took it from the frame, secured it back onto the board with brown gummed tape and lifted out a little colour here and there (see page 106). I lightened areas with the use of white acrylic ink (see page 78) applied directly, and also mixed watercolour paint with white acrylic ink to brighten some of the pinks and greens to freshen things up.

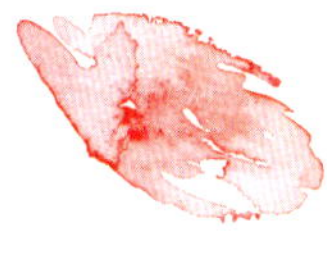

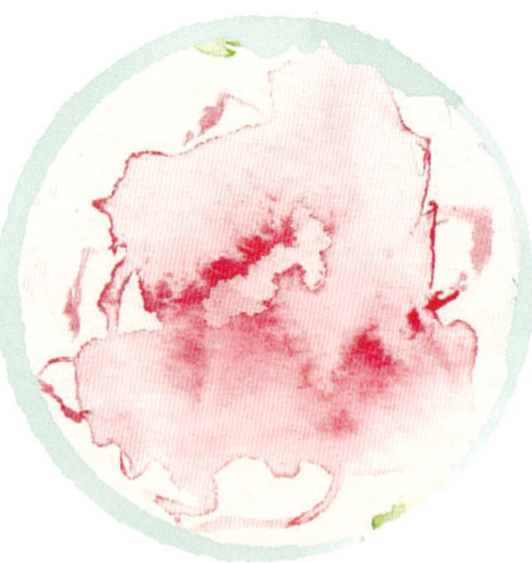

BACKRUNS

The texture on this rose is almost completely made up of backruns – the frilly texture that forms is almost impossible to paint without looking laboured – but the backruns do it for you!

Painting *Mother's Day Bouquet from Geri*

This painting is a perfect example of how one person's problem is another person's gold. So often artists get frustrated with backruns – sometimes called cauliflowers or blooms. Not me, no – I think they are blooming marvellous. In fact, they help easily create some of the petal and leaf shapes in my loose and lively approach to painting. The texture and patterns they naturally produce take the work out of detail.

Not only do I embrace any backruns which may accidentally occur, I will often deliberately encourage them to form by dropping clean water into an already drying wash.

If a backrun appears somewhere where you really would have preferred it not to, place one of the other elements over this – not to try to cover the whole backrun necessarily, but to distract the eye a little. Often what you see as an error, no one even notices – until you tell them.

Often I ask my learners the question 'where do we start?' their answer is most often 'with the background?' – I seldom do this – I mostly begin with the subject. Dare to be different.

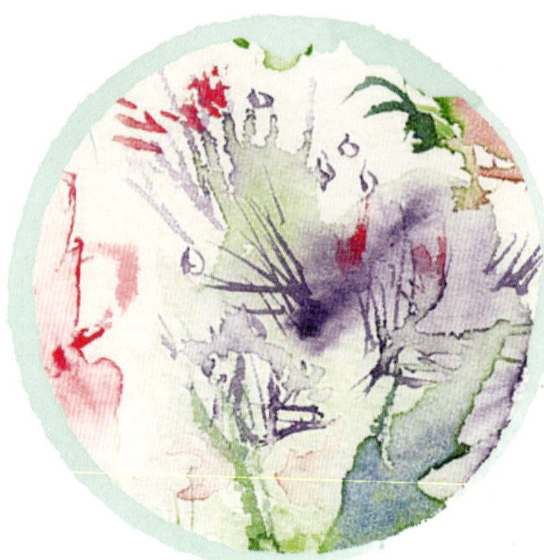

IMPLIED DETAIL

Fine marks were made with the tip of the rigger brush to suggest detail over looser underlying marks.

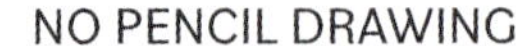

NO PENCIL DRAWING

The detail shows where I went straight in with a brush to keep this nice and loose.

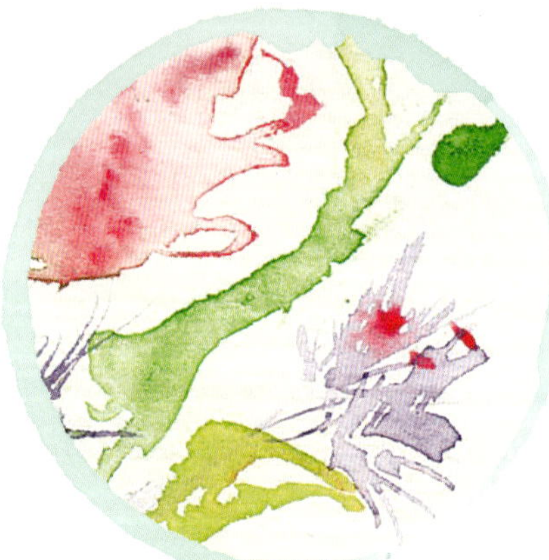

STEMS

I dropped clean water into this area when the green paint was partially dry – this created interesting textures.

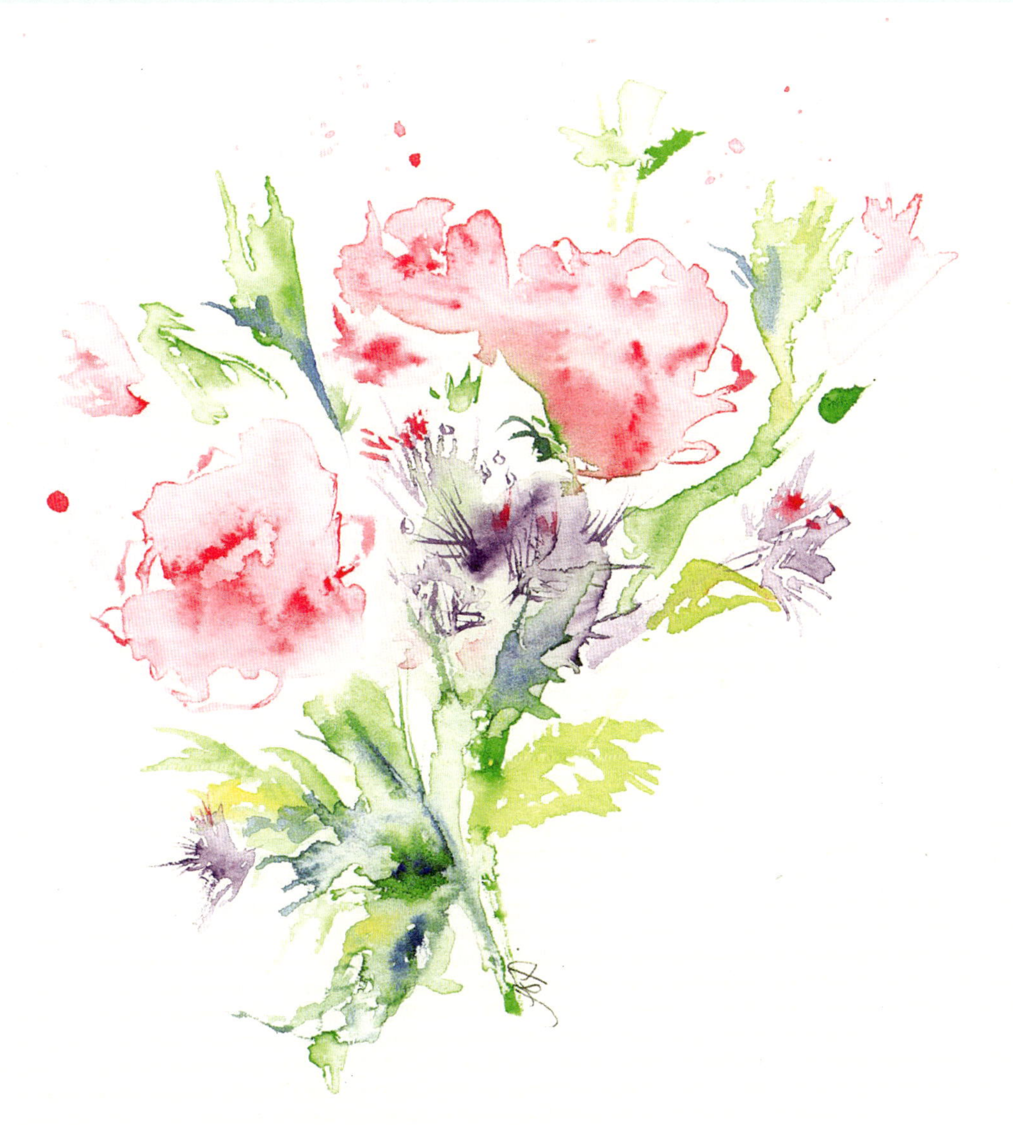

MOTHER'S DAY BOUQUET FROM GERI
15 x 15cm (6 x 6in)

The finished result is lovely and fresh. I opted to omit the
vase that these were in so as not to detract from such a
beautiful spray of flowers. I made sure to leave plenty of white
space around the bouquet and didn't think that it required a
background colour at all.

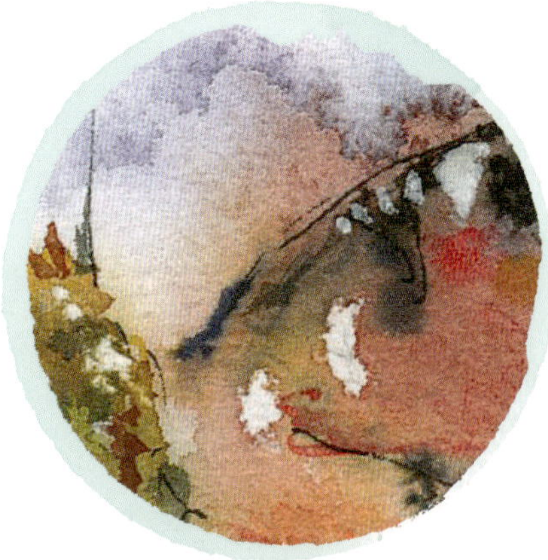

MOVEMENT

I wanted to create a sense of movement within this painting. Using plenty of water and encouraging colours to bleed outwards helped with this.

Painting *Peacock Butterfly On Blackthorn Blossom*

There's something about the purity of white flowers, they are so pretty. The mass of tiny white flowers is a big reason why I love blackthorn blossom – and I also love the wildlife it attracts. The flowers of the blackthorn produce nectar and are a valuable food source for the equally beautiful peacock butterfly.

I like to include insects alongside my flower paintings, and try to make them appropriate to the flower. In particular, the jewel-like colours of butterflies and other insects often mean they beautifully complement the petals of the flowers.

This mixed-media painting involved combinations of many techniques detailed elsewhere in the book, including wet into wet, wet on dry, wax resist, pen and wash, inks and salt.

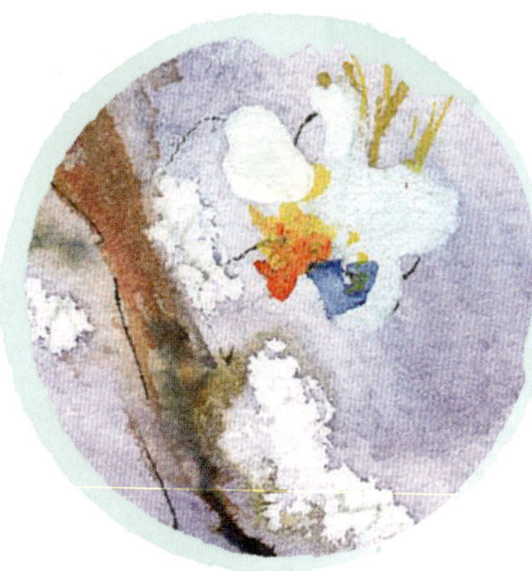

TWO WHITES

A good example of how there's more than one way to produce white – here you can see both wax resist and white ink giving subtly different results.

WET ON DRY

Here is a close-up of the peacock wing patterns where I have dared to go darker for more contrast and vibrancy. The underlying red colour was quite light, so I layered bolder red over the top wet on dry for added 'pop'.

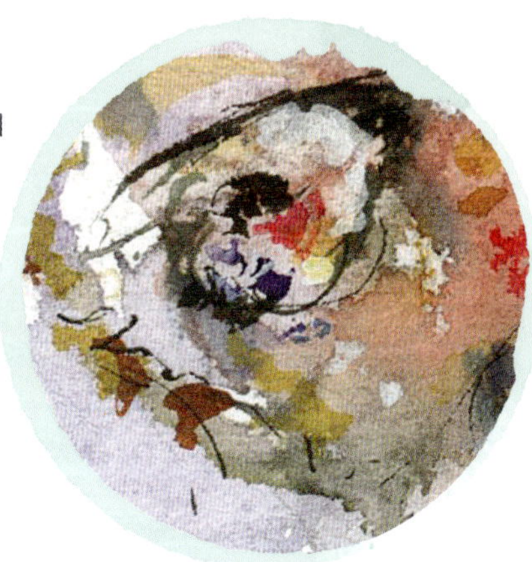

PEN AND WASH

Black Parker ink was used for fine detail – the sharp lines on the butterfly bring the soft watercolour into focus.

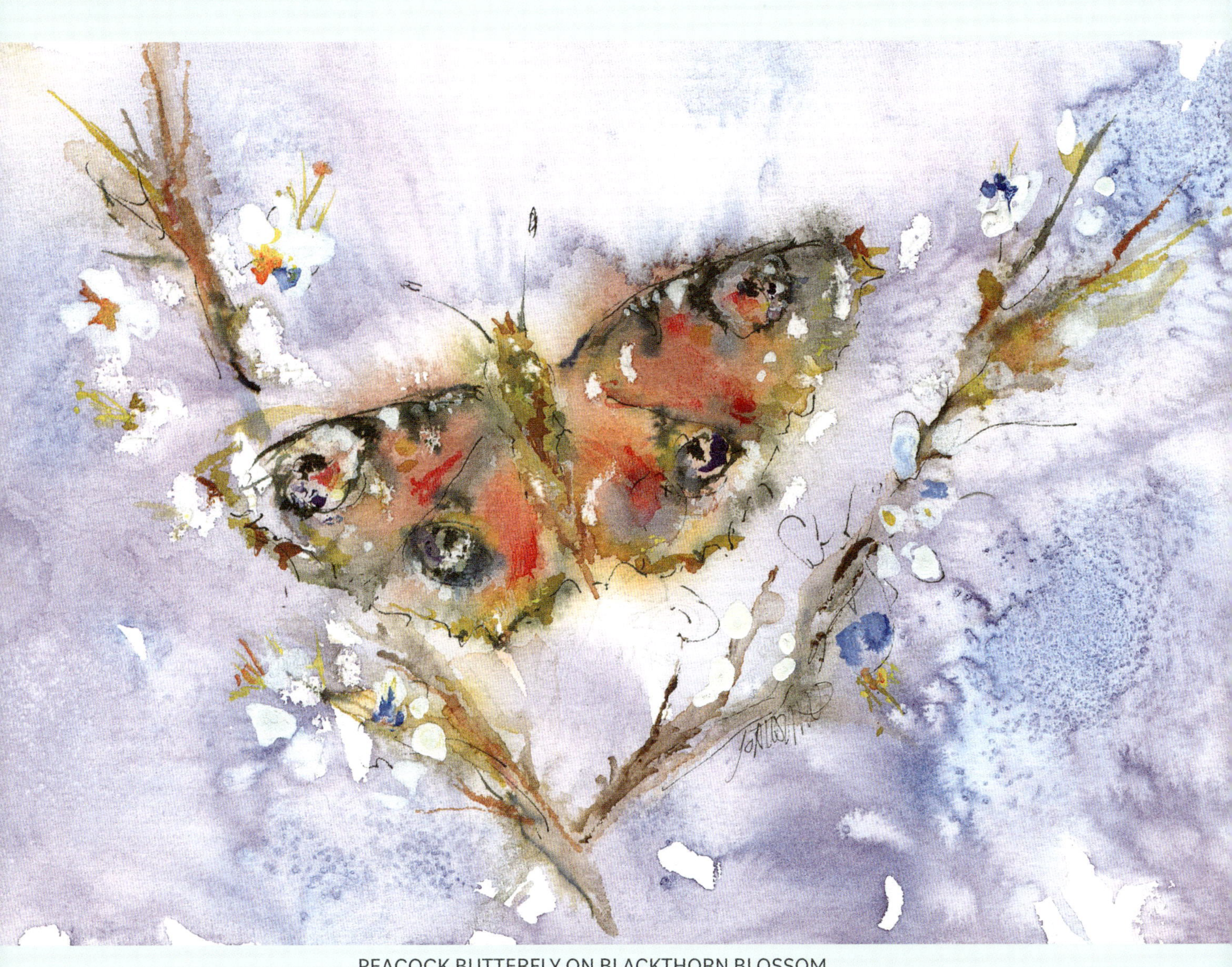

PEACOCK BUTTERFLY ON BLACKTHORN BLOSSOM
25.5 x 18cm (10 x 7in)

Watercolour
& beyond

There are thousands and thousands of different flowers; far too many to try to cover in just one book – though as you'll see, I've tried! This part of the book aims to give you lots of ideas and teach you new techniques, with which you can play, experiment and use to paint whichever flower you particularly love.

Over these pages you'll find exercises that show you how to include new media like inks, wax and metal leaf in your painting, along with ideas and inspiration for using and combining the techniques explained earlier in new and interesting ways.

Of course, if you wish, you can simply pick your favourite flower from the list and have a go at it exactly as described by following the steps.

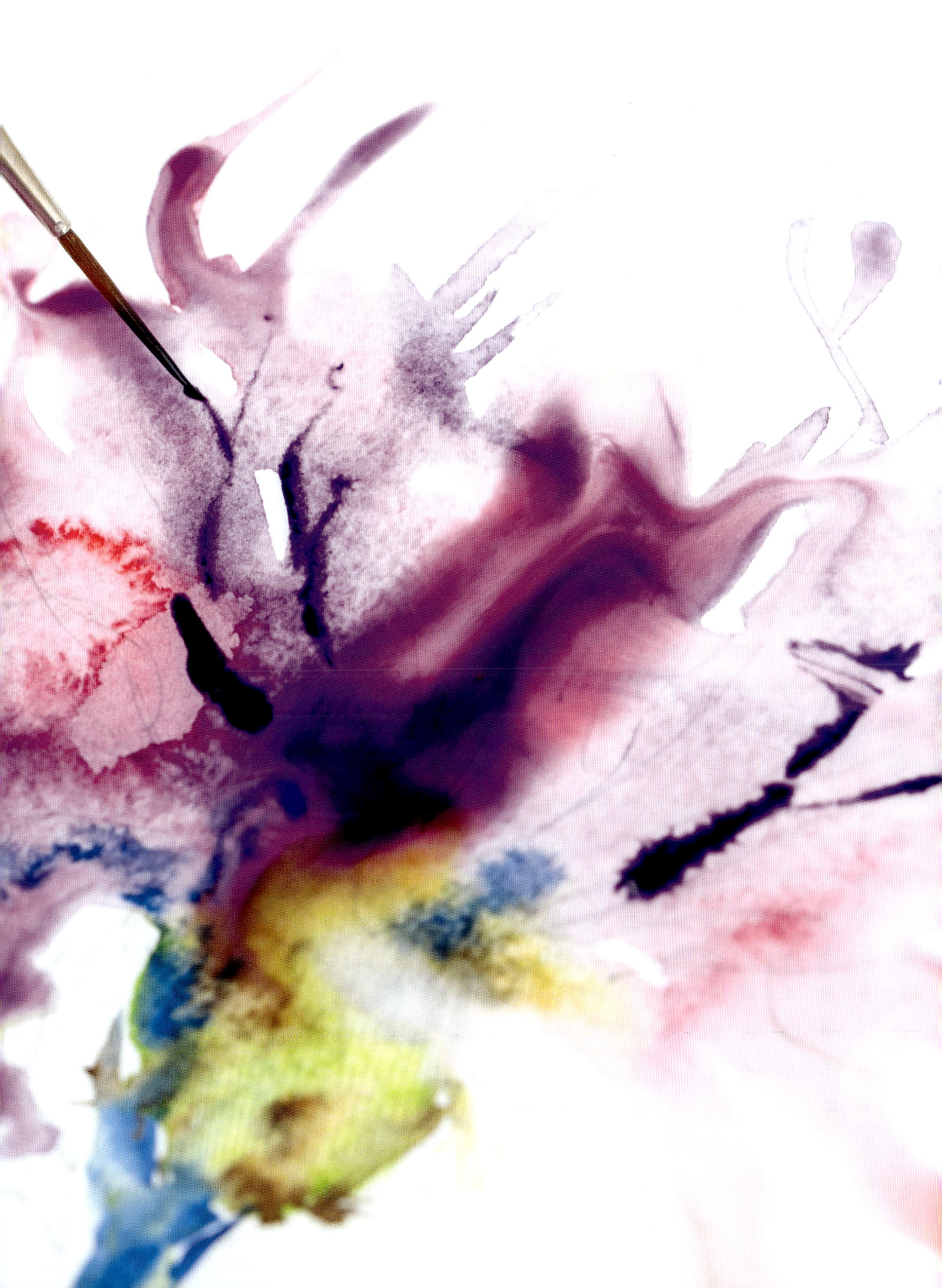

Daisy

I have to start this part of the book with my favourite flower, which can be found everywhere on the planet except Antarctica. Believe it or not, they are edible, too!

When starting out, it can be difficult to work out how to paint white flowers – the trick is often to let the paper do the work.

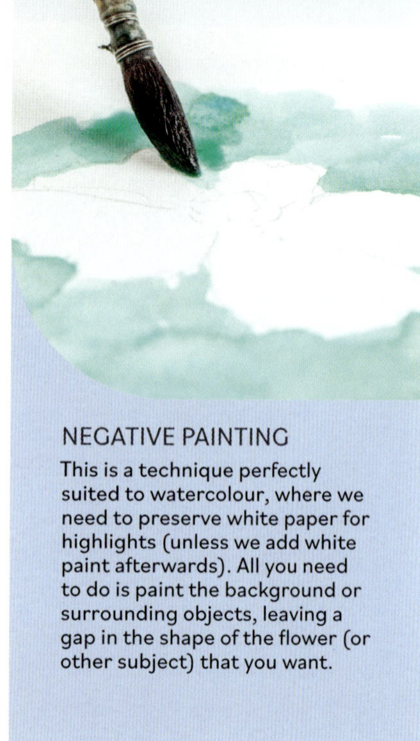

NEGATIVE PAINTING

This is a technique perfectly suited to watercolour, where we need to preserve white paper for highlights (unless we add white paint afterwards). All you need to do is paint the background or surrounding objects, leaving a gap in the shape of the flower (or other subject) that you want.

Negative and positive painting

'Negative painting' is simply painting around an area to suggest its shape, rather than what might seem more familiar – painting the object itself. It's a great way to paint white flowers.

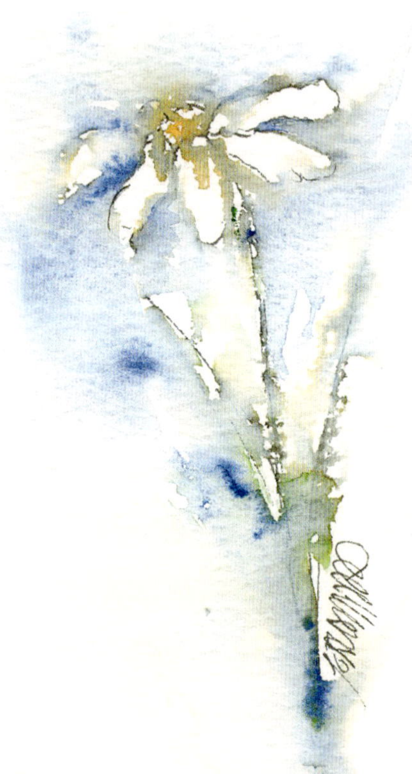

POSITIVE SHAPE

Here, the petals of the daisy have been drawn out with a watersoluble fineliner pen (see page 82), and filled in with some paint – though some white remains as highlight.

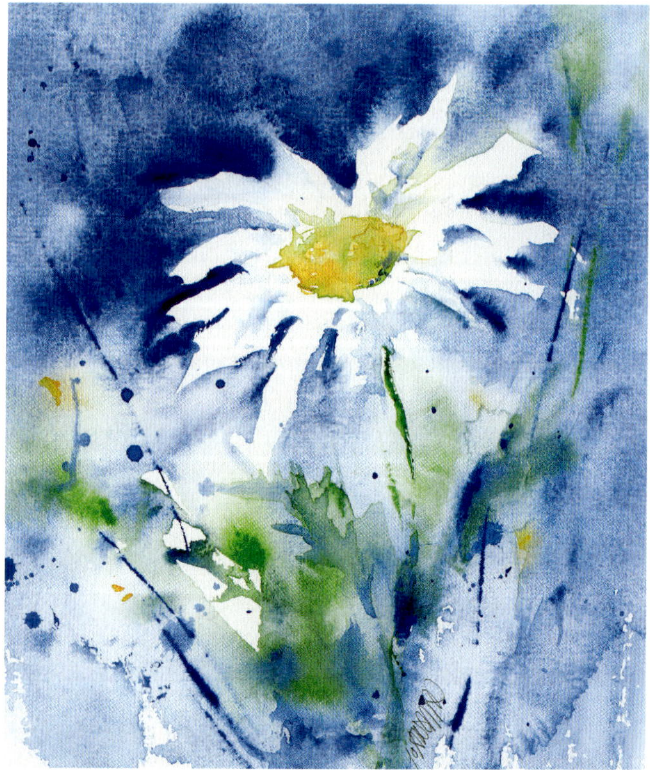

NEGATIVE SHAPE

The petals of this white daisy have to be left as pure white paper, so we use negative painting to add a rich blue background which allows the daisy shape to stand out.

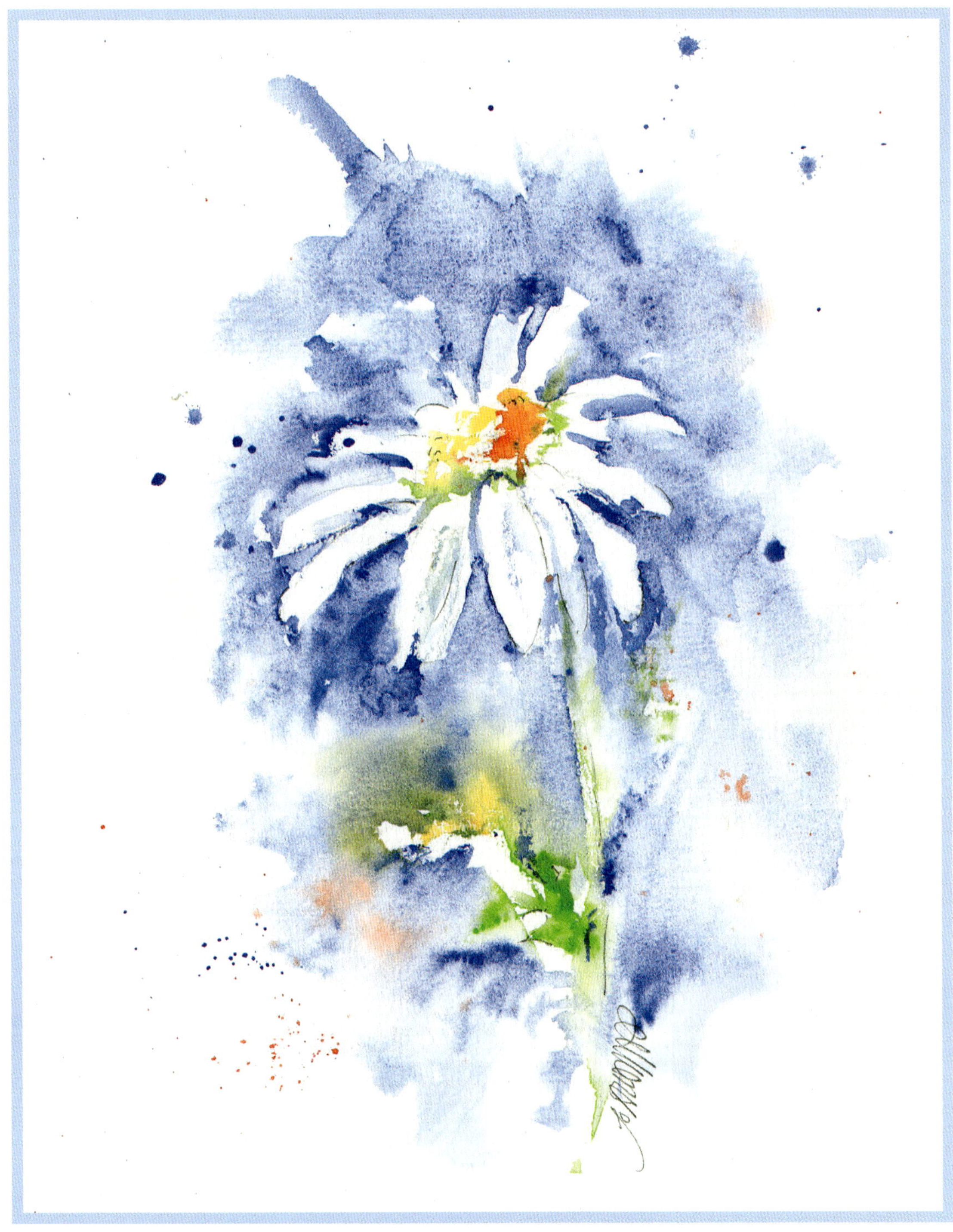

DAISY IN WATERCOLOUR AND PEN
18 x 25.5cm (7 x 10in)

Painted using the negative painting technique, this watercolour
also used an archival fineliner pen – a Sakura Pigma Micron 005
in black – to help add definition to the petals.

Painting in negative

For the freshest result, we should use the white of the paper rather than white paint, and one way to preserving it for white flowers is to carefully paint the background around the area, revealing the white flower.

You can then enhance the white flower with more detail, by painting the centre and any shadows with 'positive painting'.

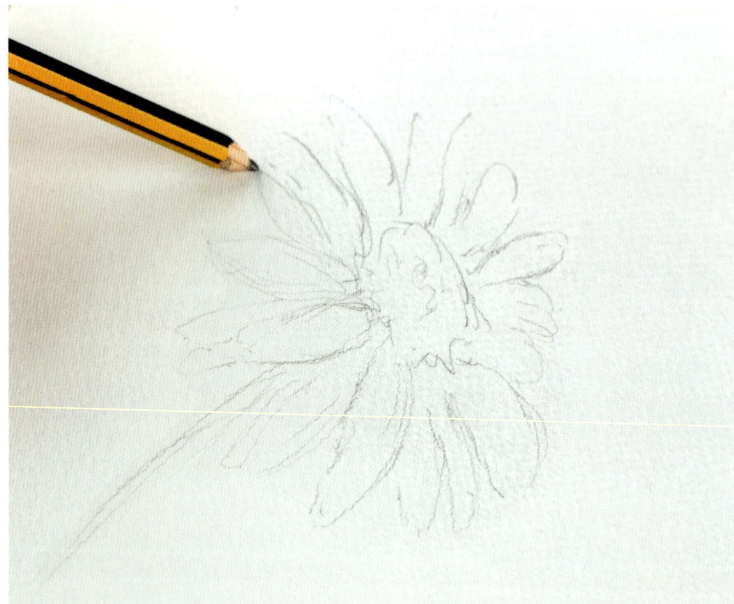

1 Draw in a light sketch with an HB pencil – it's easier to paint up to a line than it is to visualize the whole flower.

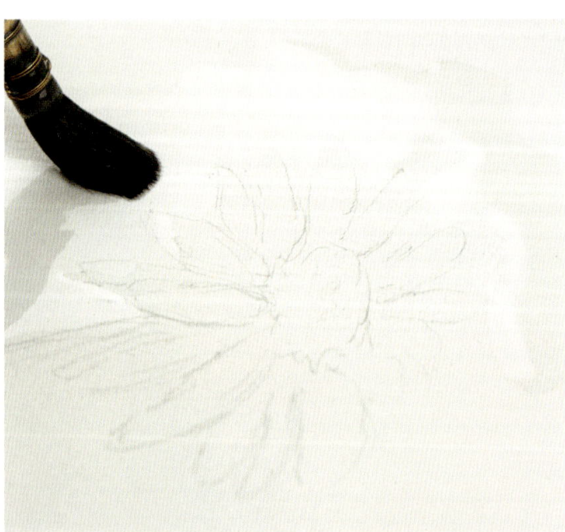

2 Use a large brush to wet all round the subject with clean water.

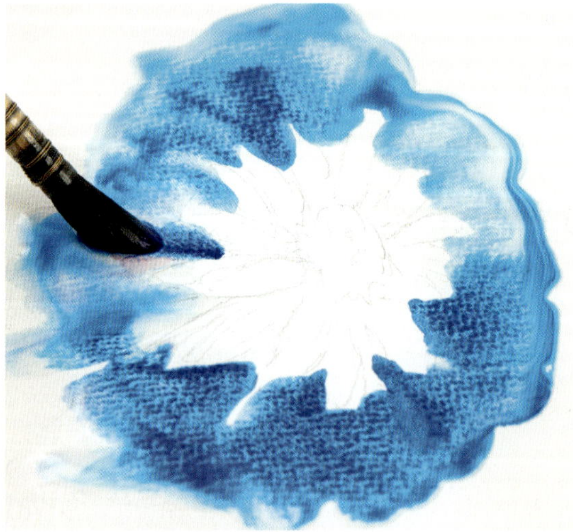

3 Drop French ultramarine and helio cerulean into the water – the paint will only flow where the paper is wet. Using strong colour will be most effective, as it will increase the contrast and make the negative area seem beautifully bright.

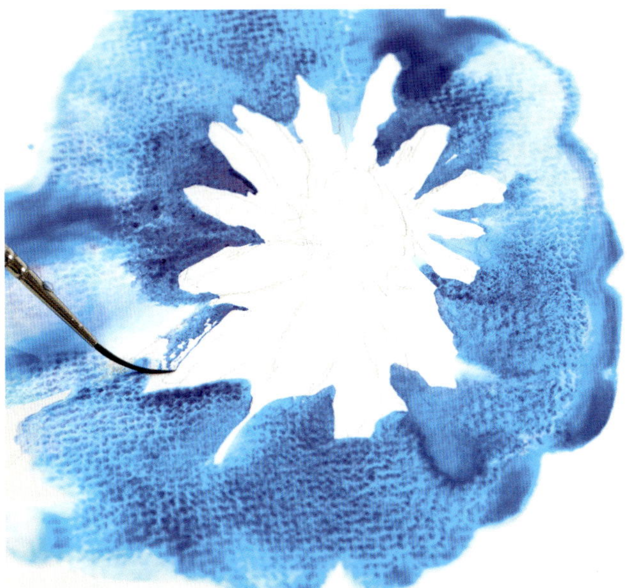

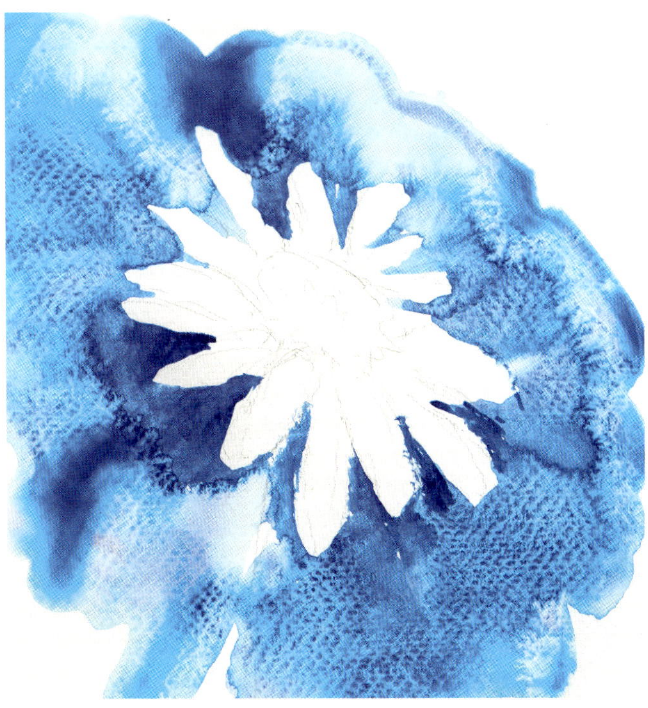

4 Swap to a small brush and use the tip to tidy the shape of the flower using the paint on the surface. Work into the spaces between some petals , but don't be too fussy – you want it to stay loose.

5 To strengthen areas and increase the tone near the edges, use the small brush to add more paint where necessary.

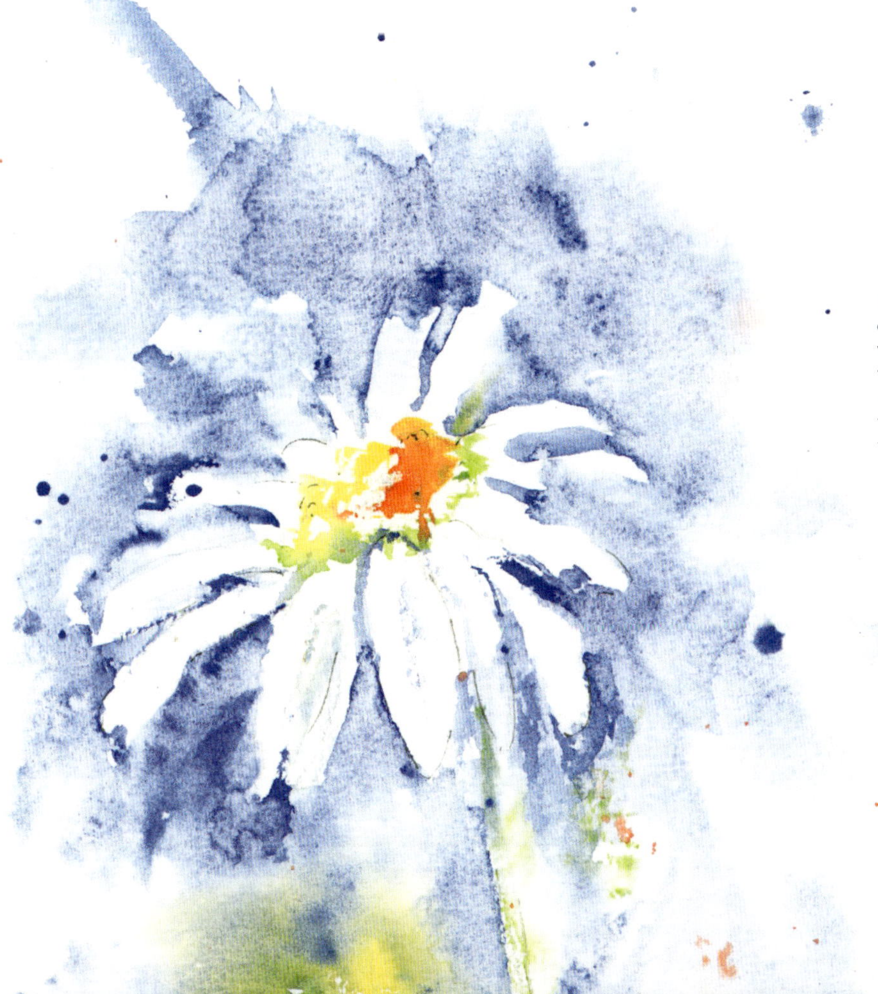

Don't be tempted to leave the resulting daisy shape pure white, however. It will look very flat and so we need to include different tones to create depth. Study a white flower like a daisy and count how many different tones are actually visible: you will spot more than you might have thought.

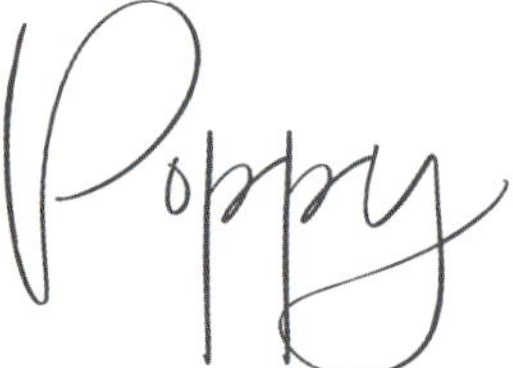

Poppy

I do love poppies, they are so cheerful and bright. For this painting I decided to use my vibrant vermilion red and then add a nice contrast to the centre, where I chose to use the black Parker ink. I was careful to avoid some areas of the paper to give some texture for the middle of the flower plus the petals.

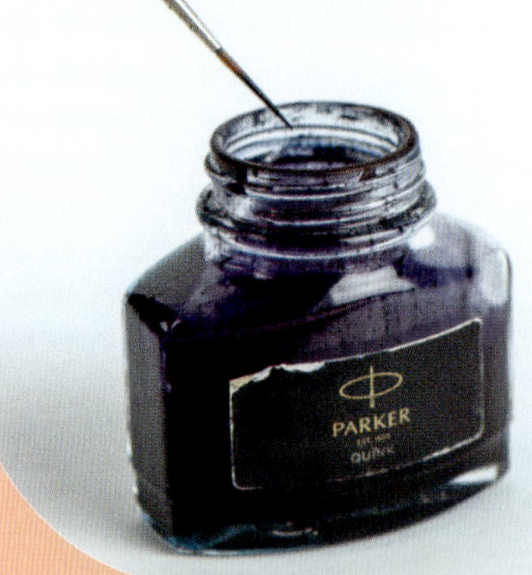

PARKER BLACK AND BLUE INKS

These I love, particularly the black which separates with water application into blues/yellow ochre tones.

Both are also excellent when I use my bleach technique (see page 98) to pull through, thus leaving a bright light mark.

Using Parker inks

I always use my best brushes with all inks as they help me to paint the shapes I need – I cannot reliably achieve this with a cheaper alternative. To avoid staining and ruining them while using inks, I ensure that I thoroughly and regularly wash them out.

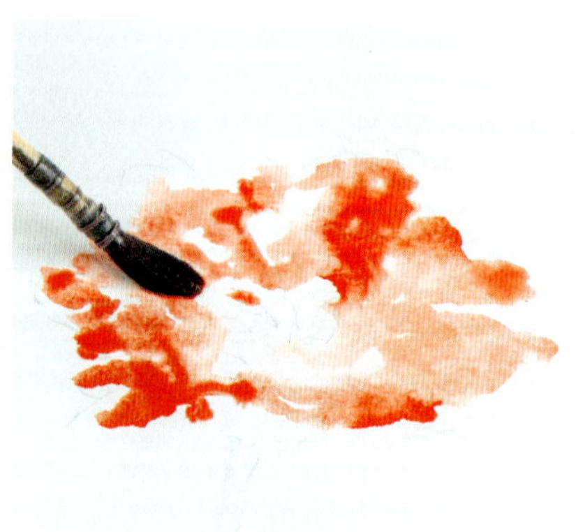

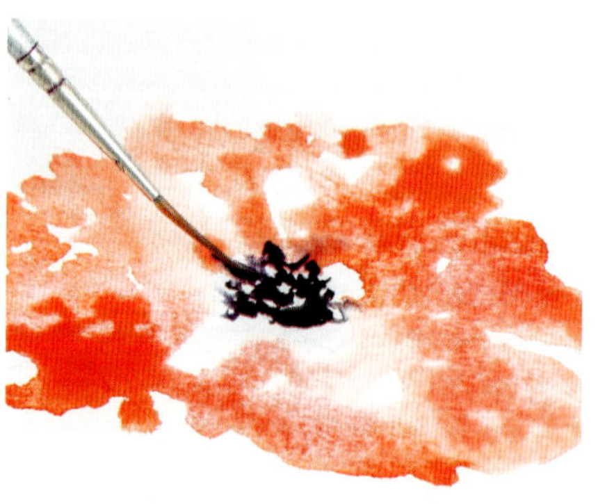

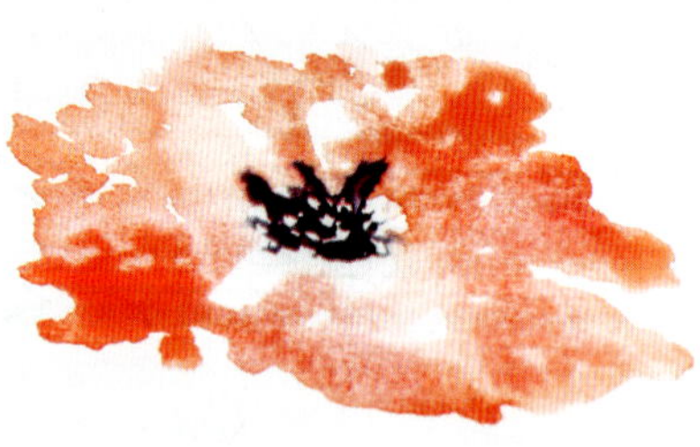

1 Use a large brush to wet the surface with clean water, then swap to the medium brush to paint in a loose poppy shape with vermilion and rose madder.

2 Use a small damp brush to add the ink to the centre, straight from the pot. The smaller brush gives you more control, and allows you to draw out a few fine marks for interest, wet into wet.

3 Avoid directing the shape too much; the ink is very strong and it is easy to overwhelm the watercolour.

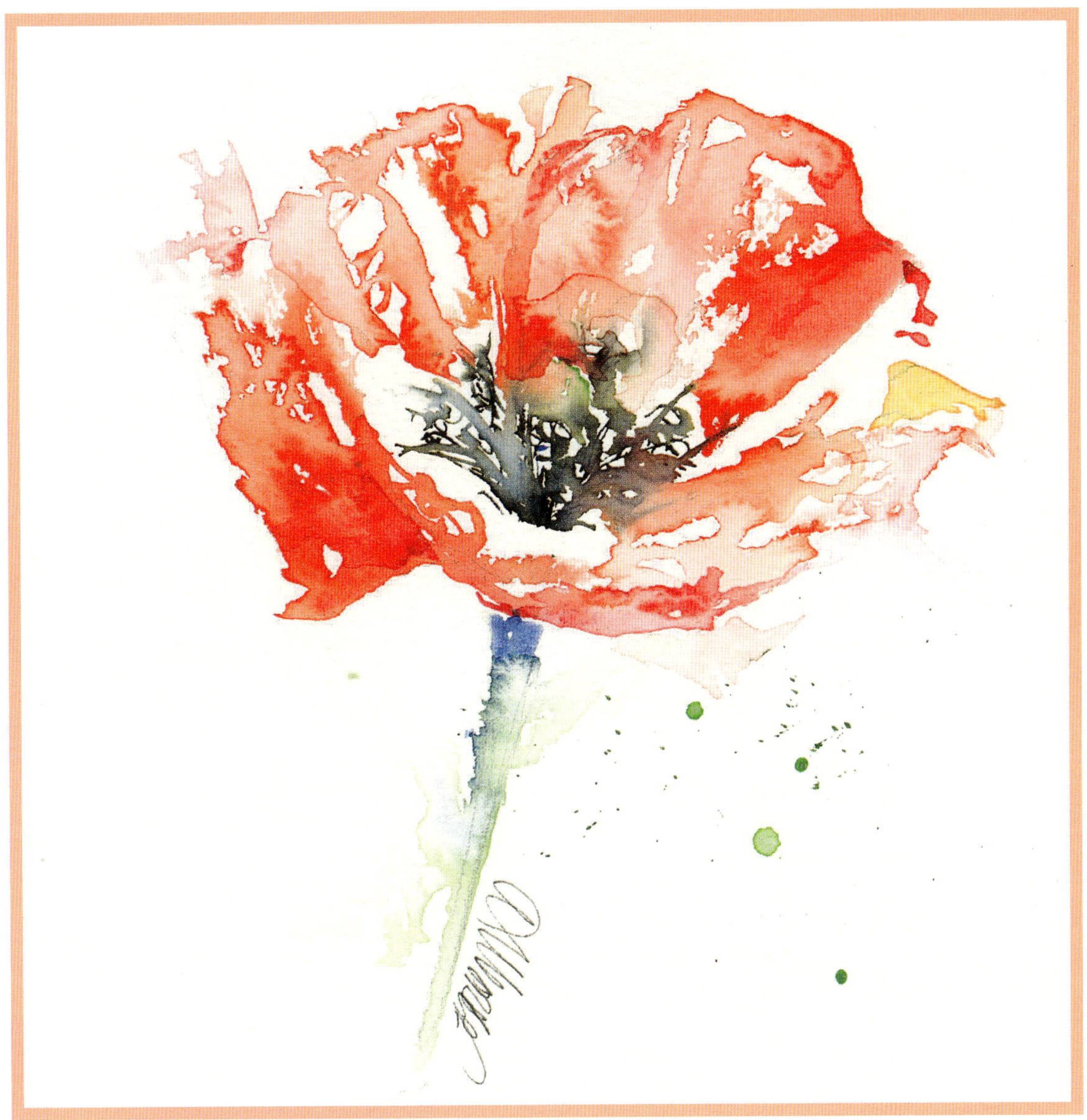

POPPY IN PARKER INK AND WATERCOLOUR
15 x 15cm (6 x 6in)

The poppy – not only a symbol for
Remembrance Day, but also used for morphine, a
powerful drug used as a painkiller.

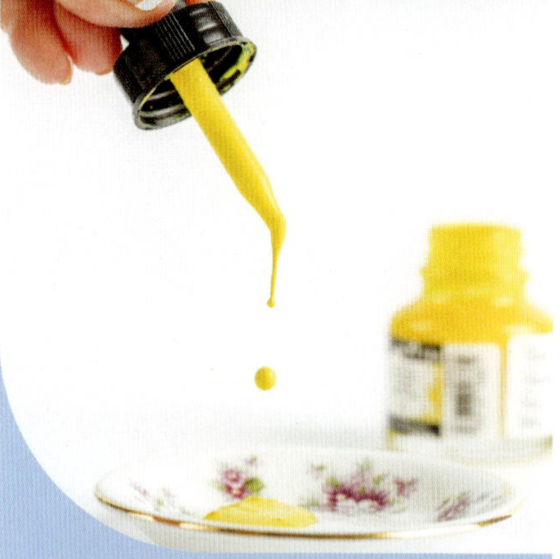

Cornflower

Commonly known as 'bachelor's button', cornflowers are pollinator-friendly and perfect for attracting butterflies, bees and other insects. The spreading rays of their flowerheads are a delight to paint.

Using acrylic inks

Acrylic inks create differing patterns to watercolours and so can make some exciting marks which cannot be achieved with watercolours alone.

Get to know what your inks do – make swatch tests to see which will react better with bleach, salt and so forth, so you can choose accordingly should you need specific results or patterns.

ACRYLIC INKS

I love the vibrancy of acrylic inks; the colours can really help a painting pop. Unlike Parker ink, which can be washed back to some extent, acrylic inks are waterproof once dry and will not lift out – once they are on, they are on.

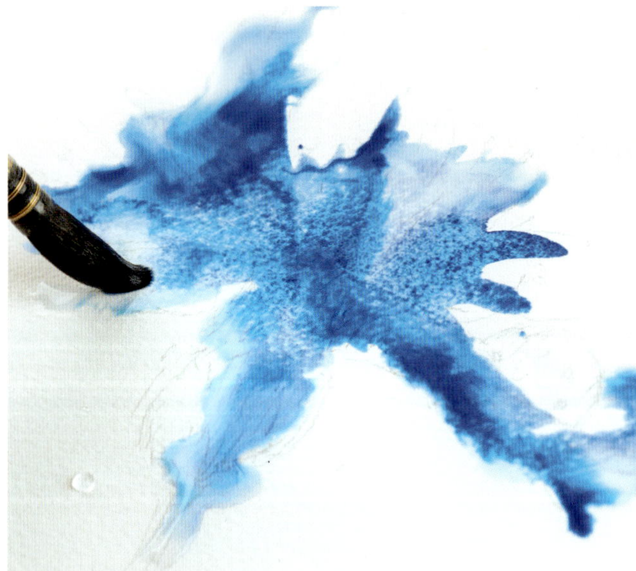

1 Make a light sketch of your cornflower and ladybird. Use the large brush to wet the surface – and don't worry about staying within the lines. Drop in French ultramarine and helio cerulean.

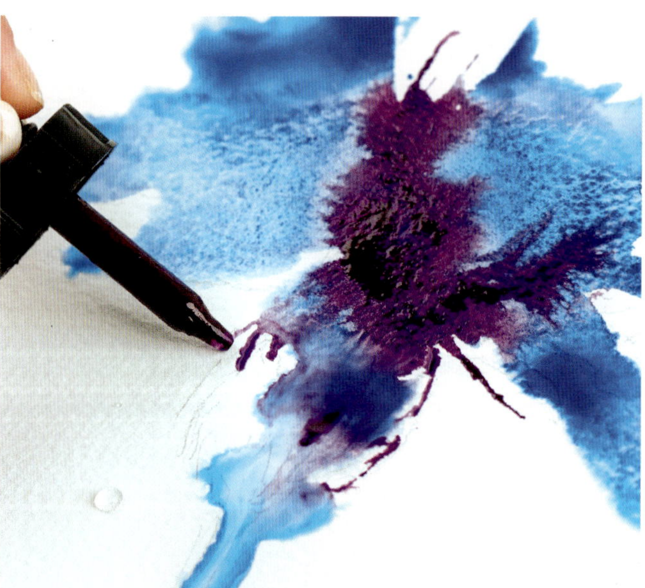

2 Apply purple lake acrylic ink using the dropper in the lid – you can use this to draw lines into the watercolour, or squeeze gently to apply larger areas. Pure ink applied like this will push wet watercolour aside, rather than mix.

Tip

When using acrylic inks, make sure you thoroughly wash out your brushes.

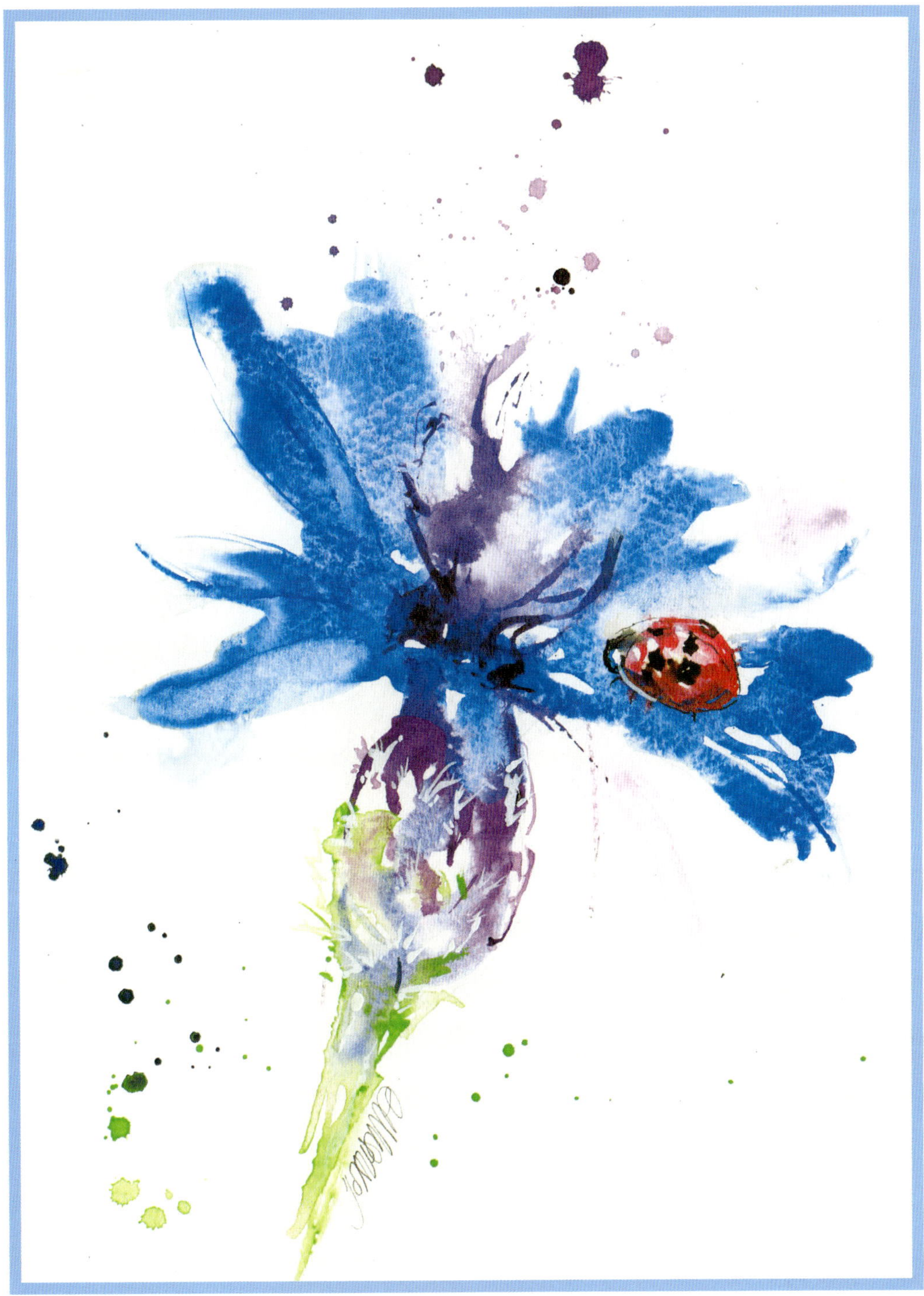

CORNFLOWER AND LADYBIRD
19 x 25.5cm (7½ x 10in)

I often use my acrylic inks alongside watercolours – as in this
example – but remain mindful as to what might occur, as they
are strong and permanent. To remedy an area covered in acrylic,
it needs to be covered; either with more inks or another opaque
medium, such as pastel.

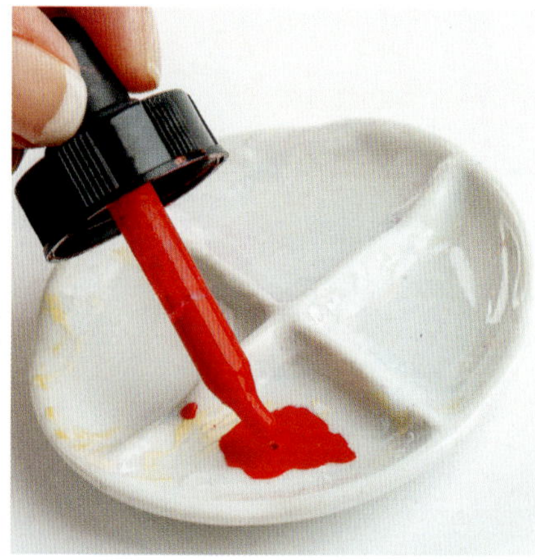

3 For more control, squeeze a little process magenta ink into a palette.

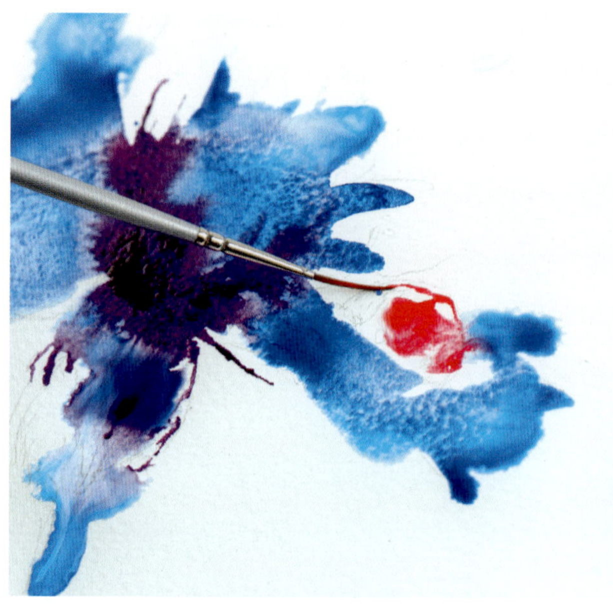

4 Use the small brush to apply the ink to the ladybird.

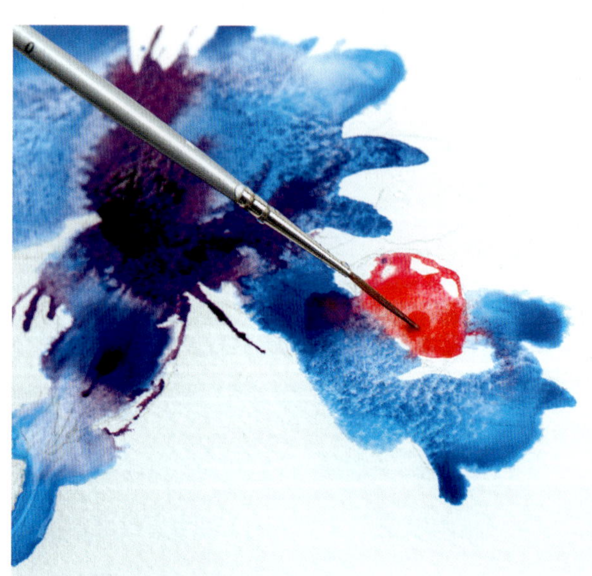

5 While the ink is wet, you can add watercolour to it, to change the colour a little. The combination of acrylic ink and watercolour will give you a result that cannot be lifted out once dry, but that will be more vibrant overall.

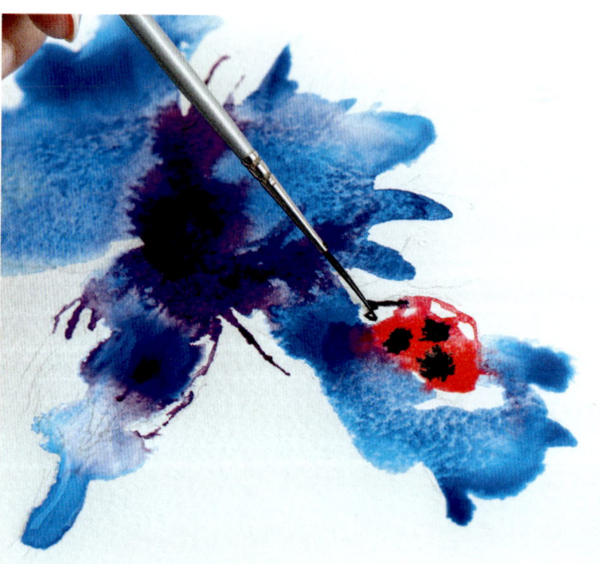

6 Pure ink can be applied. Parker Quink (calligraphy ink) can also be used alongside acrylic inks and watercolour – here applied to paint the head and spots of the ladybird.

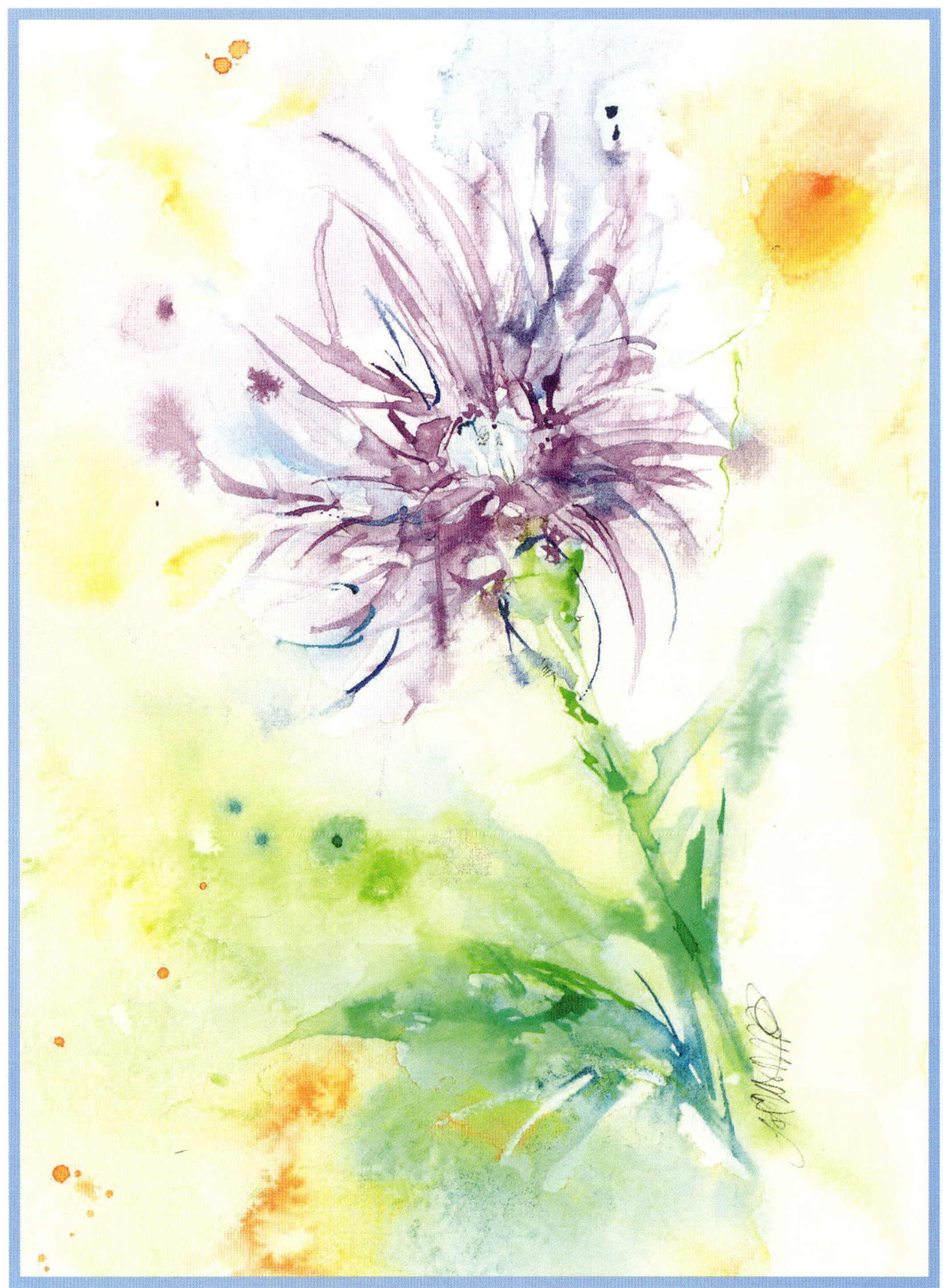

ELABORATE CORNFLOWER
12.5 x 20cm (5 x 8in)

Used alongside watercolours, the strength of inks can create high contrast easily. Sometimes I don't even plan when or where I'll use acrylic inks, and just add them to a painting along the way. This is fine so long as you understand the differing qualities of the inks you're using.

Tulips

Rather than taking all my watercolour materials with me for working outdoors, I often take just a few pens or pencils and a small pad. Among my favourites are my watersoluble pens which are available in so many vibrant colours – perfect for the clean, bright impact of tulips.

Using watersoluble pens

No paints, no water, no brushes, no water pots, these pens are convenient and great for creating quick references that you can take back to the studio and work up into roughs for future paintings. You can also use them for artworks in their own right, or alongside watercolour in a technique called line and wash.

Pen work cannot easily be corrected and it is best to lean into this rather than spend time being fussy. I usually go straight in with these pens - that is, with no outline pencil sketch beforehand. This helps to loosen up a picture and teaches you to work with what you have got: nothing needs to be perfect.

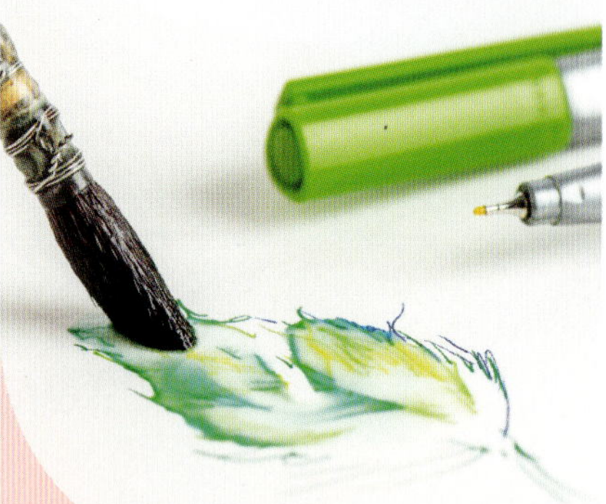

COLOURED PENS

Very convenient for sketching, coloured pens are portable and dry almost immediately. When buying yourself a set, look for watersoluble ones so that they will do two jobs for the price of one. I use Staedtler triplus fineliners.

There are a number of different ways you can use watercolour pens:

- Dry, to draw
- Wetted after sketch is finished
- Used to add detail to finished watercolour.

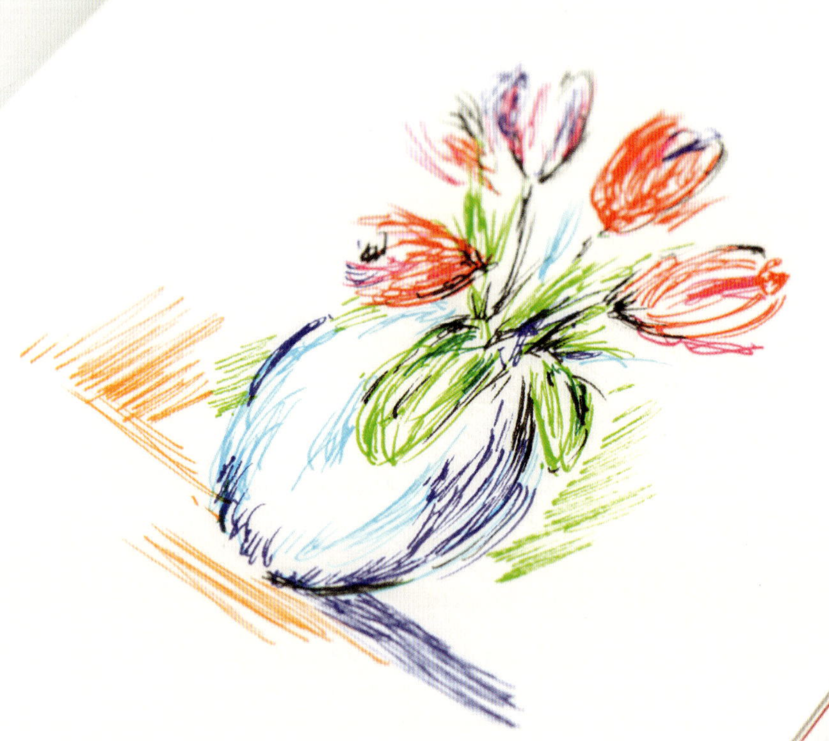

PURE PEN WORK

Traditional pen and wash, also called line and wash, involves drawing a pen drawing first, then adding colour using watercolour. With coloured pens, you can create a coloured drawing that you can enhance using just clean water, like the example opposite.

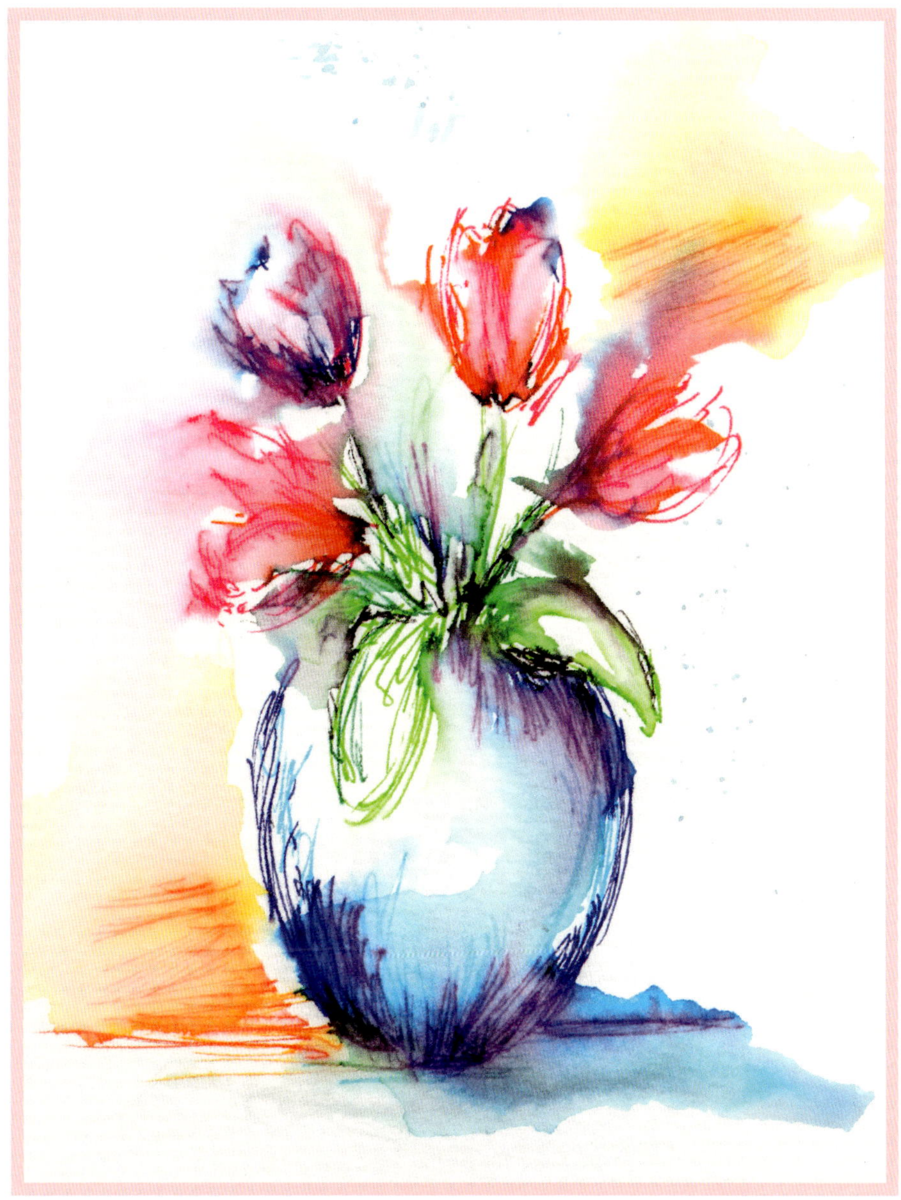

VIBRANT TULIPS
12 x 15cm (4¾ x 6in)

Wherever I go, I will not be without my Staedtler Triplus Fineliners – these pens always give the same feeling of childlike excitement, like a kid playing around with colours, no care, just pure fun!

These tulips in a vase were created really quickly: I scribbled with a selection of my pens and then wetted them. I then lifted some of the wet colour to create some of the looser marks. Some dissipated more than others, creating fascinating 'lost and found' edges as lines vary between being distinct and softening away.

Adding water to a dry sketch

Why not try taking these pens out with a small sketchbook to gather ideas, and adding water when you're back at home? After sketching in the field, we can add water to loosen up those tight lines. Use a brush appropriate in size for your sketch – for a big sketch, use a big brush; and for a small sketch, a small brush.

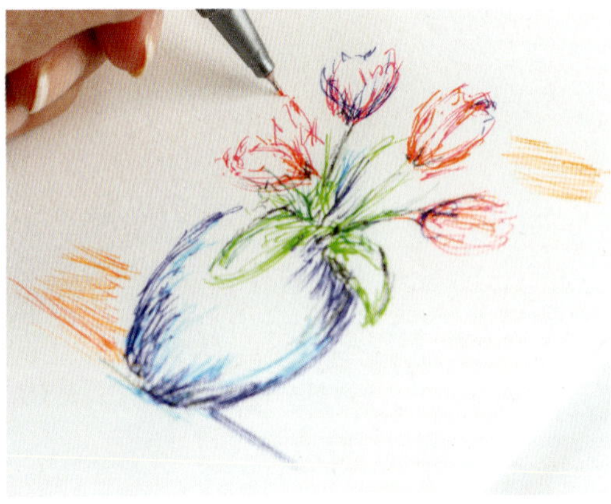

1 These pens come in a rainbow of colours, but don't worry about getting the colours exact when creating your sketch. Lean into the bright, bold colours and don't worry so much about realism.

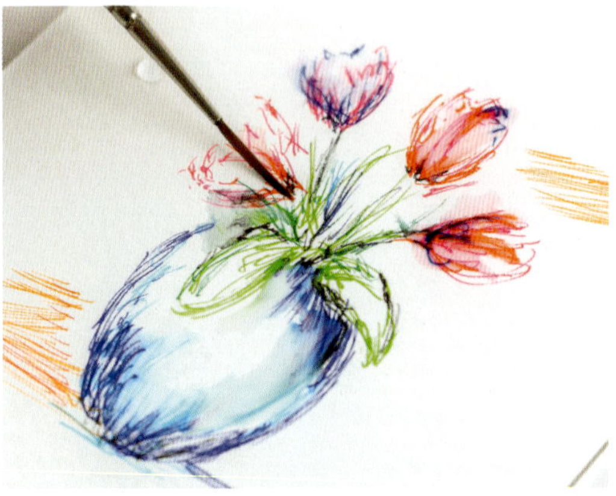

2 Wet the sketch with a damp brush – you don't need much water to activate the ink.

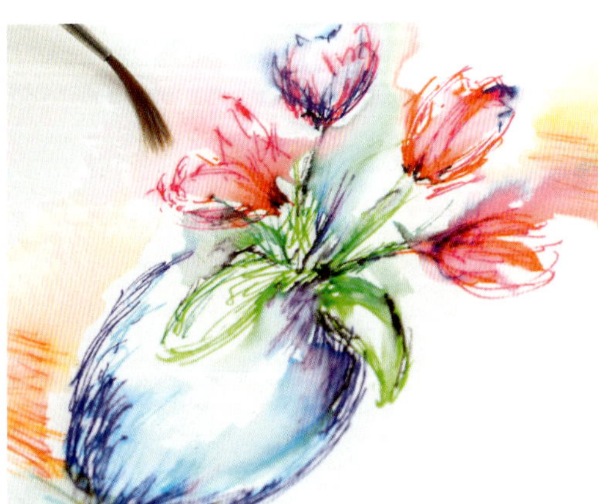

3 Leave some areas clean and dry, but don't be afraid to let colours bleed into another area.

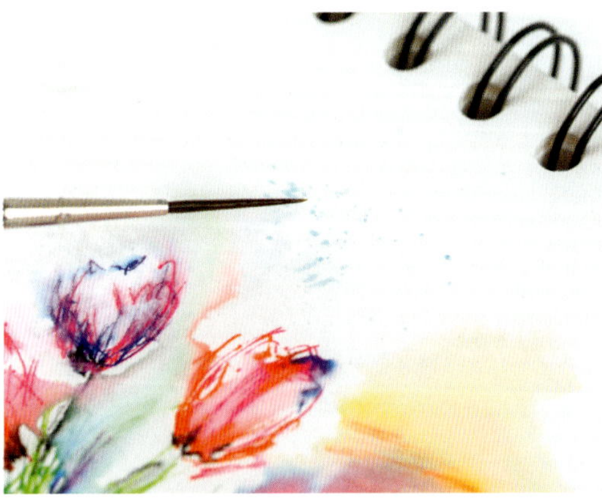

4 You can pick up wet ink from the surface with the brush, then gently tap the brush above the surface to spatter some ink onto the paper.

Adding pen detail to dry watercolour

After laying in loose washes, we usually tighten and tidy things up with wet on dry painting to bring out detail and add contrasting hard edges – but we can use pens for this. Be careful not to over-tighten things.

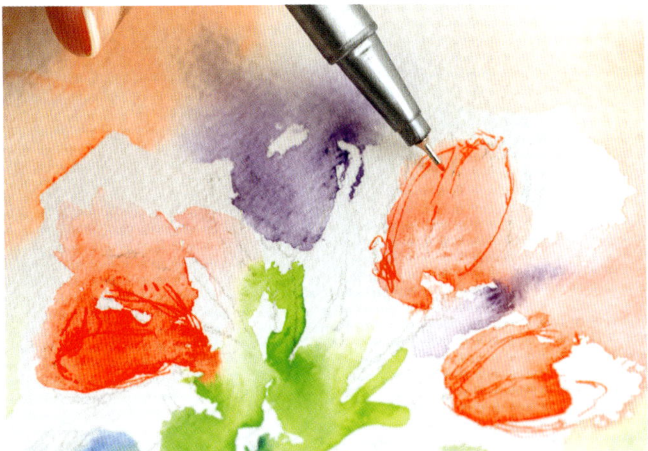

REFINING
You can use similar colours to refine loose edges created in watercolour.

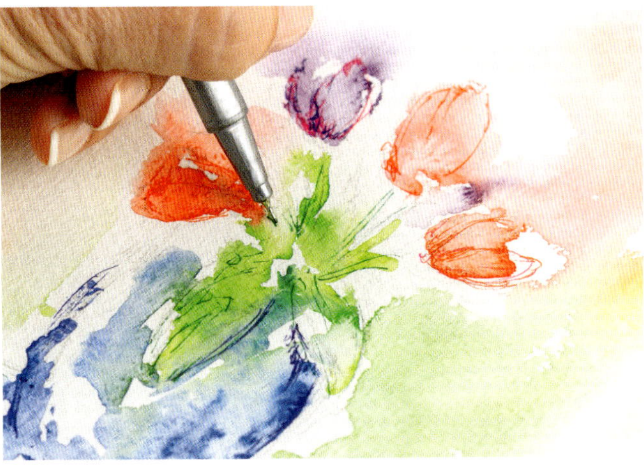

BLACK FOR CLARITY
Add black sparingly to pick out very fine details than are impractical to add with a brush and watercolour paint.

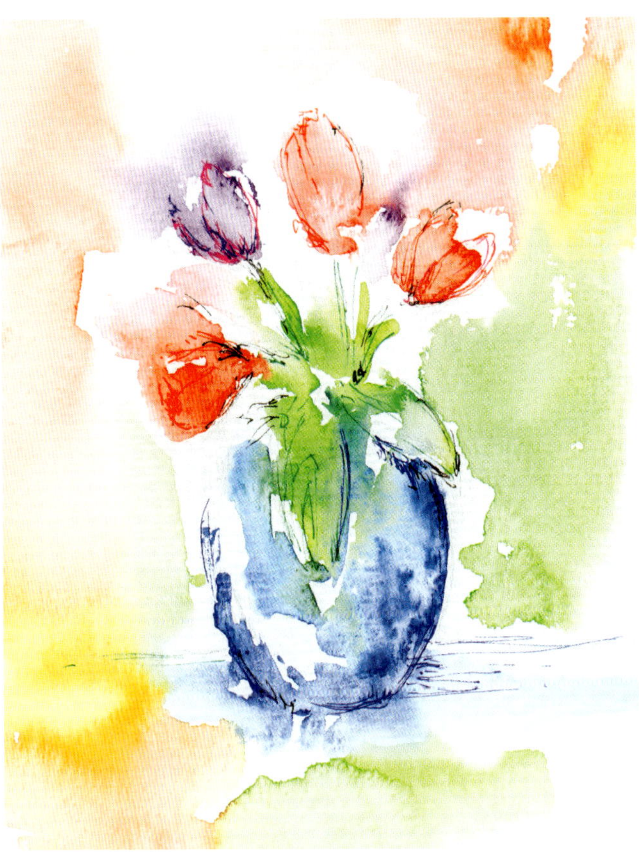

OPTICAL MIXING
If you don't have a matching or similar colour to an area, you can 'mix' pens by adding lots of small marks next to each other. From a distance, the colours appear to blend. Red and blue will mix optically to appear purple, for example.

Strawberry

Wild strawberry flowers are tiny but nevertheless beautiful. Very simple flowers like this rarely get as much attention as more showy ones, so I wanted to give them some time in the sun. Some metal leaf is a great way to really draw the eye.

Even humble subjects can make great paintings. I thought I would include a snail alongside this strawberry – perhaps sometimes unpopular with flower lovers, but they benefit our gardens by breaking down dead plants, leaves and decaying matter and recycling nutrients back into the soil. Snails also serve as a great food source for other wildlife such as birds and hedgehogs.

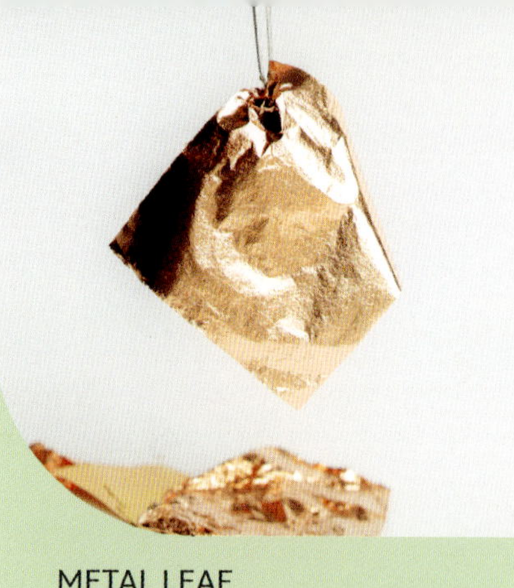

METAL LEAF
Available in many different colours, these are very fine sheets of metallic material that can be added easily to watercolour to provide a striking contrast.

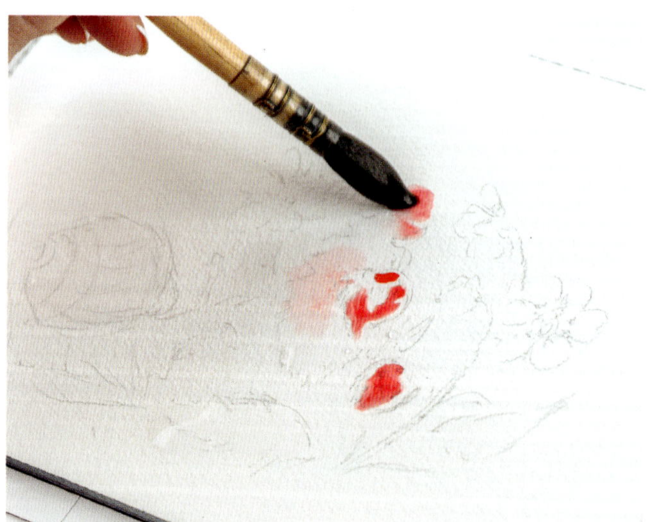

1 Use an HB pencil to lightly sketch in the basic shapes. Wet the main subejct areas - the snail, leaves, fruits and flowerheads - with the large brush and clean water. Paint the strawberry fruits with rose madder, then drop in vermilion.

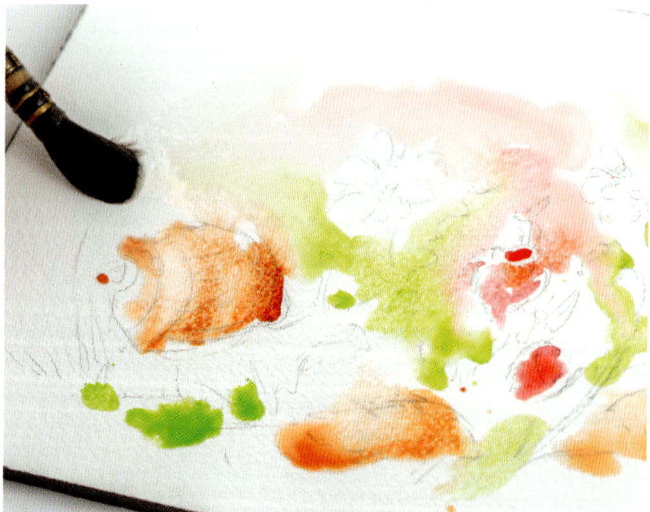

2 Use burnt sienna to paint the dead leaves, and also to paint the curves on the snail's shell. Paint the fresh leaves with May green, then bring in fresh water from the background to let the colour fade outwards.

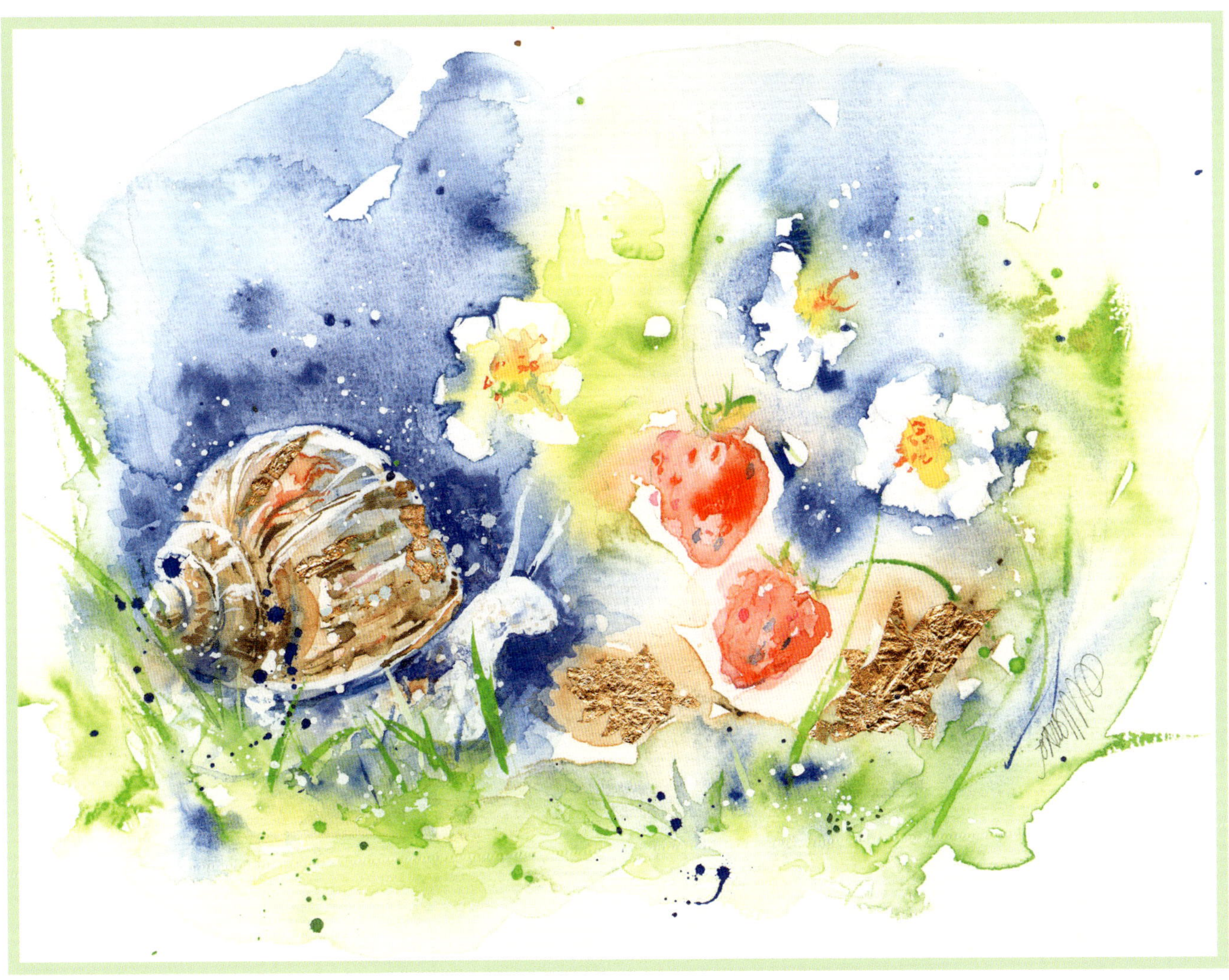

STRAWBERRIES AND SNAIL WITH BRONZE LEAF
23 x 15cm (9 x 6in)

I wanted to include the snail to complement the strawberry
flowers. I decided that his shell would also look great with some
enhancements with the gold leaf and to then balance this within the
painting, I also added a couple of leaves in the foreground too.

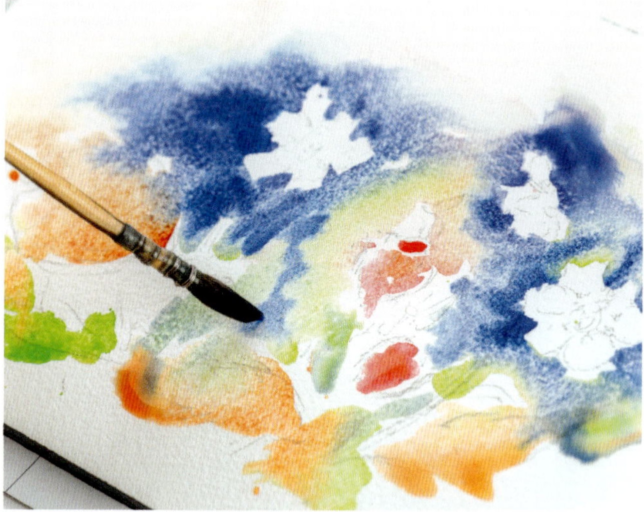

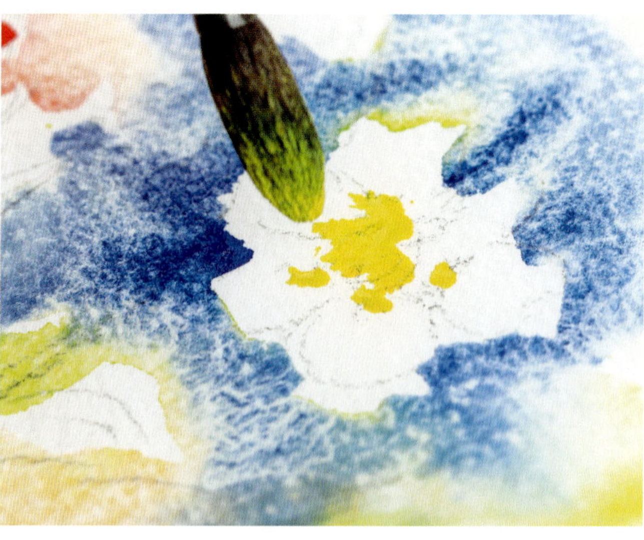

3 To help the pale strawberry flowers pop out, we need bold background colours. Add French ultramarine wet into wet.

4 Add vanadium yellow to the flower centres.

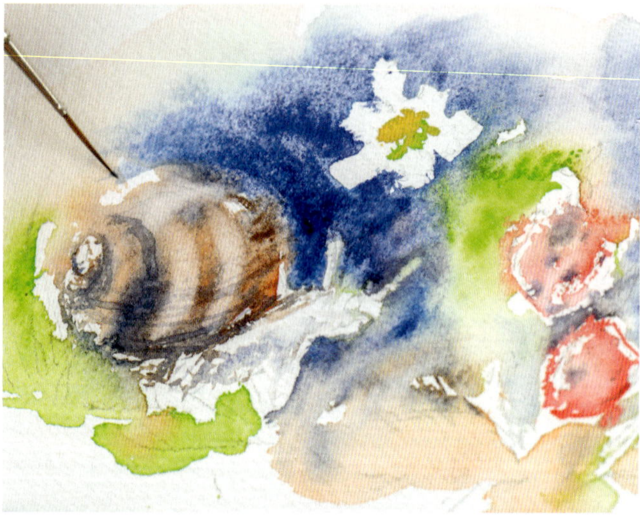

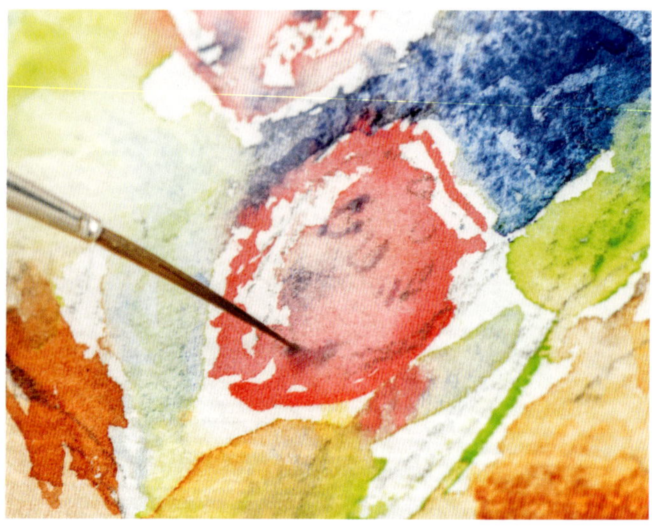

5 Using the small brush, paint the markings on the snail's shell with burnt umber. Add French ultramarine under the shell for shadow, and a dark mix of burnt umber and French ultramarine for details.

6 Add detail to the leaves with the dark mix, then use rose madder and vermilion to develop the strawberry fruits, letting the colours mix on the paper. Once the fruits are nearly dry, use the dark mix to add some small dots.

Tip

You'll need to judge the wetness of the paper – it needs to be dry enough for the marks to stay where you put them, but damp enough to bleed slightly.

Adding bronze leaf

The process of adding bronze leaf to the surface is very simple,
and well worth experimenting with.

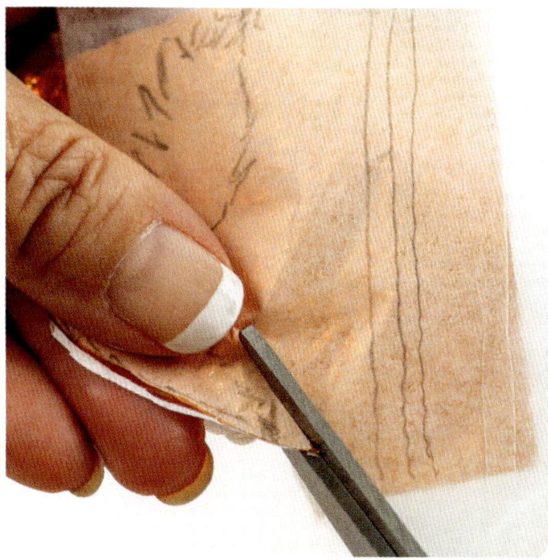

7 Draw the shapes you want to add bronze leaf to
on the backing paper using an HB pencil, then cut
out the shapes with scissors.

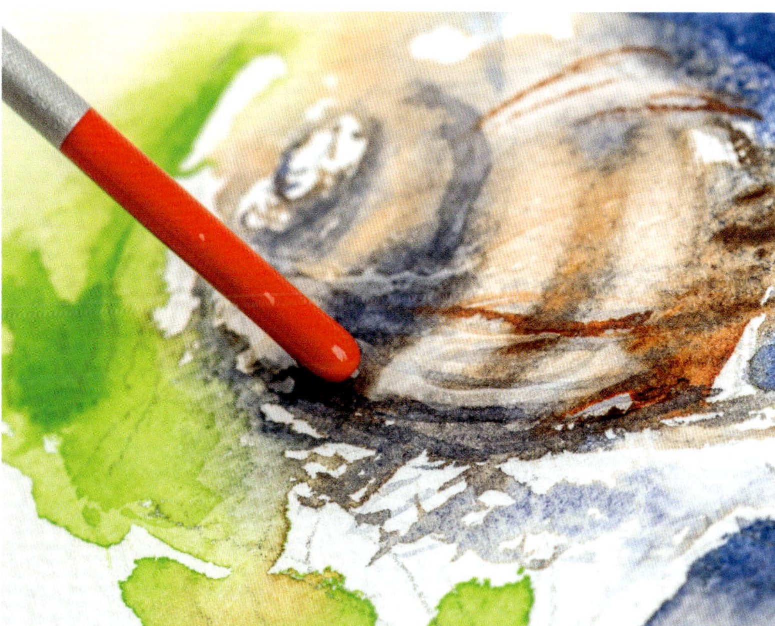

8 Dip the end of the small brush into PVA glue
and use it to draw the marks on the paper. I'm
placing bronze leaf on the snail's shell and
dead leaves.

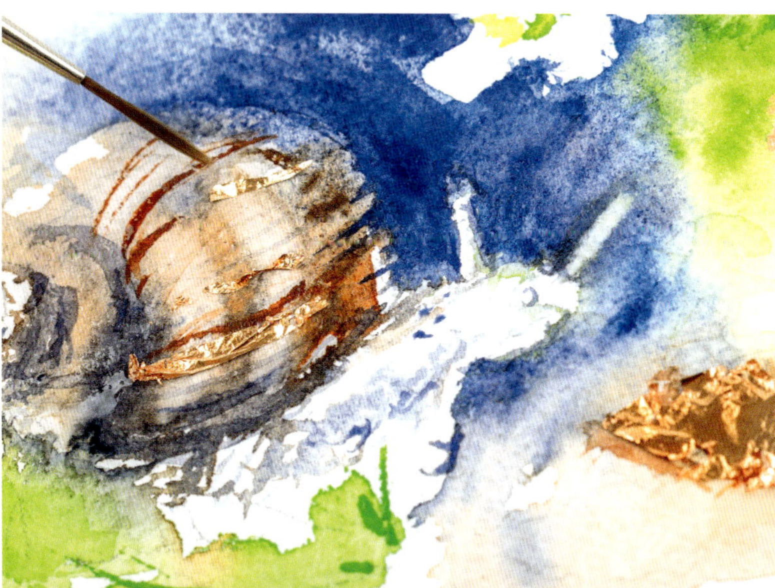

9 Working one piece at a time, remove the
backing from the metal leaf and use tweezers to
place it on the glue.

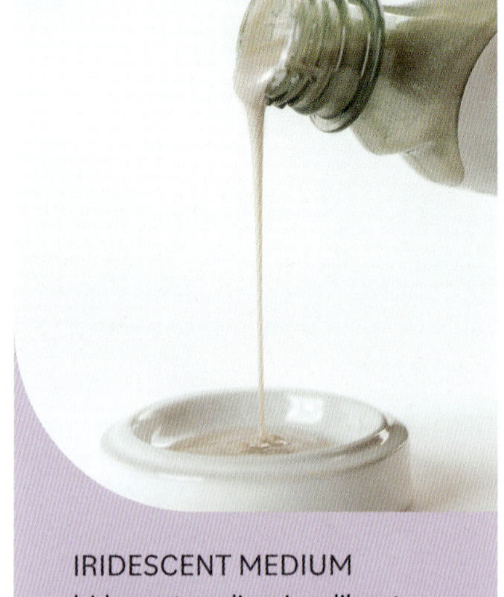

Meadow sage

Simple, understated flowers like meadow sage can benefit from a complementary subject to share the limelight. I think it best to make these appropriate to the flower. Dragonflies like this beautiful example are often drawn to meadow sage as their tiny florets attract their prey. When I saw this combination, I knew I just had to paint it.

Using iridescent medium on dry paintings

As well as being mixed with paint, iridescent medium can be used on its own, applied over an already-dried colour to give it a little sparkle.

Pick the medium up with a damp brush and apply exactly as you would any other paint. Always wash your brush thoroughly and change your water after using iridescent medium, or it will make your next painting sparkly, too!

IRIDESCENT MEDIUM

Iridescent medium is a diluent that can be mixed with watercolour in a tinting saucer to give a sparkly iridescent quality to whichever colour you like. Note that it will change the characteristics of your watercolour if used like this – making it thicker and less fluid. The way you use it all depends on what effect you're after.

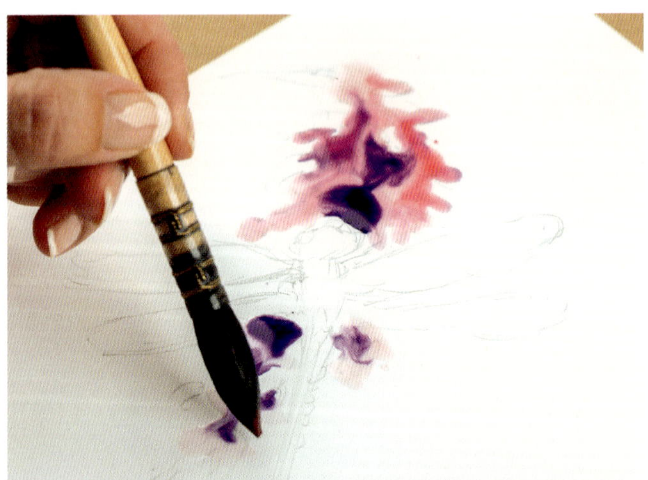

1 Establish the meadow sage by wetting the surface and dropping in rose madder and Schmincke violet using a large brush. Avoid overcomplicating the flowerhead; just aim for an impression.

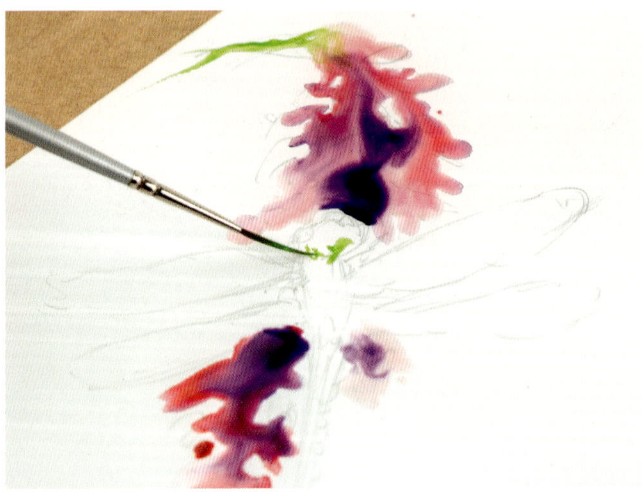

2 Add May green for the stem with the small brush. Use the same colour for the dragonfly's eyes.

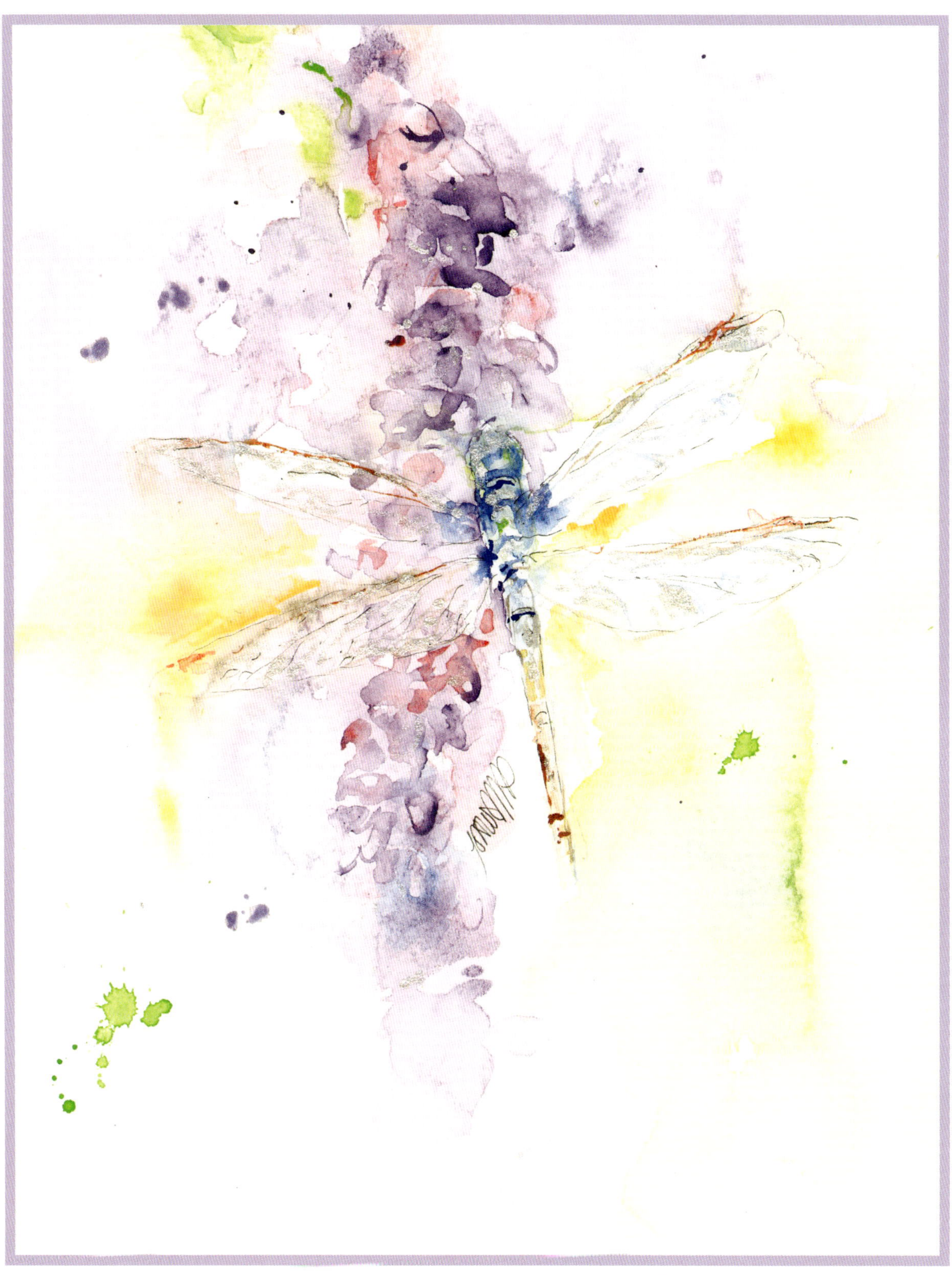

MEADOW SAGE AND DRAGONFLY
18 x 25.5cm (7 x 10in)

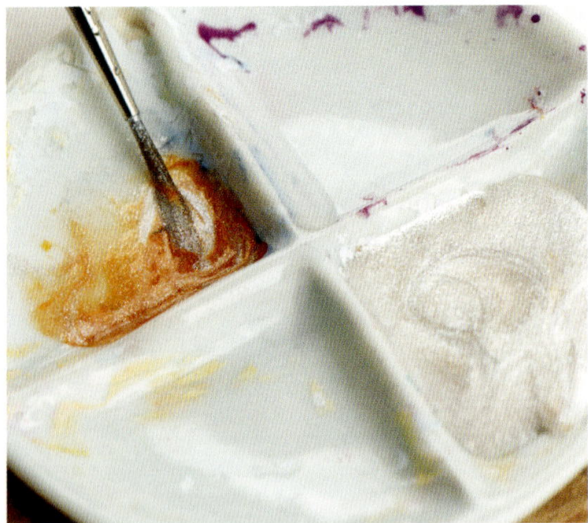

3 Mix burnt sienna and yellow ochre in a tinting saucer, then add roughly the same amount of iridescent medium as paint. The exact proportions don't really matter: just remember that the more medium you add, the more sparkly the result will be, and the thicker the paint will feel.

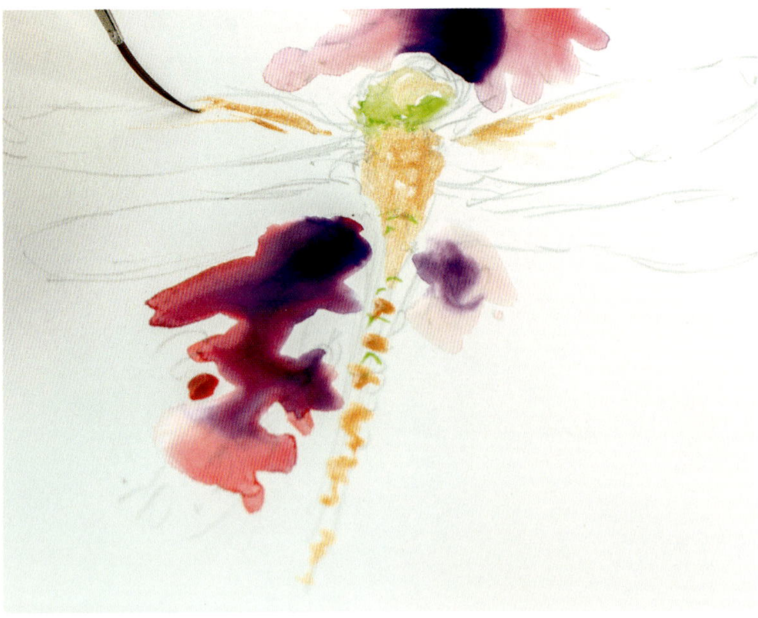

4 Use the brush to pick out alternate body segments with the mix, then the inner parts of the wings, as shown.

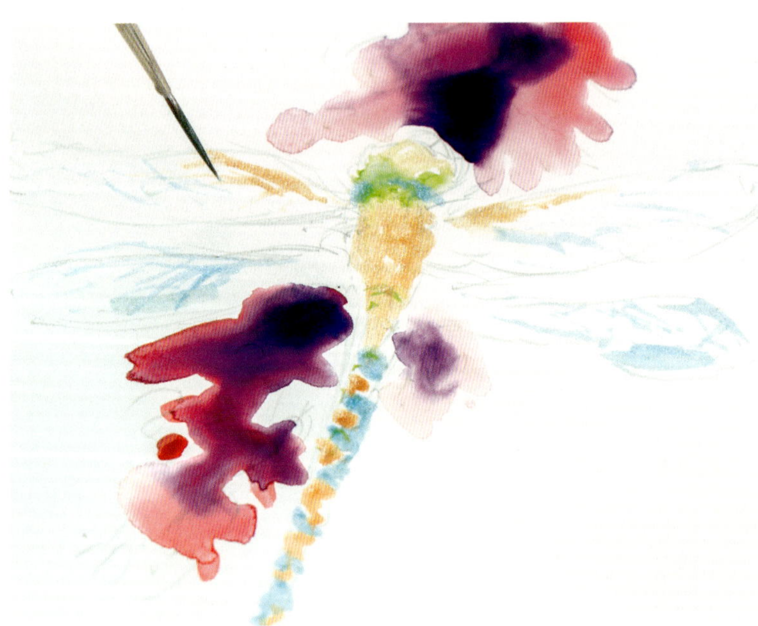

5 Iridescent medium will tint your paints, too. Here I've added some to helio cerulean for the dragonfly's body and wings, and you can see that it's made it a paler colour.

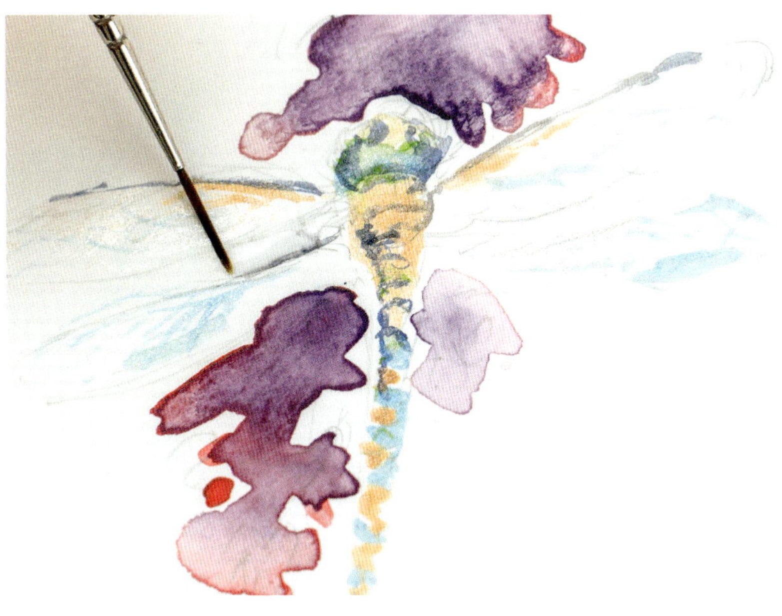

6 Iridescent medium looks very effective against a contrasting dark, so add some dark marks using a mix of French ultramarine and burnt sienna.

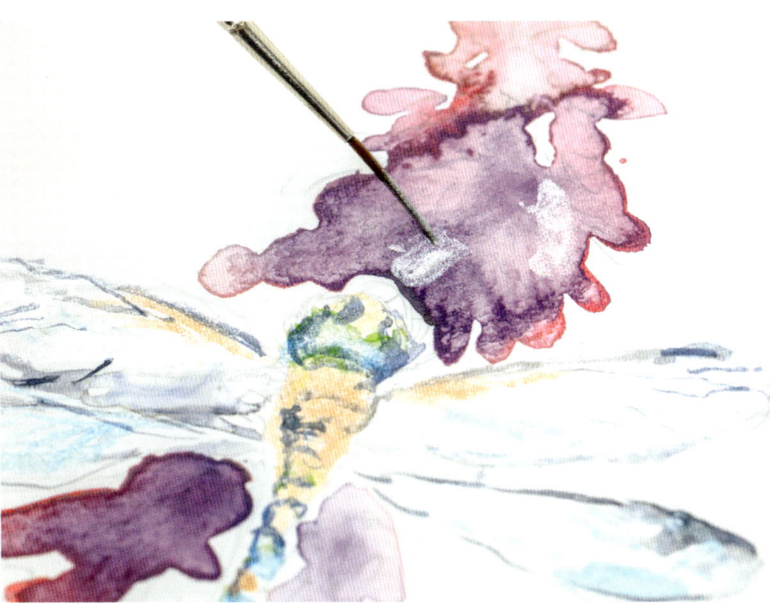

7 The medium can be used neat, on its own, too. This is great for adding an attention-grabbing shimmer to areas.

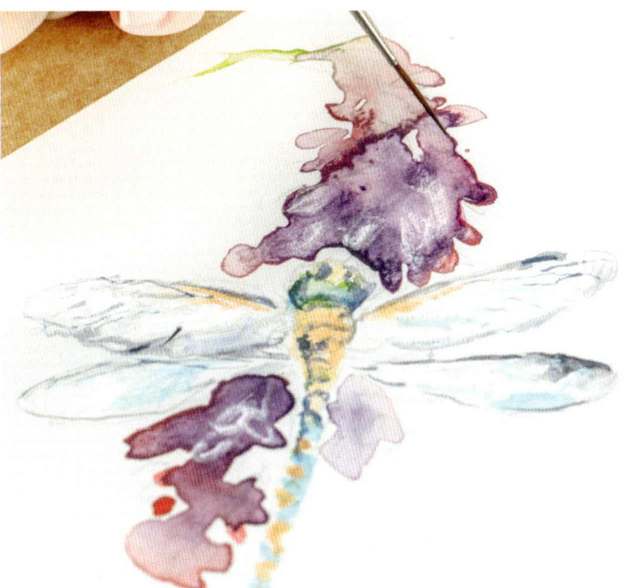

8 Pick out some details and highlights on both the meadow sage and dragonfly. The use of these light glazes of iridescent medium will help to unify the painting.

Waterlily

Water lilies are beautiful floating flowers which not only provide shelter for insects but improve our water quality too as they can absorb polluting nutrients. I often see these beautiful flowers on my walks with my dog Alfie when we visit a local pond and so I've photographed them to use for my painting projects many times.

Using gum arabic

Watercolours look glossy when wet but of course dry to a matt finish. To retain that glossy effect, I have found gum arabic to be extremely useful on subjects like water - perfect for contrasting the water with the delicate petals of the waterlily.

Gum arabic can be added wherever you want a sheen - and it's as simple as painting it directly onto the surface.

GUM ARABIC

This viscous gum can be used to make colours look glossy and shiny even after they have dried, perfect when something needs to appear wet.

It can also be used to help lift out paint, giving a softer effect than masking fluid.

Always ensure that you change your water once you have used this as it can contaminate your water and can add gloss where it is not required.

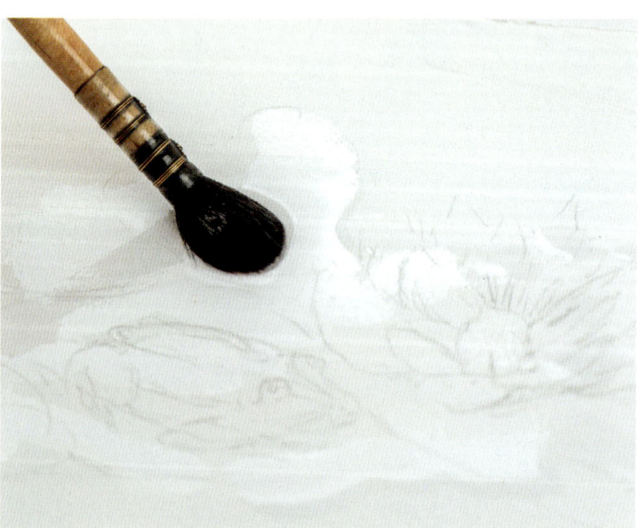

1 Use an HB pencil to lightly sketch in the lily flower, pads and frog. Using the large brush, wet the whole surface of the water.

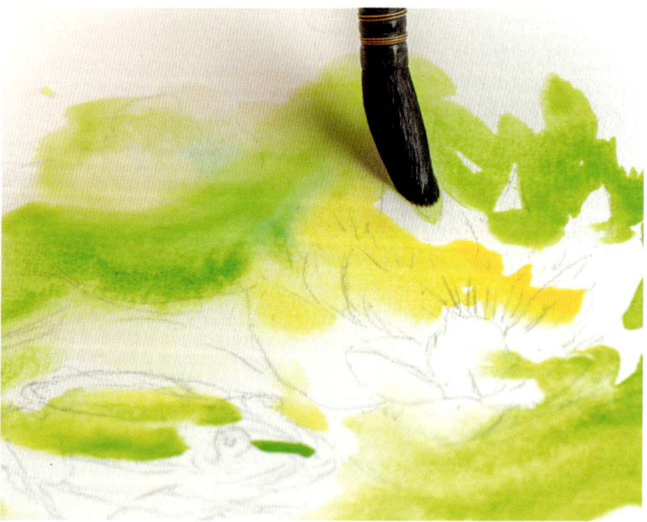

2 Paint around the lily flower with vanadium yellow, leaving plenty of white space, then add the greenery wet into wet with May green, working mostly around the frog. Use the shape of the large brush to help get the sharp angles in between the petals.

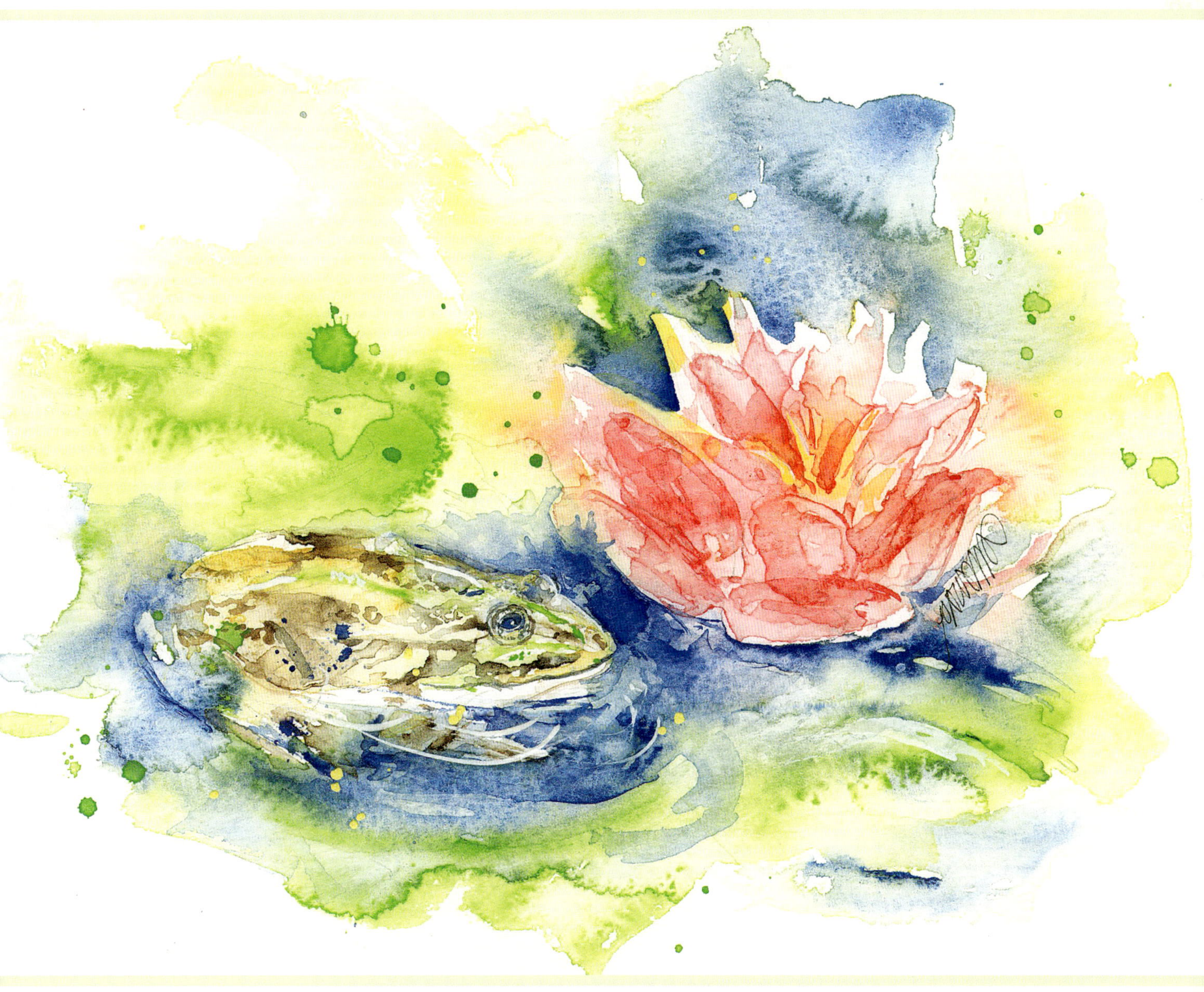

WATERLILY AND FROG

25.5 x 18cm (10 x 7in)

Frogs are helpful to our flowers and plants as they will eat the
many insects that harm them, so are great pest controllers.

I see a lot of waterlilies on my walks, and I'm always drawn to
their clean shapes and little pops of colour.

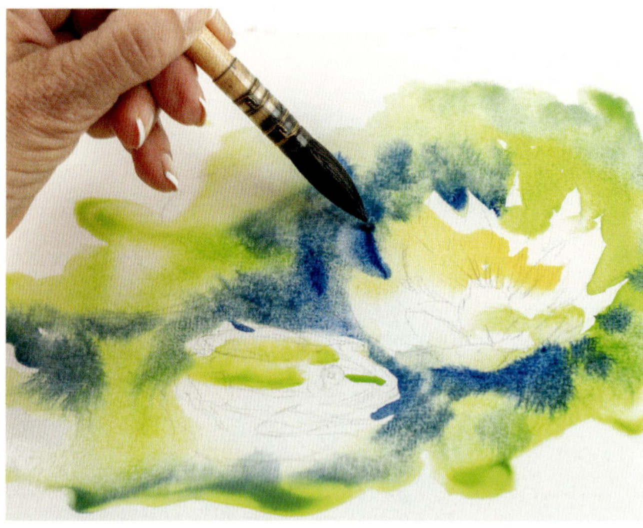

3 Add French ultramarine wet into wet for shading, again using the shape of the large brush to help retain the shapes of the flowers.

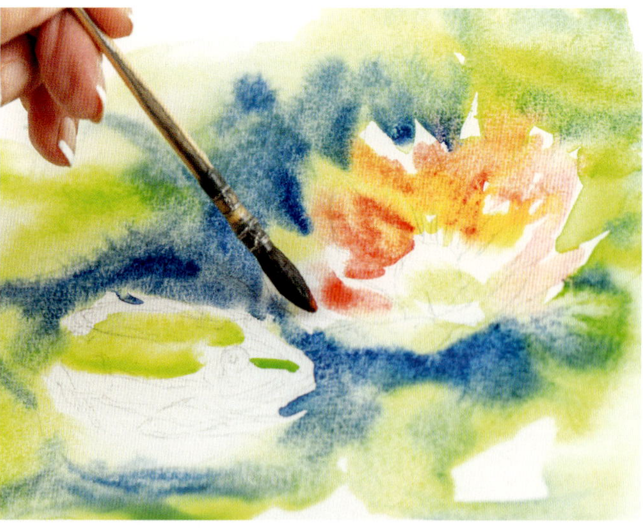

4 Swap to the medium brush and use rose madder to paint the lily petals. Allow the colour to bleed into the yellow, but leave white space between the pink and green to keep things clean.

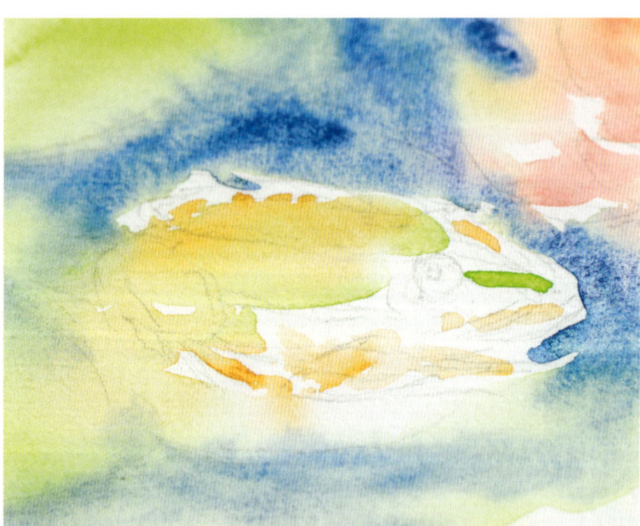

5 Use yellow ochre to add markings to the frog's back, then allow the painting to dry completely.

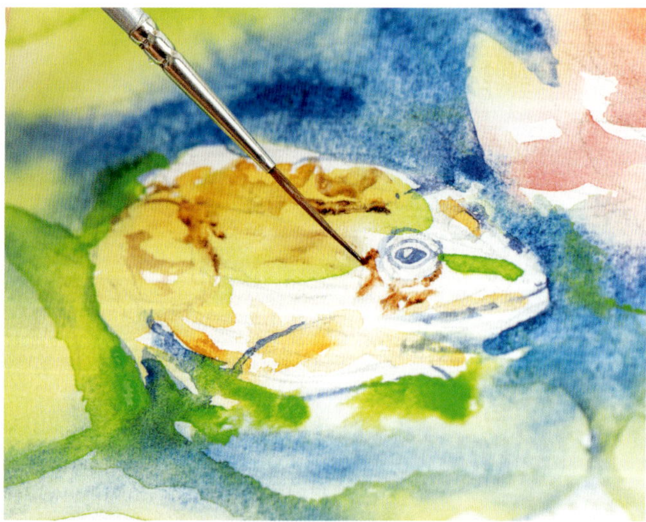

6 Use the small brush to paint the eyes on the frog using a dark mix of French ultramarine with a little burnt umber, then add a subtle outline to refine the shape, blending it outwards with clean water. Use burnt umber to add further markings and detail.

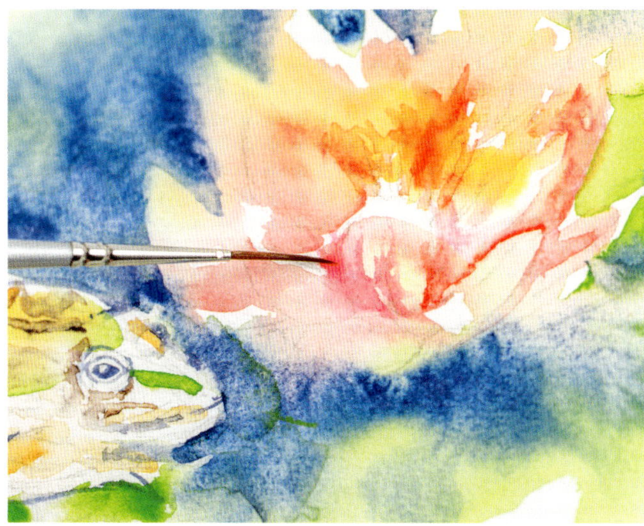

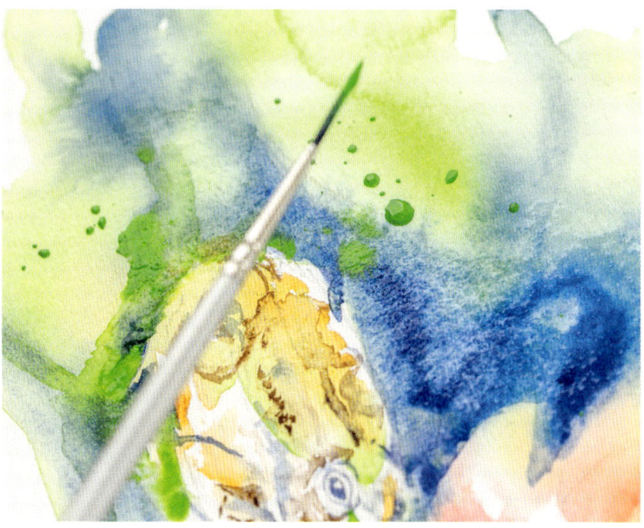

7 Develop the centre of the flower using rose madder. You're aiming to suggest the stamens (the pollen-producing stalks) by adding shadow around them, leaving them as yellow.

8 Add a few spatters of May green by loading the brush and flicking it at the surface. Allow to dry completely.

Adding gloss with gum arabic

This is also a good way to subtly integrate different parts of a painting, and I thought the wet look of a frog's skin could also be achieved using this diluent.

9 Pour a little gum arabic into a dish, and paint it onto the surface where you would like a glossy effect on the finished painting - in this case, on the frog, and the lily pad on the front right.

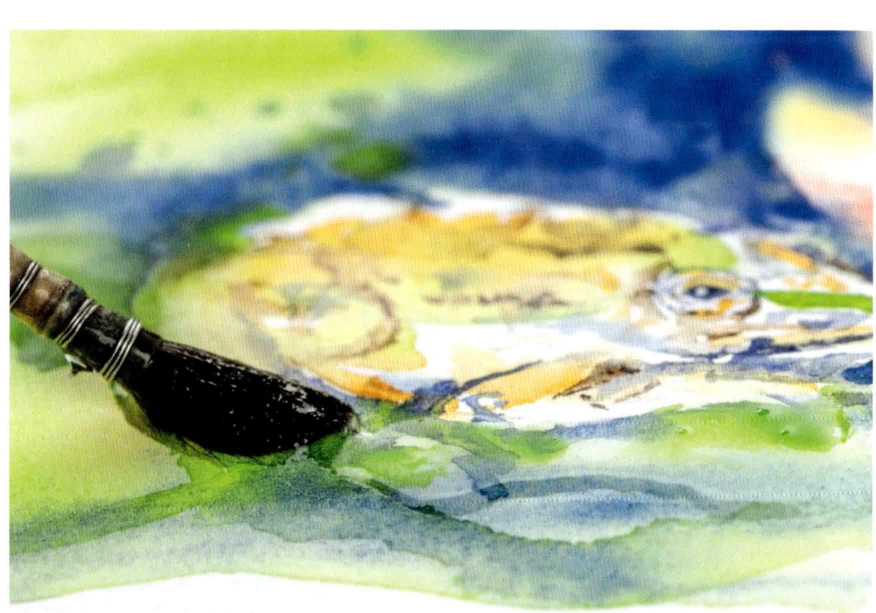

Dandelion clock

Another magical memory from our childhoods – the dandelion clock, who has not blown one of these to play the game where apparently the number of breaths taken will tell you the time... only to see the magical fairy-like seeds float in the air.

BLEACH

Experiment with your inks before committing to a painting. Bleach will work better with some inks than others, and particularly well with Parker blue ink.

When using bleach, keep washing your brush to avoid damaging the hairs.

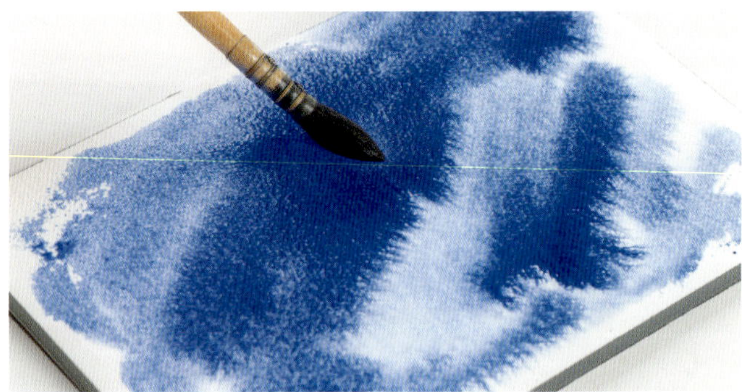

1 Wet the whole surface with clean water using a large brush, then lay in a wash of Parker blue ink. Make sure you get quite a strong, varied tone.

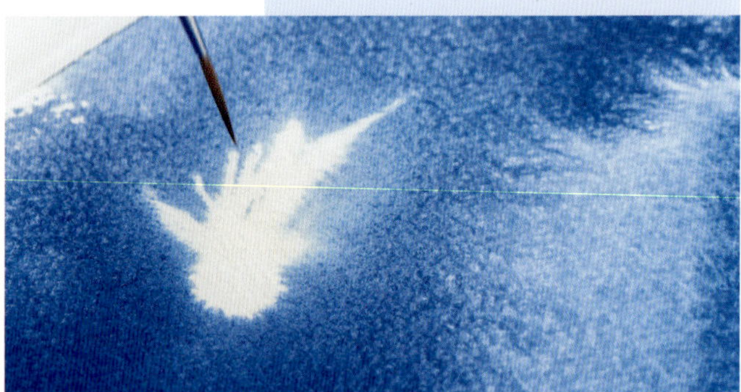

2 Pour a small amount of bleach into a glass container. You can use this just like paint – pick it up on your small brush and begin drawing fine lines out from a central point. While wet, the effect will be soft.

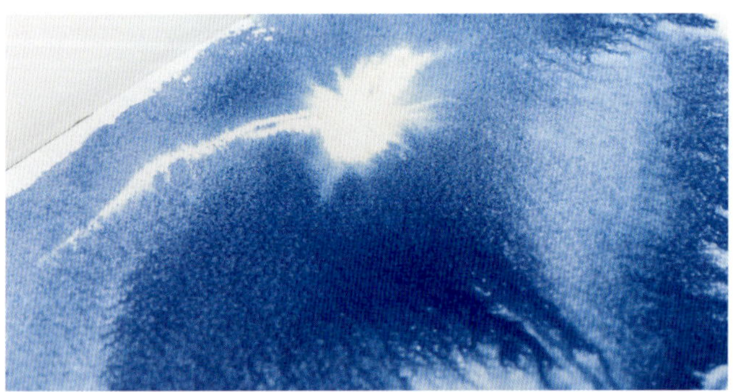

3 Continue working round the central point, building up an overlapping circular mass of lines with one longer line as a stem.

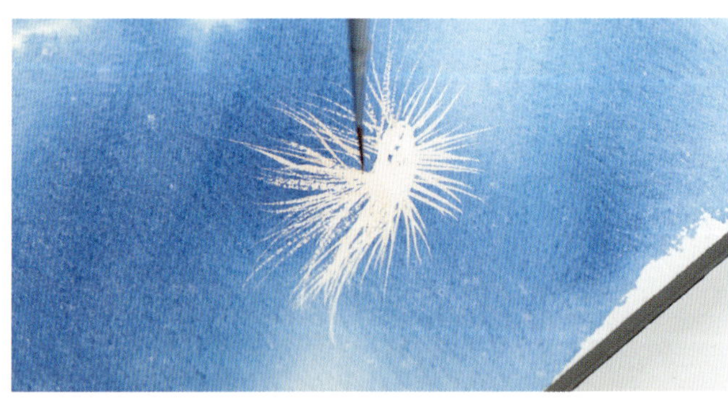

4 When the ink has dried, repeat the process to make a clearer foreground dandelion clock.

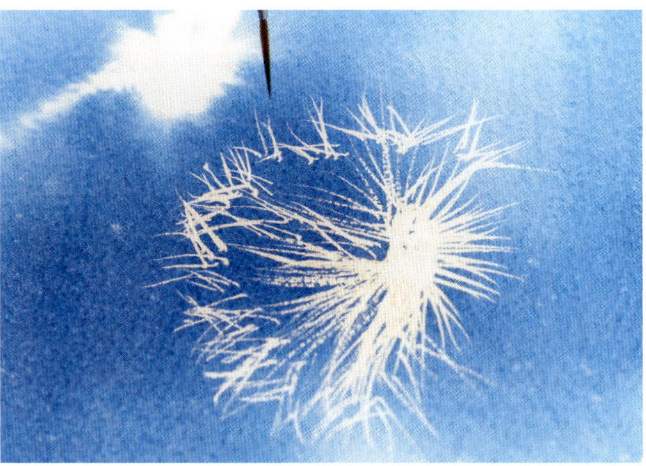

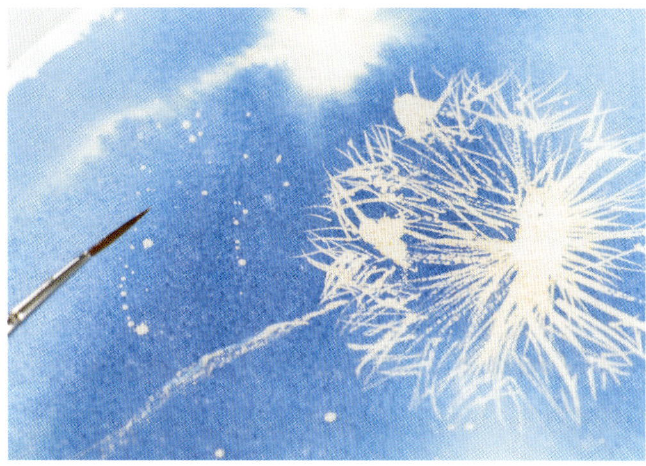

5 At the ends of the lines, add shorter lines at angles, to create the effect of the seedheads.

6 Draw out one long stem. Use a light touch, and barely any bleach on the brush to get a textural finish – then add a light spatter of bleach to finish.

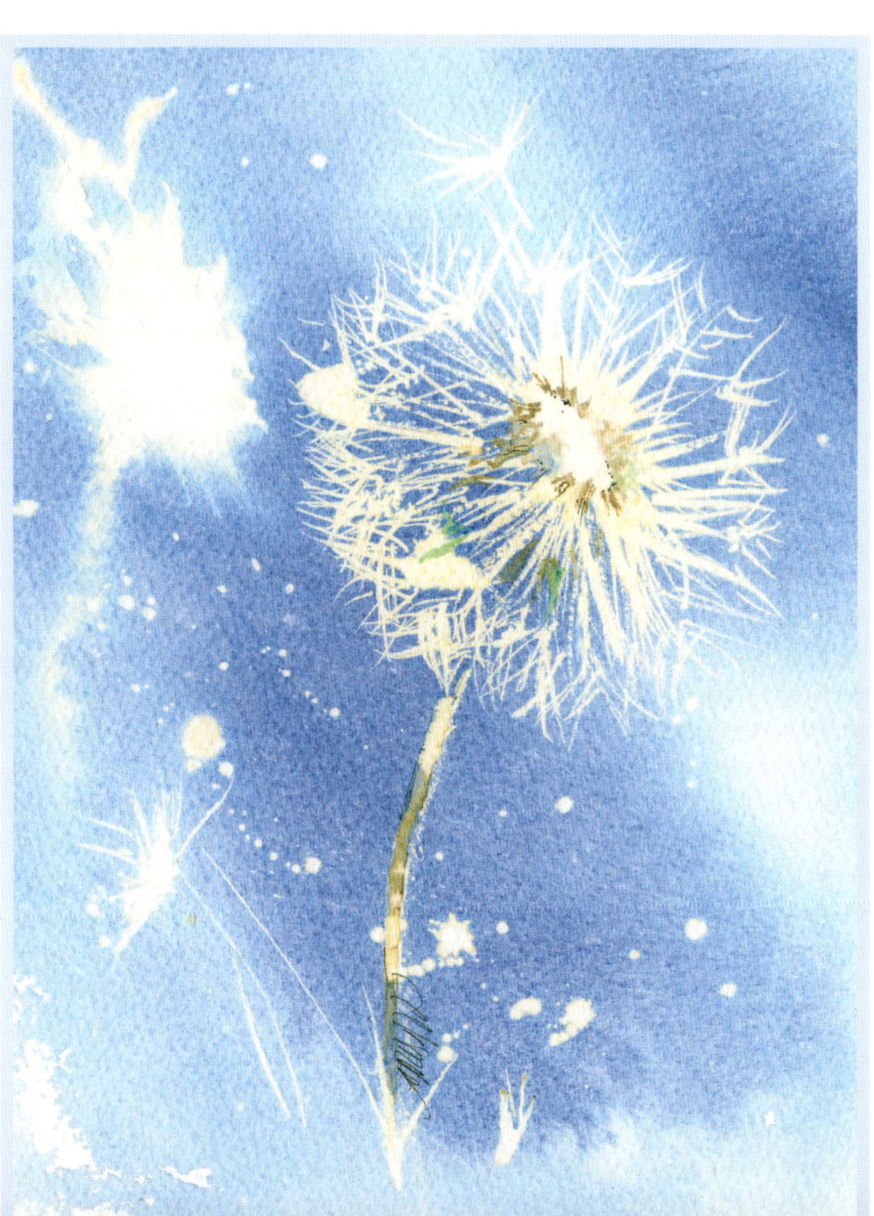

DANDELION CLOCK WITH WATERCOLOUR AND BLEACH
18 x 25.5cm (7 x 10in)

I am not a great fan of using masking fluid; I much prefer wax to reserve white as it is more rugged. Neither would have worked for this project owing to its delicacy, but I knew that the bleach would be a perfect combination with the Parker ink, as I know how well this pulls out against the pigment to reveal the white paper underneath.

I had so much fun seeing how immediate the effects were and even spattered some bleach for good measure to demonstrate some movement. I then added just the slightest hint of colour using some calligraphy inks (see page 132).

Cherry blossom

Cherry blossom is stunning, and happily I have lots of this in my own garden to serve as inspiration. I love the colours and when I see my tree flowering after a long winter, it reminds me the spring is coming.

The brightness of spring sunshine on their petals demanded a vibrant finish – and my way of using watercolour pencils meant I could also suggest the distinctive texture of the pollen.

I have used Derwent watercolour pencils here (the silver cases are because my much-treasured set is an older design) but there are lots of excellent options.

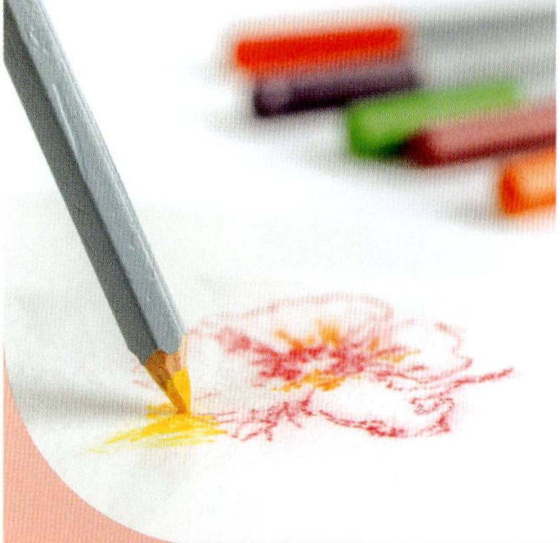

WATERCOLOUR PENCILS

These can be used dry for additional detail or scraped into a wet wash for varying effects.

When used dry, the marks made with watercolour pencils are very faint (see step 1), but when used on wet paper – as shown above – the marks are very bold and strong.

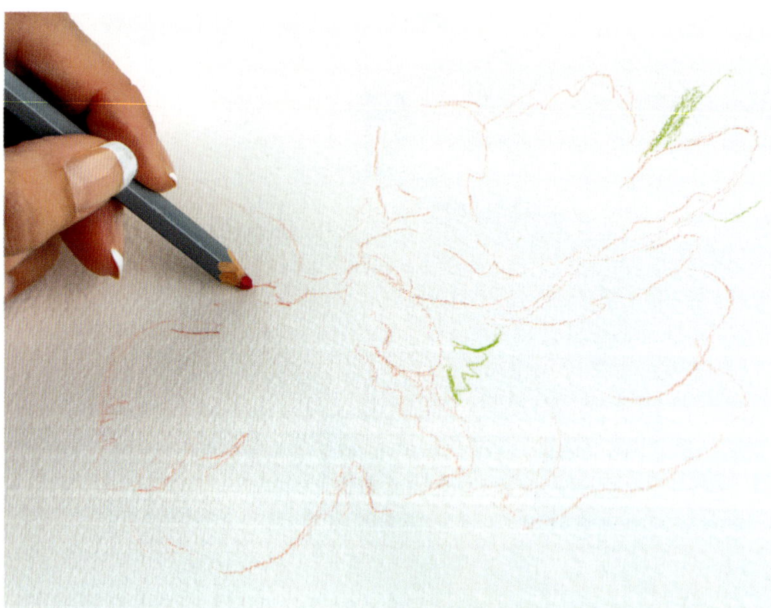

1 Use crimson lake 20 watercolour pencil to outline the petals, and pick out some green areas with grass green 47.

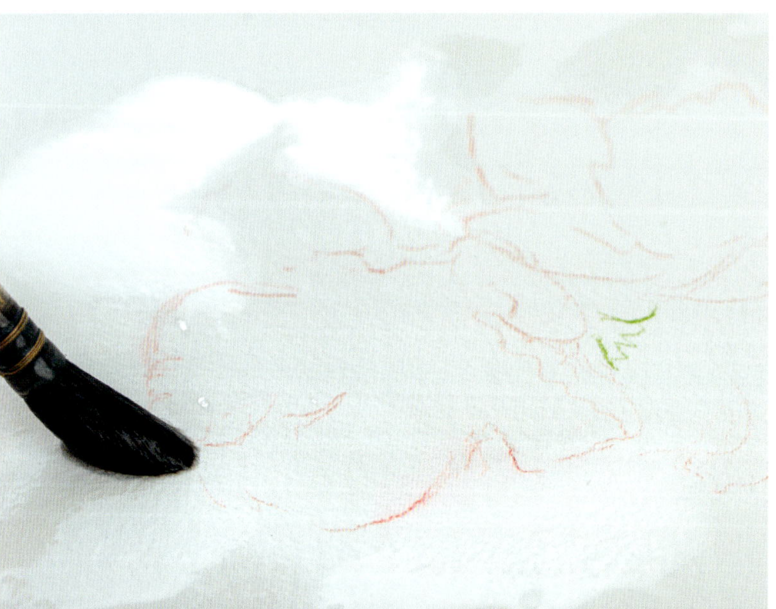

2 Use a large brush to wet the background, working up to, but not over, the edges of the petals.

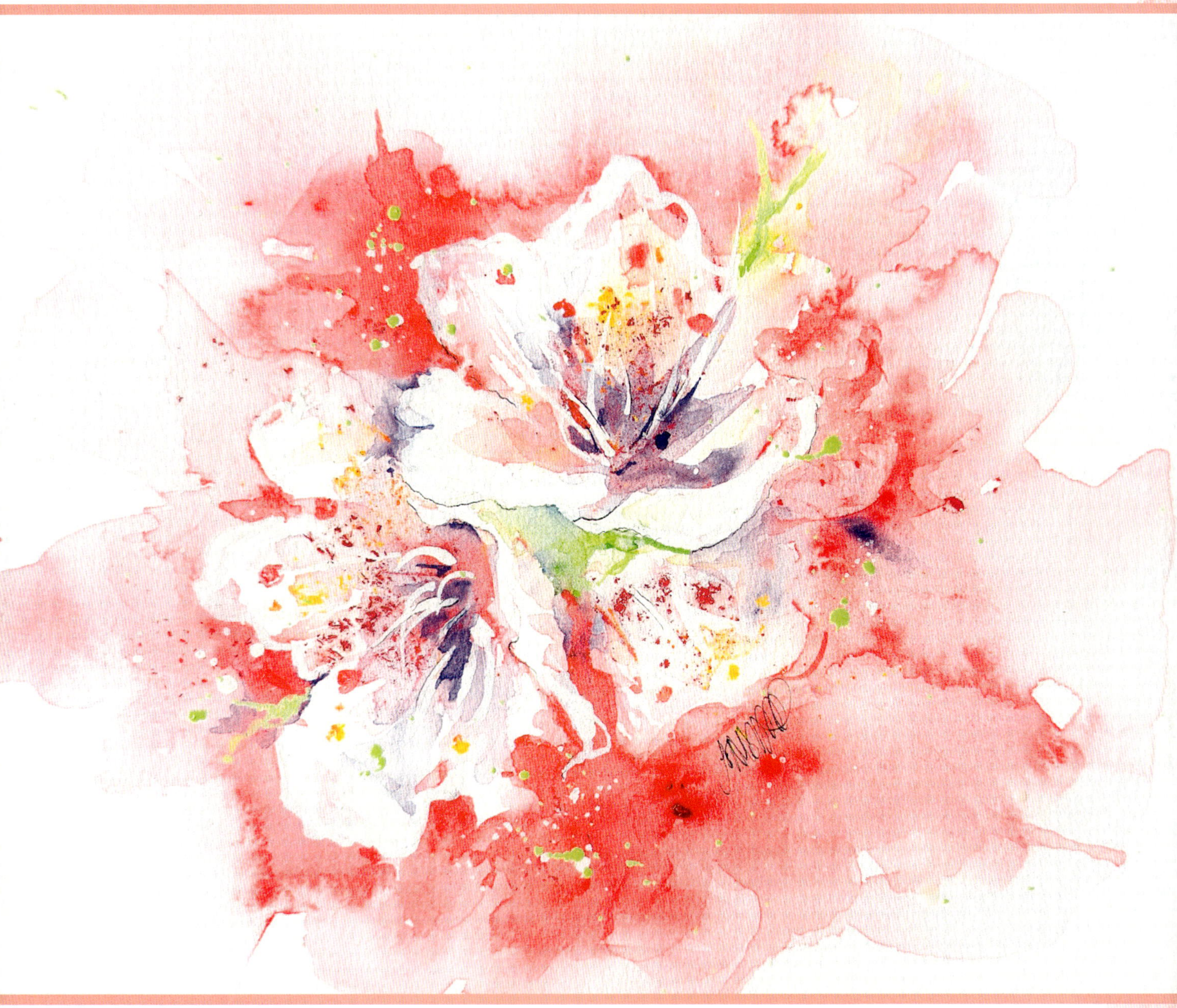

CHERRY BLOSSOM #1
25.5 x 18cm (10 x 7in)

Outlines made in watercolour pencil will partly dissolve
into the wet paint when it's added, while shavings of the
pencil lead added into the wet surface will create impact
and texture.

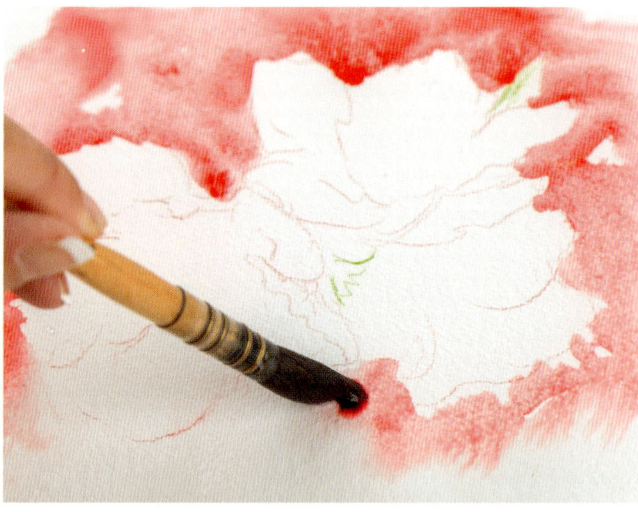

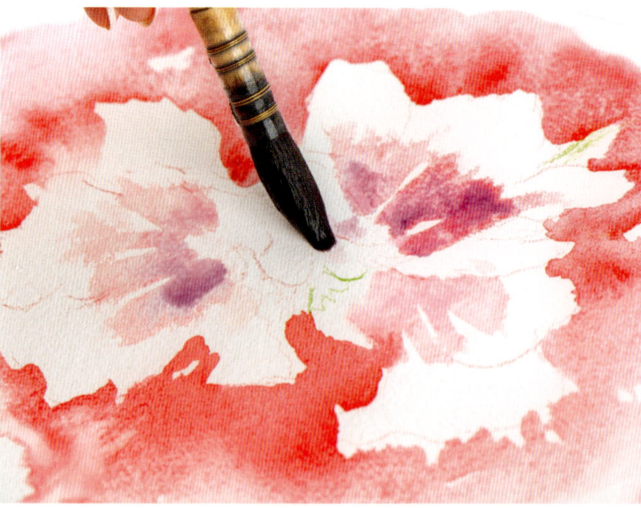

3 Working wet into wet, lay in rose madder with the large brush, working up to the edges of the watercolour pencil.

4 Still using rose madder and the large brush, add some marks in the centres of the blossoms, then add a little Schmincke violet wet into wet.

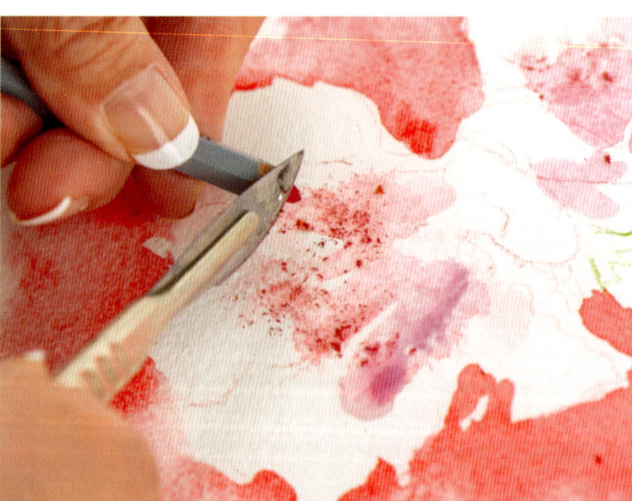

5 Hold the crimson lake 20 pencil near to the centre of the blossom, and use a craft knife to gently scrape the coloured lead of the pencil onto the wet paper.

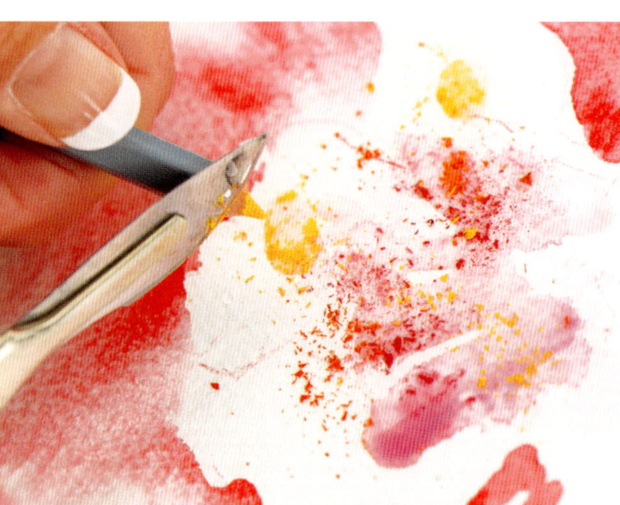

6 Repeat the process with orange chrome 10 and deep cadmium 6 pencils.

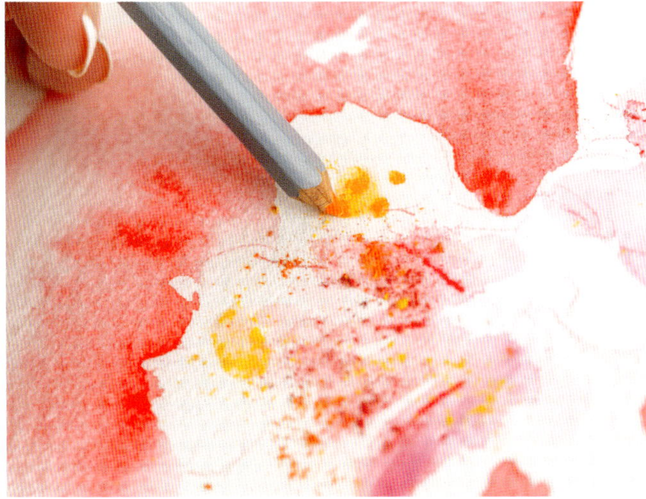

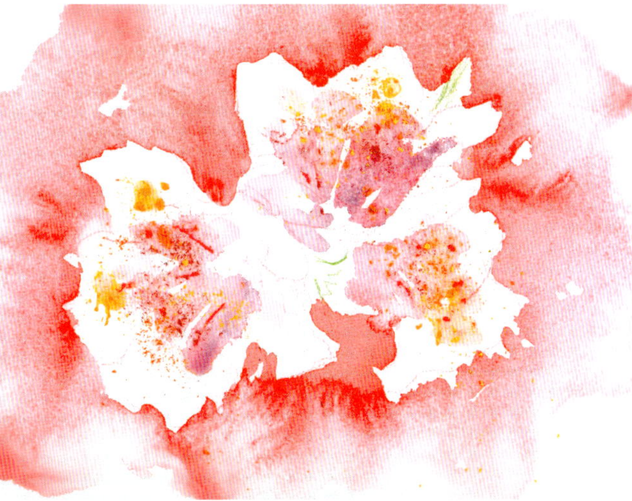

7 Use the pencils to add just a few fine stamens in the wet centres – you won't need to press at all hard.

The finished effect has a lot of impact. You can now develop the rest of the painting to ensure it's balanced, as shown in the finished example on page 101.

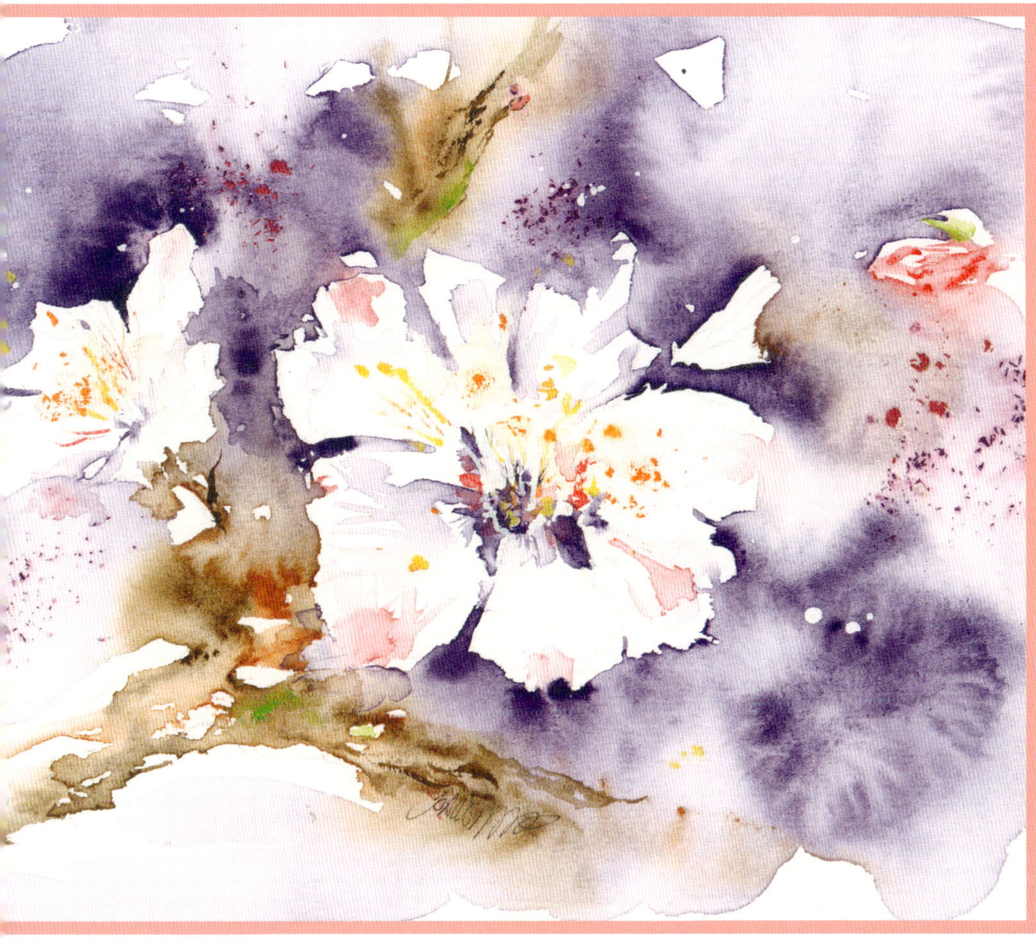

CHERRY BLOSSOM #2

25.5 x 18cm (10 x 7in)

Another take on cherry blossom which uses the same technique, but here I've also scraped the pencil shavings into the background.

Sunflower

Yellow is such a joyful colour – known to release our happy hormones, stimulating feelings of optimism and positivity. I thought this flower would be the ideal candidate for some of my Schmincke bronzing powder. Aqua Bronze is great for sunflowers because it allows you to emulate the texture of the massed seeds at the sunflower's centre.

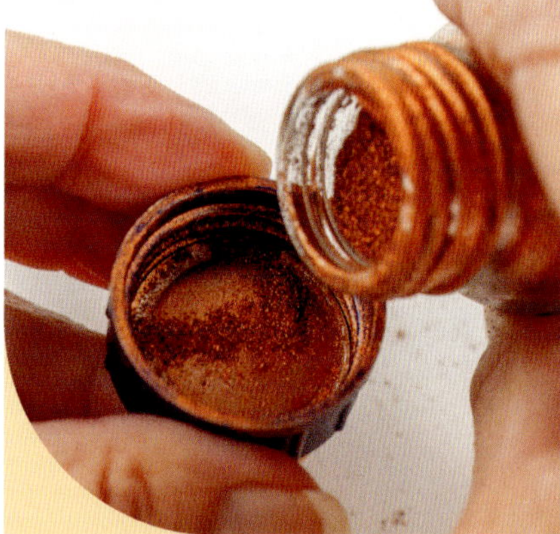

AQUA BRONZE
These powders are called 'Aqua Bronze' or bronzing powders, but are available in a variety of colours. The one I'm using here is copper Aqua Bronze.

They are fantastic to add shimmering effects to any painted subject.

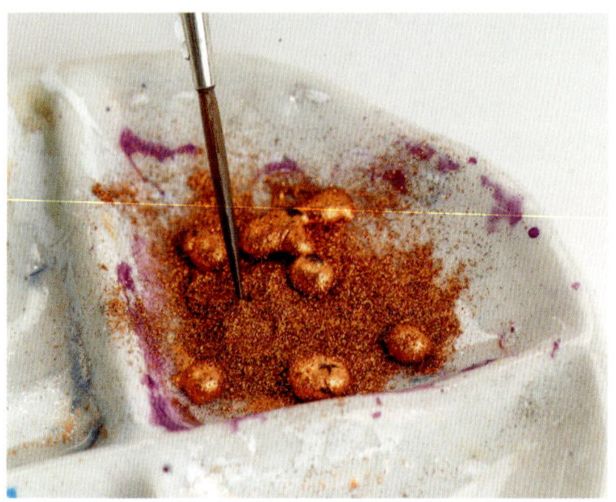

1 Tip the powder into a mixing saucer – you only need a little. Add a few drops of clean water with a brush, and gently stir to mix it.

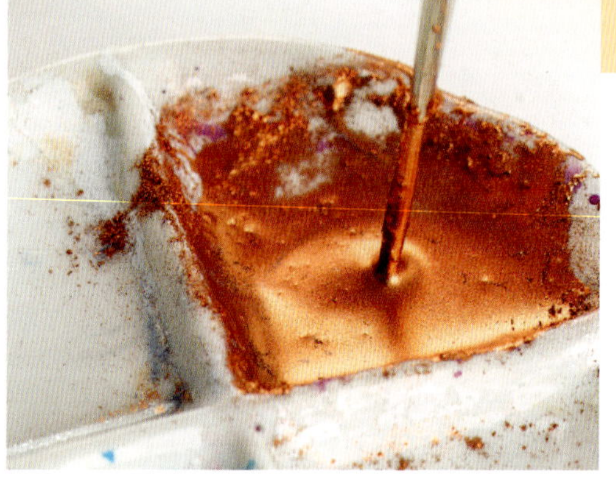

2 The powder will dissolve into the water, a bit like coffee granules, to make a shimmery liquid. The correct consistency is fairly thick. It should move fluidly, but not drip from your brush.

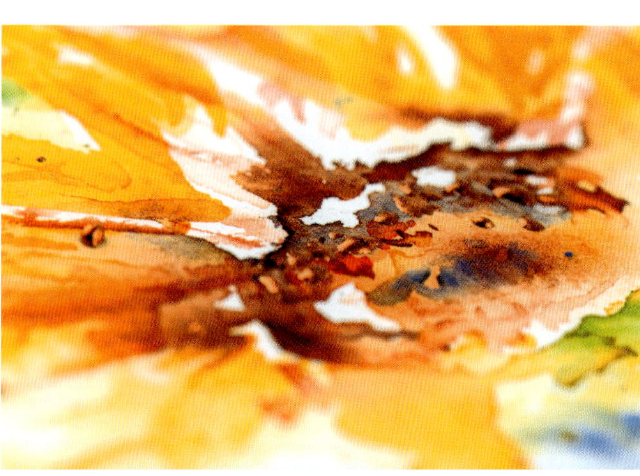

3 You can now apply it to your dry painting. Less is more! It can be applied in large brushstrokes, small dots (which will stay raised when they dry), or even spattered on.

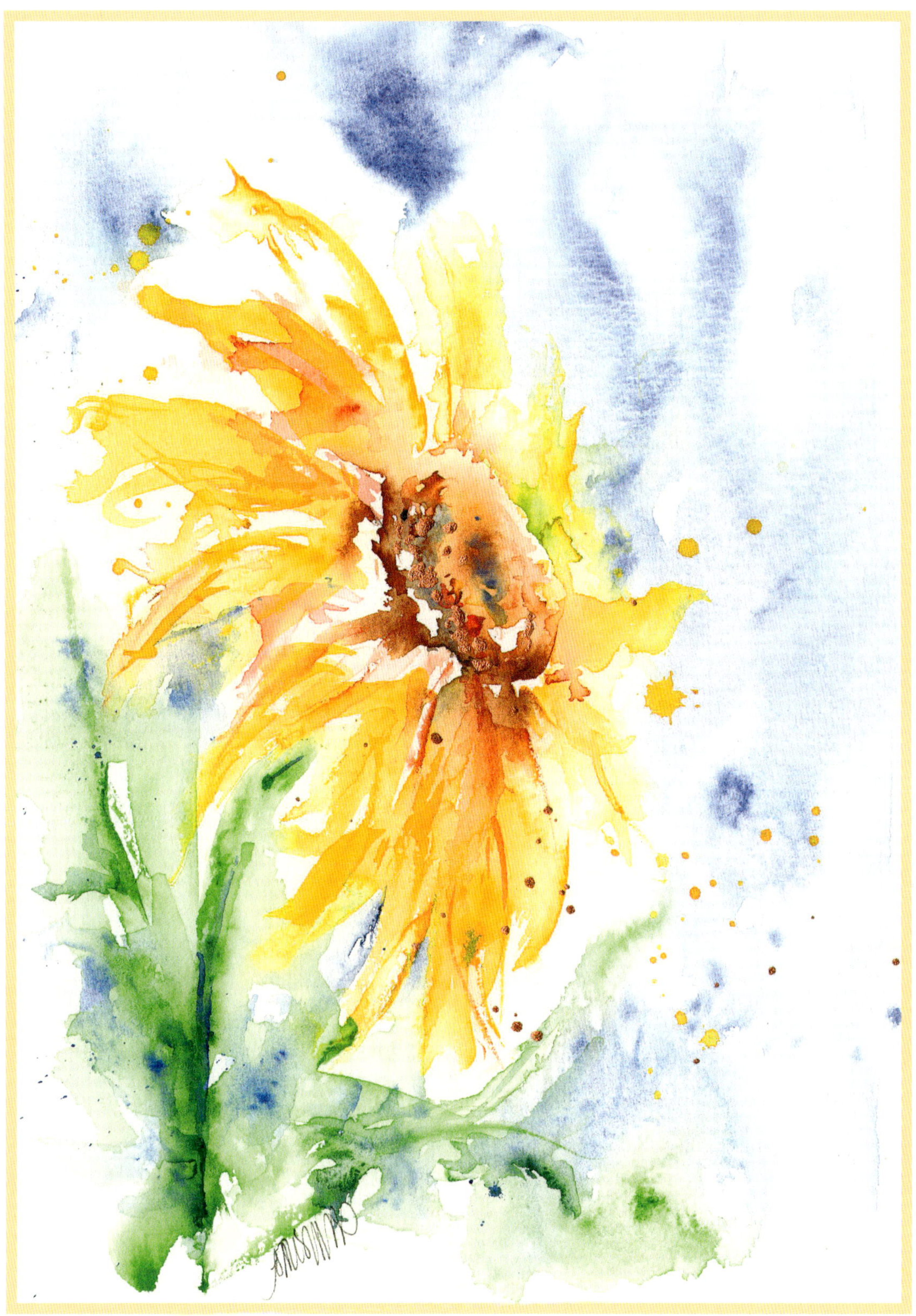

SUNFLOWER
18 x 25.5cm (7 x 10in)

A sunflower will turn its head towards the sun, and some
varieties can reach heights of more than 4.75m (16ft)!

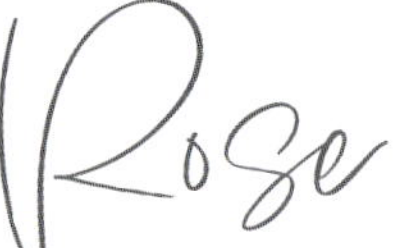

Rose

All varieties of rose are so very stunning, no wonder the whole world loves them. This iconic and ever-popular flower is wonderfully enjoyable to paint.

LIFTING OUT
A technique that requires stiff bristles for control. The 6mm (¼in) flat synthetic brush is ideal.

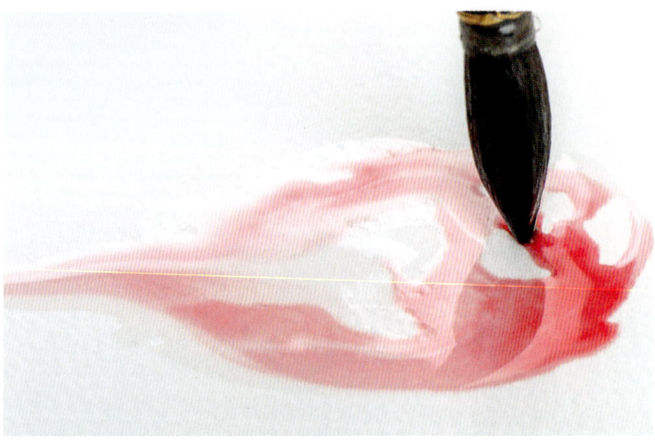

1 Use the large brush to paint a loosely oval shape of clean water, with plenty of gaps of clean paper left within. Still using the large brush, drop in rose madder by touching the tip of the loaded brush to the water here and there.

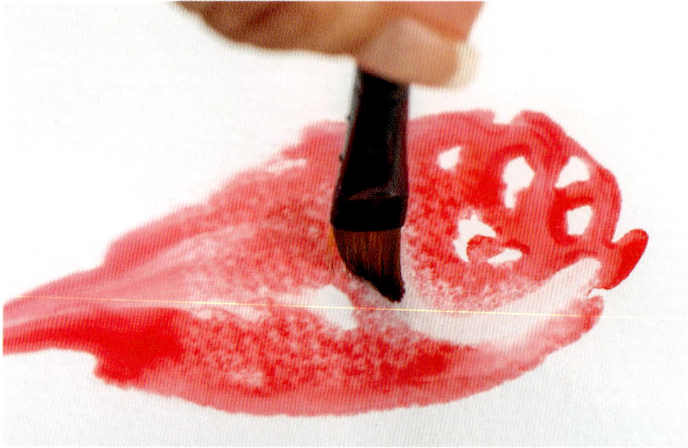

2 While the paint is wet, you can draw the tip of the flat brush over the surface and it will draw up (or 'lift out') the wet paint, leaving a thin, pale gap.

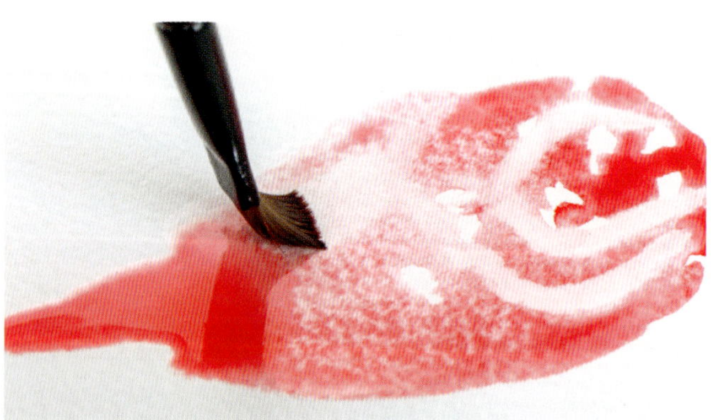

3 You can draw the brush around, and also flatten it to draw out larger amounts, creating large pale petals.

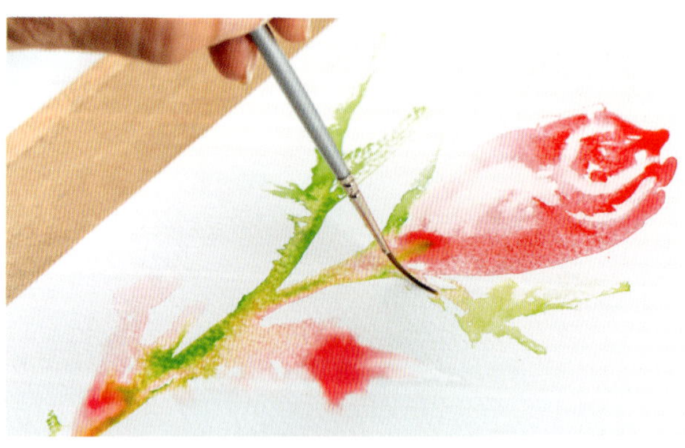

4 While the paint remains wet, you can use the small brush to add more paint to strengthen shadows, creating more contrast against the lifted-out parts.

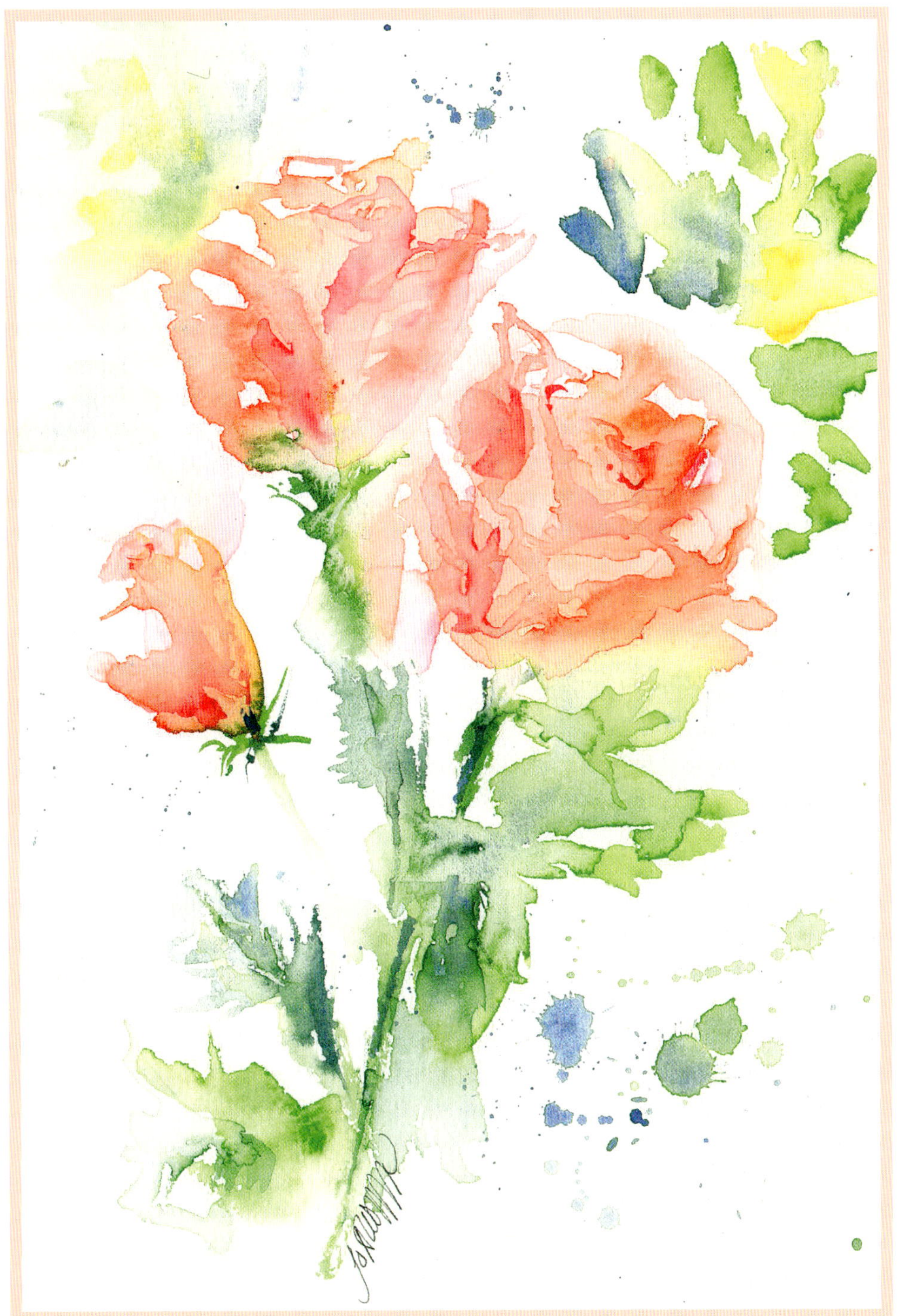

PINK ROSES

18 x 25.5cm (7 x 10in)

A development on the technque shown opposite, here I have retained the light areas with negative painting (see page 72) as well as lifting out for a different effect.

There are hundreds of varieties of rose, and so they are ideal for painting experimentation. All varieties of rose are edible, would you believe? I would rather admire than eat them, personally!

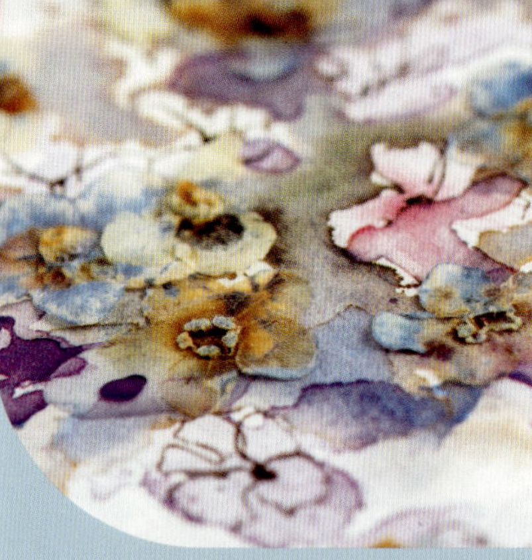

Forget-me-nots

Mixed media involves using two or more different materials – perhaps pen and wash, or watercolour with pastels – but can involve fabric, paper, or dried flowers.

I thought the addition of some real dried flowers would look fabulous combined with this simple purple flower painting. They add another dimension – quite literally – with their varying textures.

COLLAGE

Adding real flowers and foliage to your artwork can be very effective.

This could also be used to your advantage to cover a multitude of sins... You could cover up an overworked area with collage and nobody would ever know - unless you tell them, that is!

If you try this out, add a few pieces where there is no error - otherwise the collaged addition will draw the eye; quite the contrary to what you want.

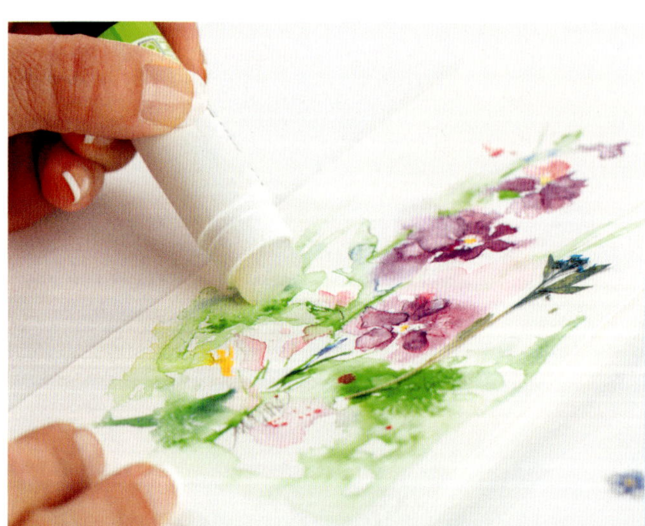

ATTACHING THE MATERIAL

Use a glue stick to attach the found materials to the surface once your painting is dry. They are often fragile, so work carefully.

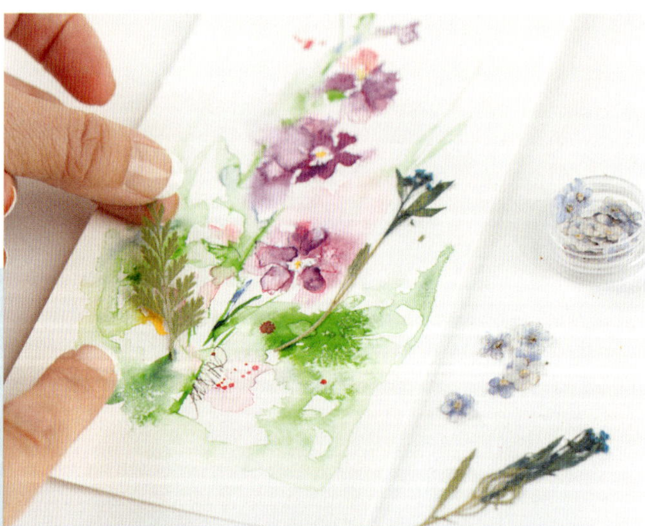

LESS IS MORE

Don't be tempted to apply too many, or you risk overwhelming the watercolour.

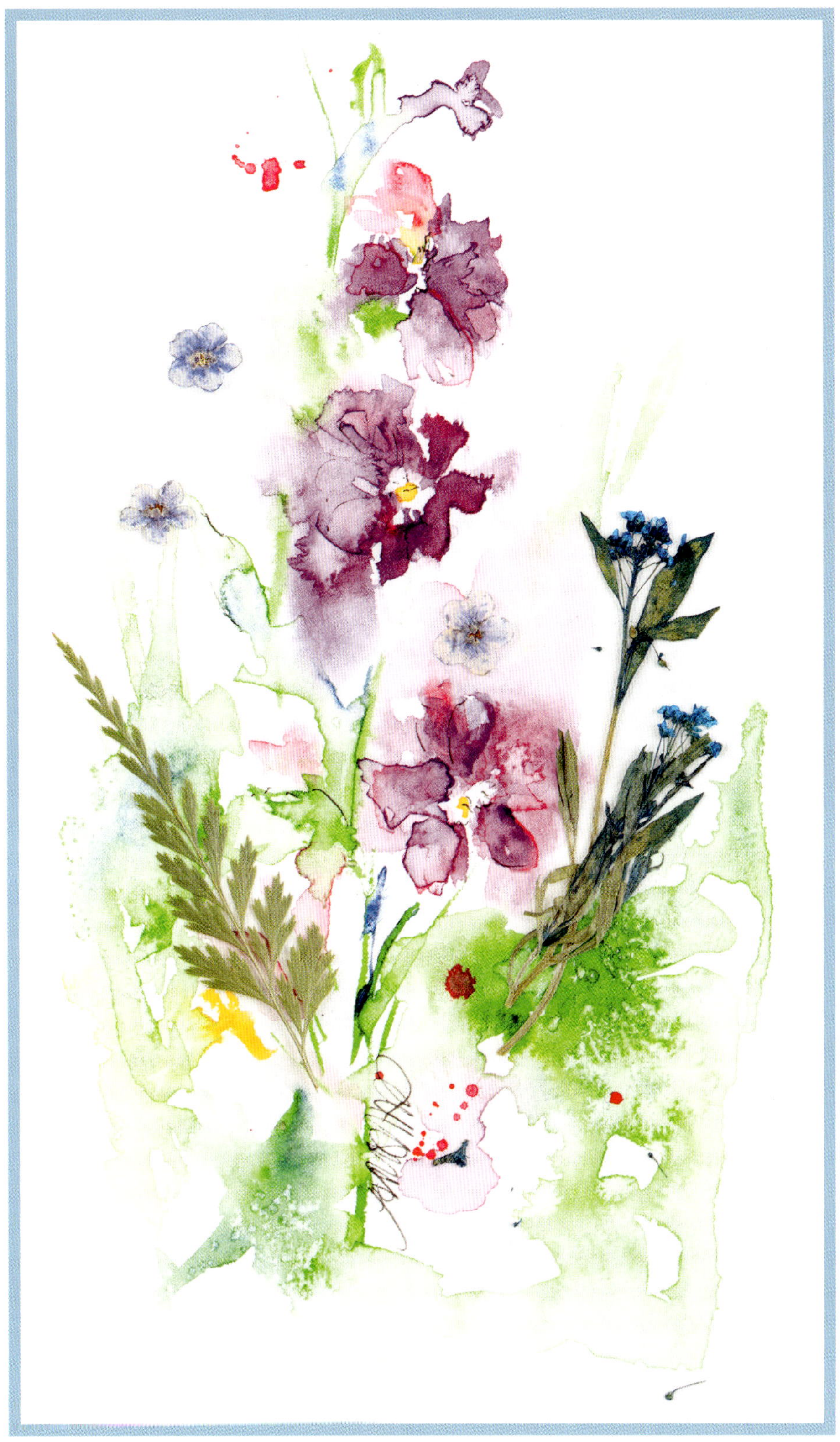

FORGET-ME-NOTS

10 x 20.5cm (4 x 8in)

Incorporating real flowerheads and leaves adds instant
detail and realism.

Knapweed

While the name does not necessarily conjure up images of beauty, I just adore the rather scruffy look of these flowers. They attract lots of insects to our gardens – and also lovely birds, such as the goldfinch, which will feast on the seeds.

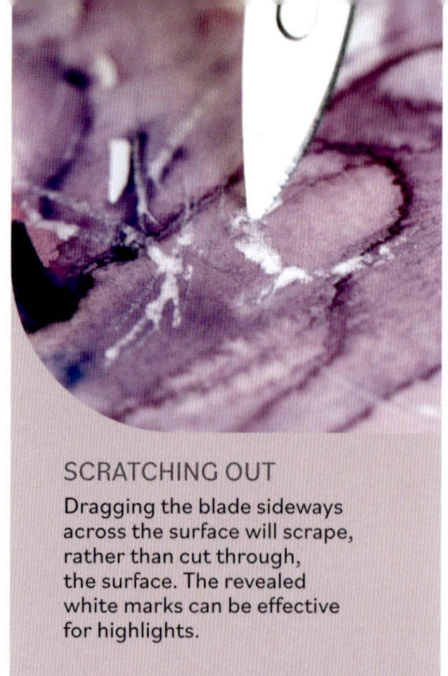

SCRATCHING OUT
Dragging the blade sideways across the surface will scrape, rather than cut through, the surface. The revealed white marks can be effective for highlights.

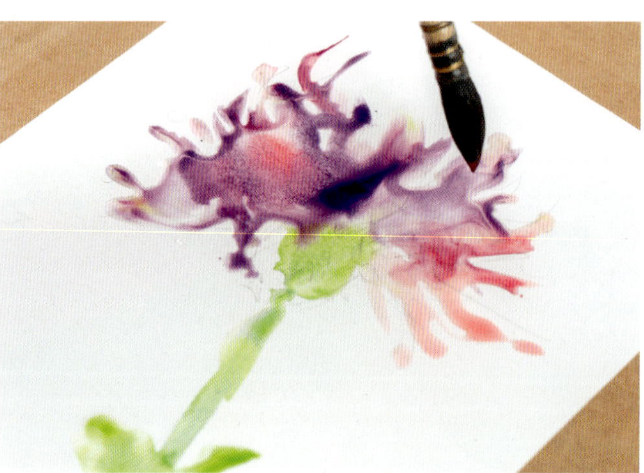

1 Sketch out the knapweed with light marks using an HB pencil. Lay clean water into the subject, then begin painting, using May green for the stem, and rose madder and Schmincke violet for the petals. Aim to make clean, simple marks with the large brush.

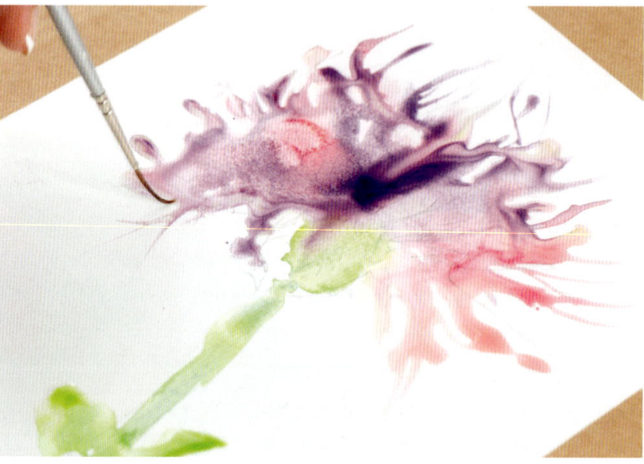

2 Swap to the small brush and use light flicking strokes to draw out the wet paint from the petals and give the characteristic look of knapweed.

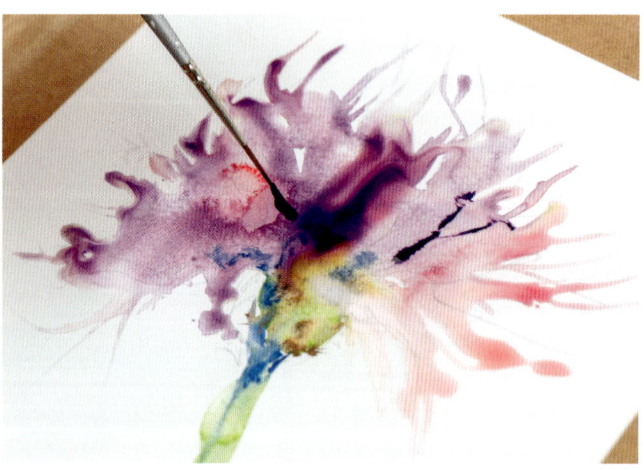

3 Still using the small brush, add French ultramarine to the stem and leaves for detail. Flick strokes of Schmincke violet inside the petals; and a mix of burnt umber and French ultramarine to bring out the detail of the bracts in the dark part of the flowerhead.

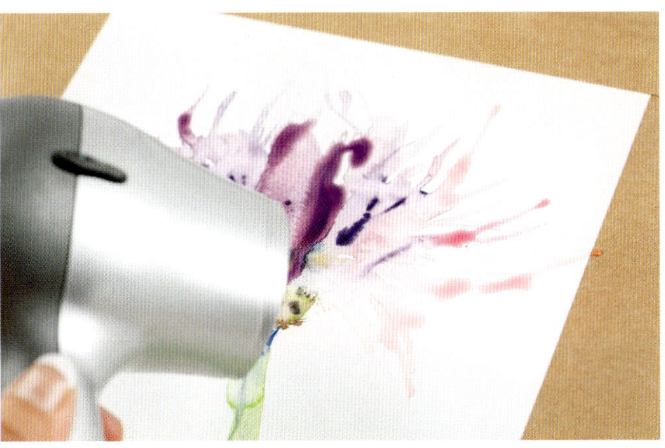

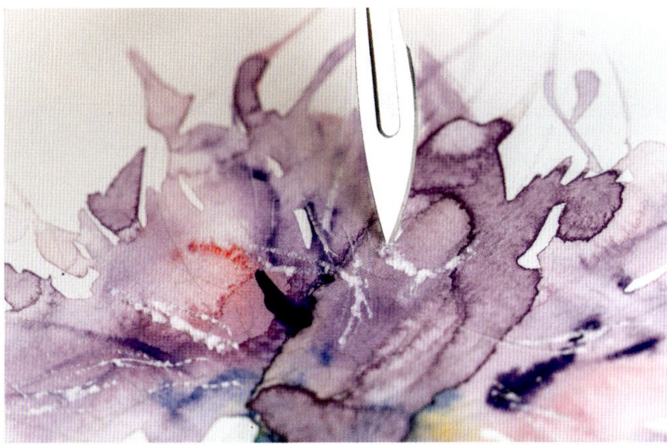

4 While the paint remains wet, use your hairdryer to push the paint out from the centre.

5 Once completely dry, use the tip of the scalpel to lightly scratch the surface. Use just enough pressure to take off the surface fibres of the paper, revealing clean white marks.

Tip

If you're unsure about using a hairdryer, or are worried about it blowing out of control, use a drinking straw to push the paint just where you want it.

Tip

Turn the painting so that you can always scratch away from your body.

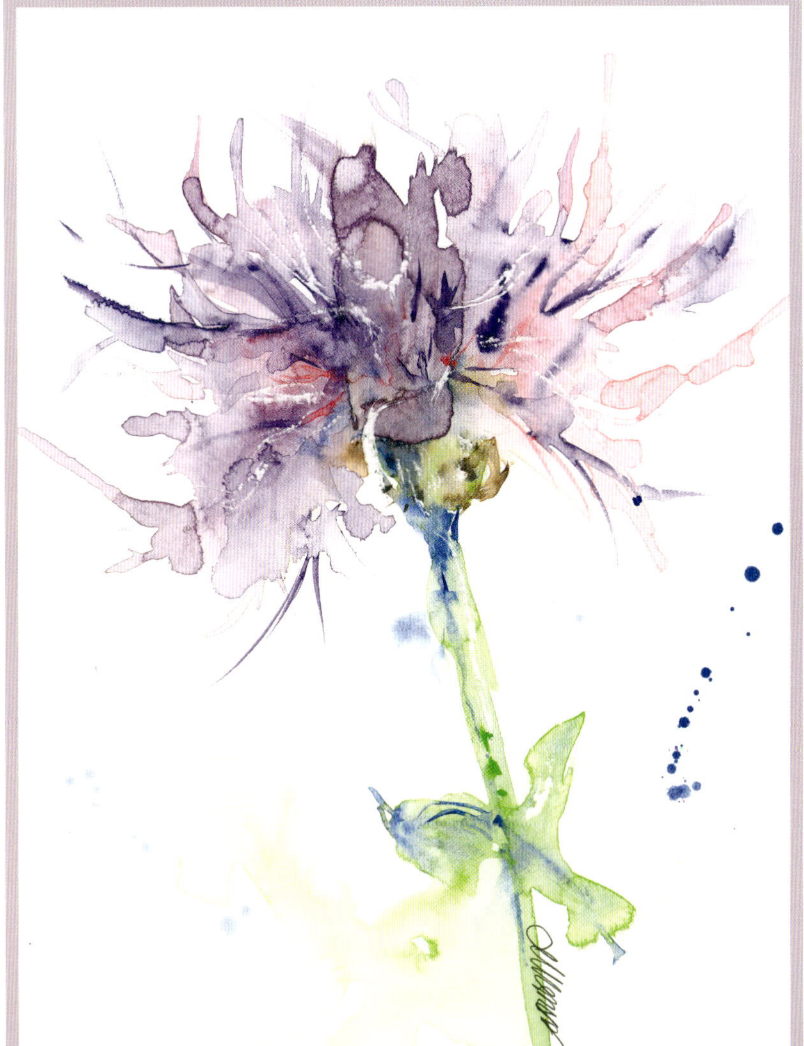

KNAPWEED
20 x 28cm (8 x 11in)

Ragged wildflowers

The technique used here, drybrush, is very useful for painting all sorts of different spiky or ragged wildflowers, such as African lily (Agapanthus). The loose flowerheads of this flower grow on long, slender stems, open in summer, and come in a variety of different colours. The globe-shaped flowers of globe thistles (Echinops) have a textural appearance that also lends itself to the drybrush technique; and closer to home, the humble thistle is also easy to paint with this technique.

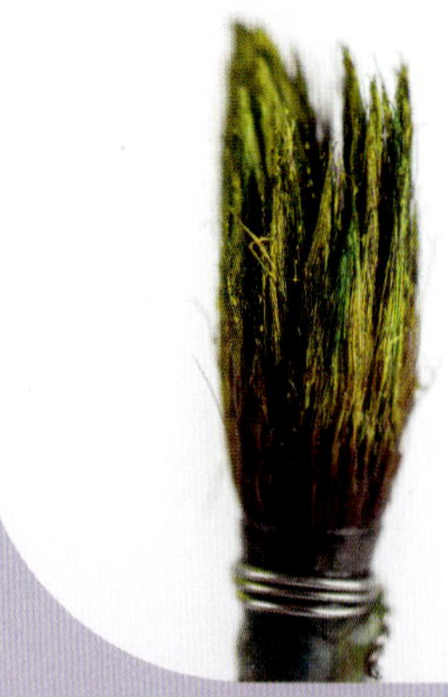

DRYBRUSH
Exactly as it sounds, for this technique, both the brush and the paper must be dry – and the paint should have only as much water added to make it workable.

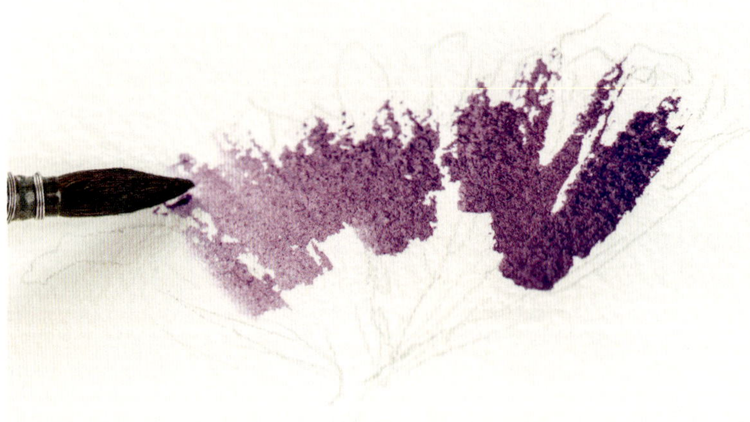

THE TECHNIQUE
Load a small dry brush with a little paint, then draw it at an angle over the surface, just skimming the paper. The aim is to end up with strokes that break up near the end.

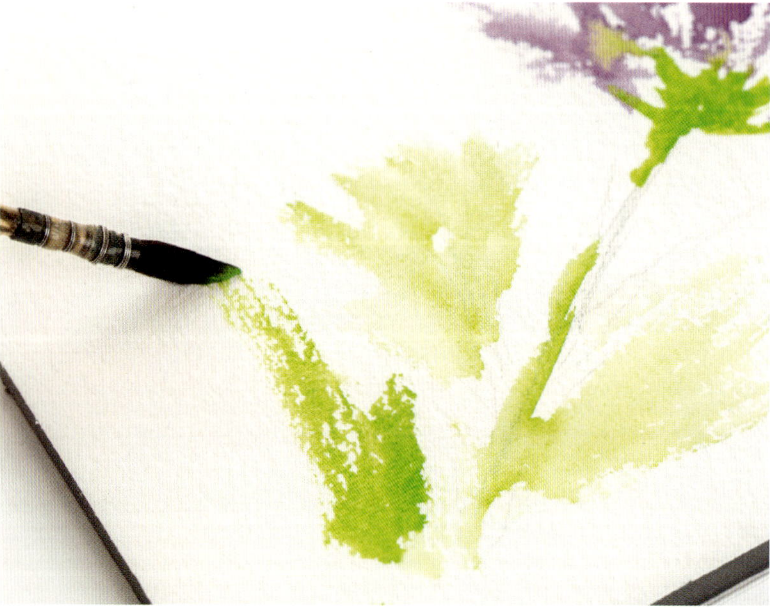

NOT JUST FOR PETALS
Drybrushing works well for leaves and stems too – and helps them not to be too bold or dominant.

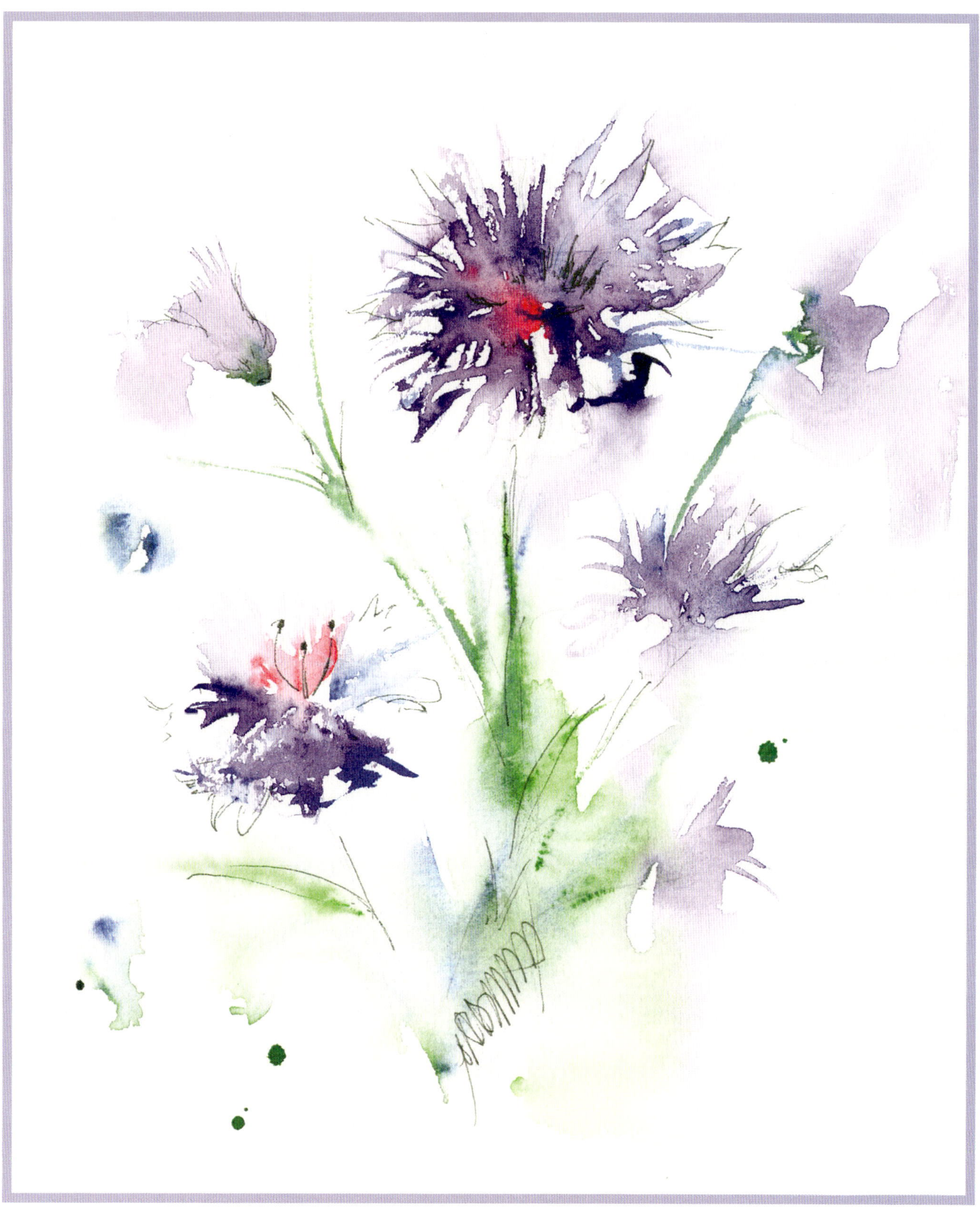

PURPLE WILDFLOWER
18 x 25.5cm (7 x 10in)

Cosmos

These belong to the same plant family, Asteraceae, as my favourites – daisies – so it is no surprise that this flower has made an appearance in my book.

Cosmos flowers come in an array of colours and can greatly differ in shape and size, so I decided to paint mine pink and use the texture medium to plump up some of the petals for a little three-dimensional effect.

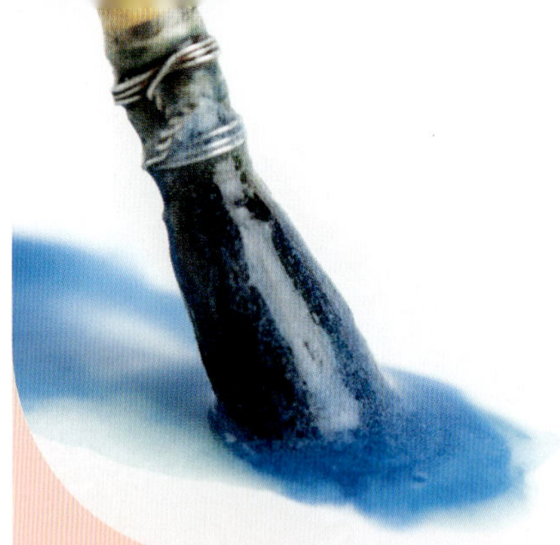

TEXTURE PASTE
This medium is fabulous to add to watercolours to give them a subtle physical texture for impasto-like effects.

Using texture paste

You can use this medium in a variety of ways. At its most basic, it is as simple as painting it on with your brushes. It will dry to leave a milky, subtle texture, after which you can paint over it. Use liberally!

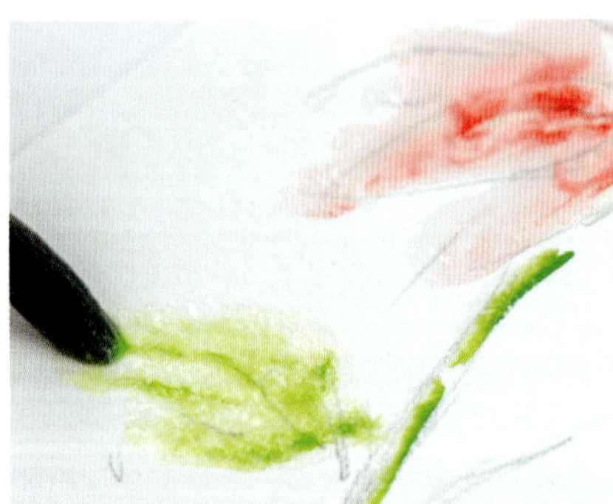

PAINTING OVER THE TOP OF DRY MEDIUM
The pigment will tend to settle in the medium, giving a stronger, darker, grainy result that doesn't flow as freely.

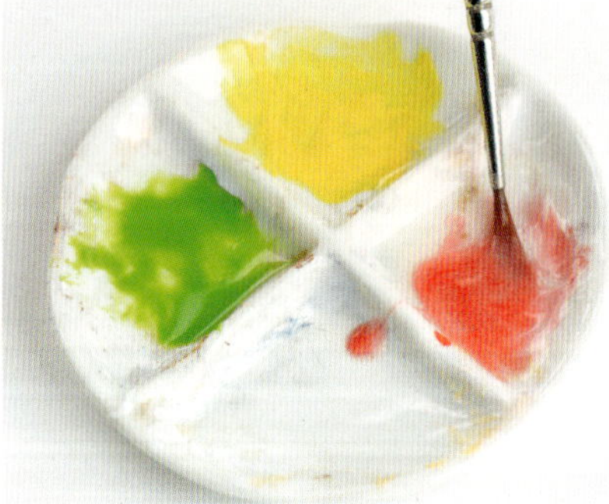

MIXING IT WITH PAINT
Prepare small wells of each colour you'll want to use, adding the paint to the texture paste. There's no need to add water to this mix; the texture paste will provide the fluidity.

You can now apply the paint to the surface using the brushes as normal. This approach results in a creamier, less grainy effect than painting over the top of the paste. This means you have a lot more control, as the paint will stay where you put it, and barely flow at all.

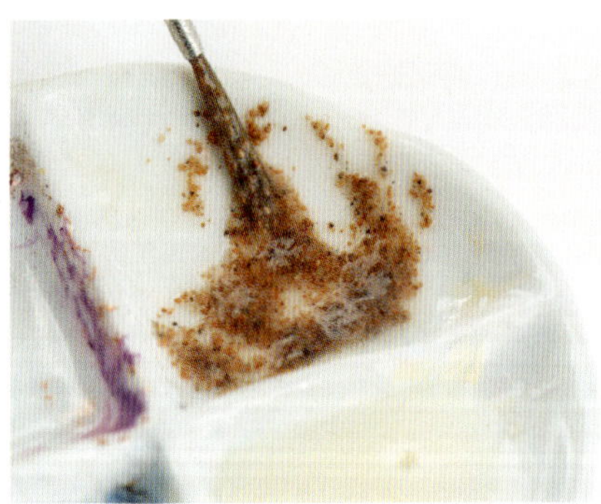

MIXING IT WITH SAND
Gently stir the sand and the medium together on a tinting saucer, then pick it up on your brush and apply it to the surface. As the medium dries, it will securely bind the sand to the surface, resulting in a definite 3D effect, ideal for very heavy textures.

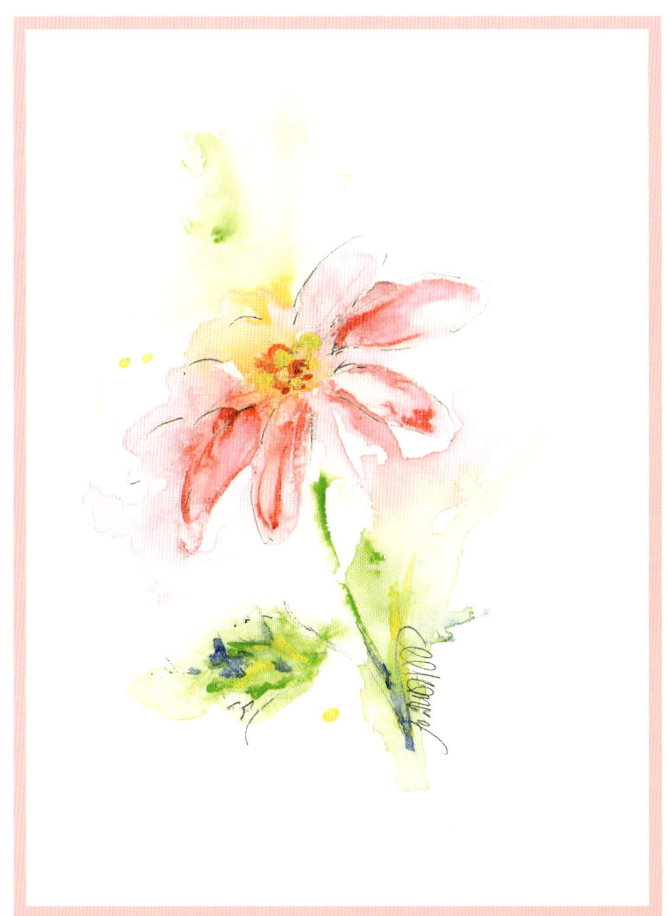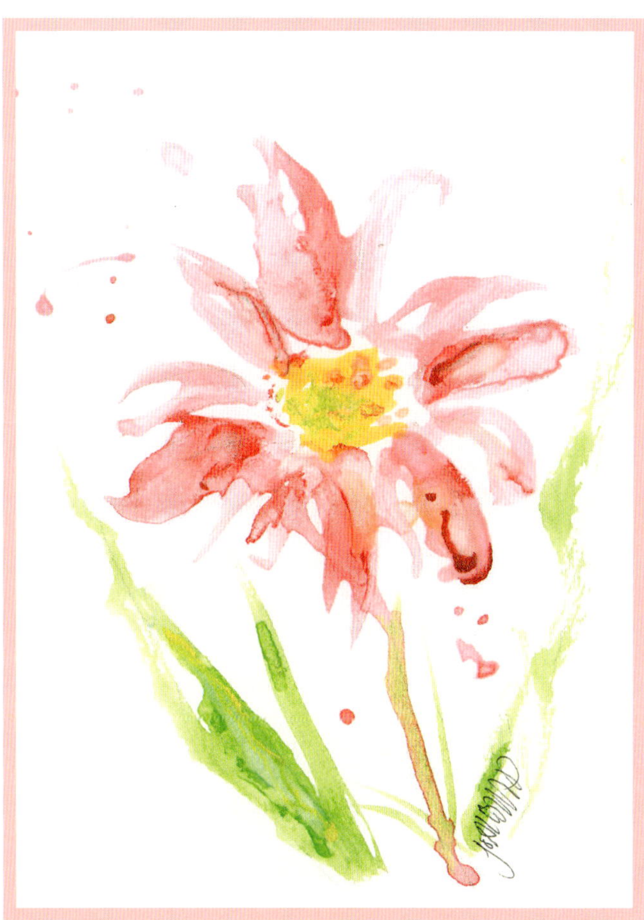

TWO COSMOS FLOWERS
Both 11.5 x 16.5cm (4½ x 6½in)

Field of poppies

When drawing a big group of poppies, bear perspective in mind. Keep larger flower heads in the foreground and consider making them not only smaller, but also less detailed in the midground and distance. This can be achieved by using wet into wet techniques so they appear softer and less clear. In contrast, poppies in the front should be larger and can contain a little more detail and brighter colours. Using wet on dry for this will enhance and bring them forwards.

Sometimes, if possible, I use cooler colours for background flowers as these are receding, and opt for warmer colours in the front so they appear to advance.

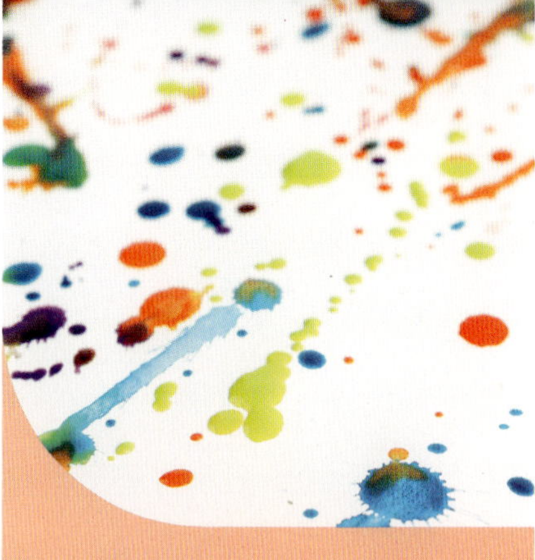

SPATTERING

Spattering is flicking droplets of paint onto the surface in a controlled – or mostly controlled! – fashion.

Load the brush with a dilute mix of paint, then flick it at the surface, releasing a spray of paint drops that add movement and dynamism to your work.

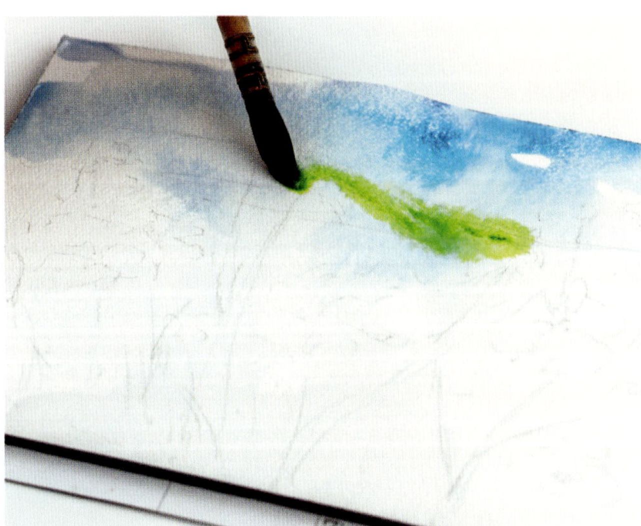

1 Use the HB pencil to lightly sketch in the main shapes. Wet the whole piece of paper using the large brush and clean water, then drop in a mix of French ultramarine and helio cerulean across the sky. Working wet into wet, lay in May green along the horizon, letting it blend into the blue. Leave gaps for the smaller poppies.

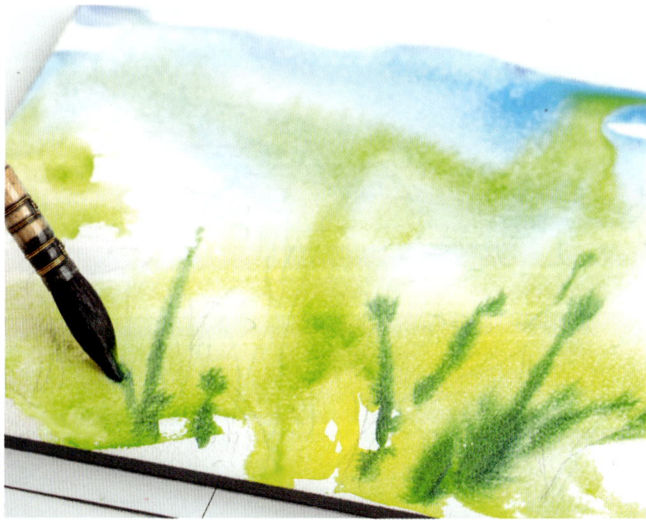

2 For the foreground, use a mix of May green and vanadium yellow, again leaving space for the larger poppies. Use the tip of the brush to add stems with a mix of French ultramarine and May green.

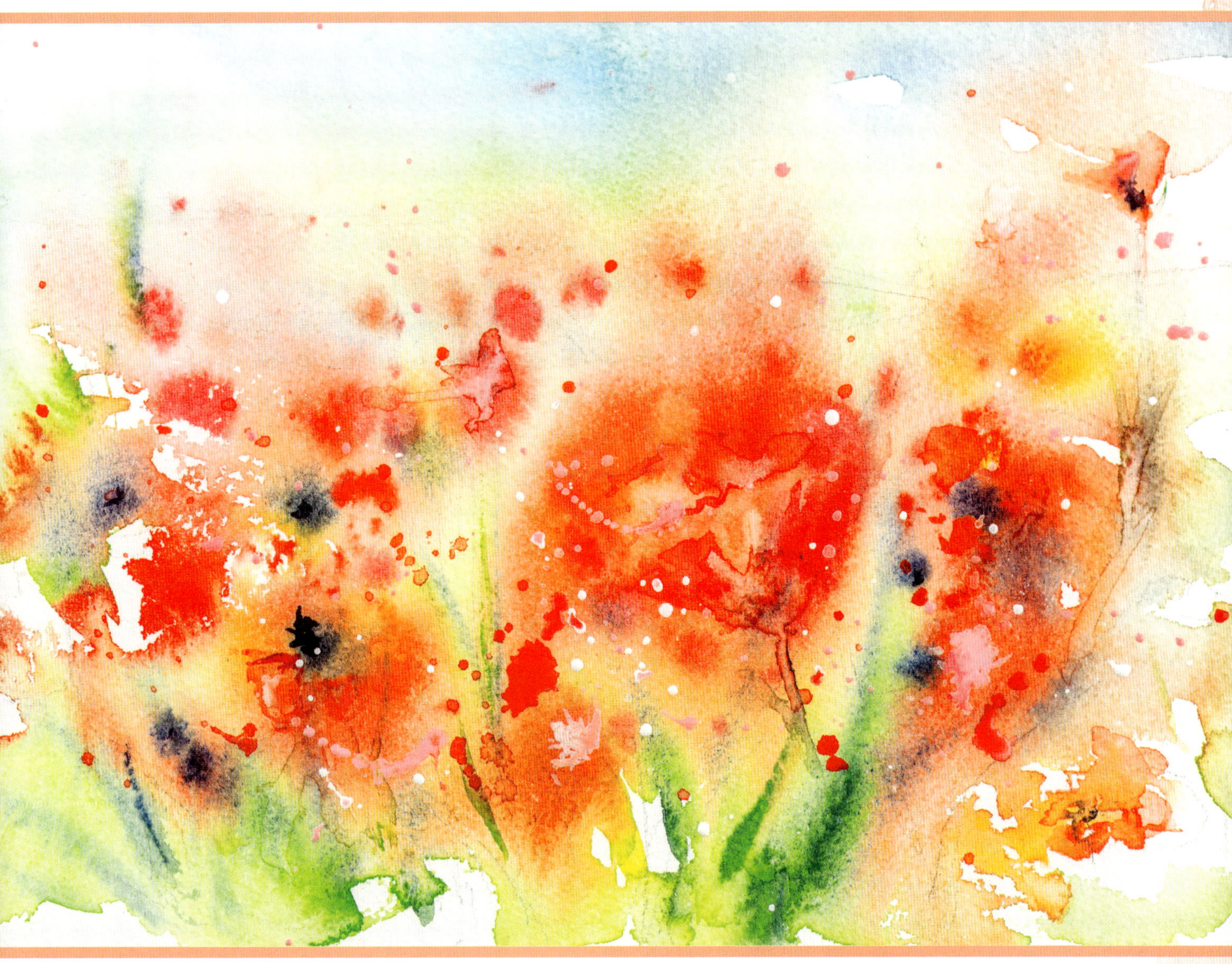

POPPY FIELD IN WATERCOLOUR AND INK
25.5 x 18cm (10 x 7in)

Tip

You can spatter onto a dry or wet surface for different effects.

- Spatters that land on a dry surface will keep their shape, and be more obvious in the finished piece.

- When working wet into wet, the spatters will soften into the surface, giving a more subtle effect.

- Try using your non-dominant hand. You'll naturally get less contrived results.

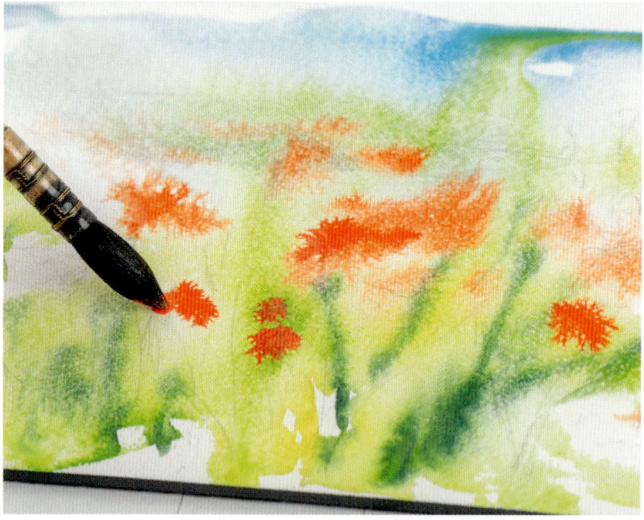

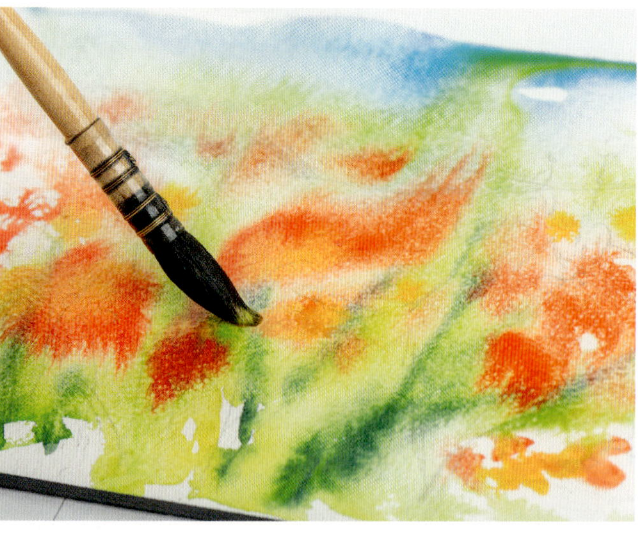

3 While the foreground remains wet, use the tip of the large brush to touch in vermilion for the poppies. Make the marks a variety of sizes, with the largest in the foreground.

4 Vary the hue with a little rose madder and vanadium yellow here and there.

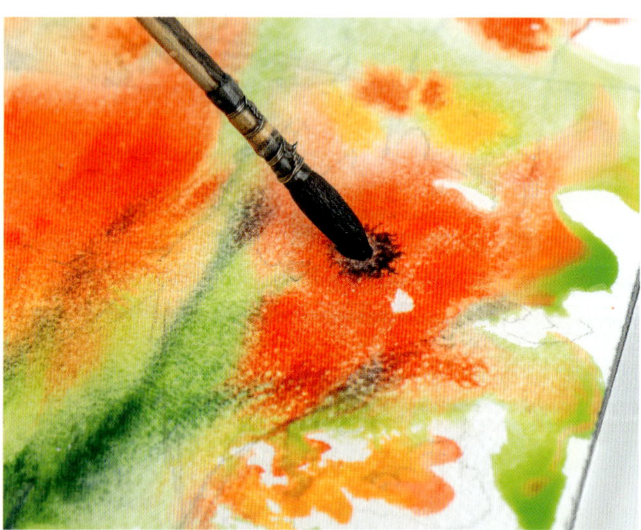

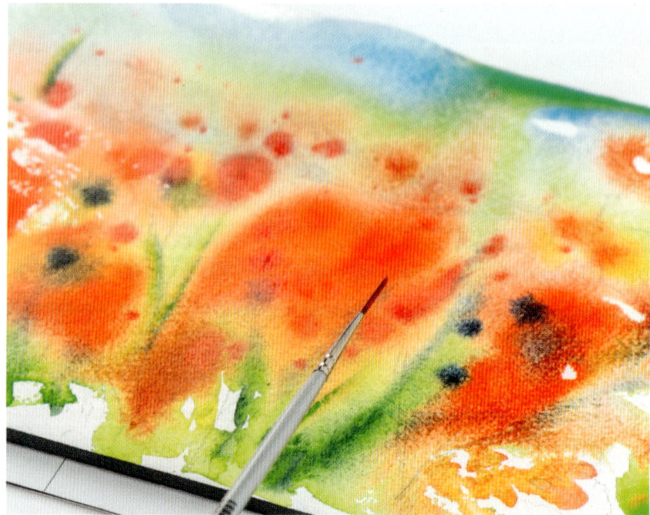

5 Change to the small brush and touch in the poppy centres using a dark mix of French ultramarine and burnt umber.

6 Pick up some rose madder on your rigger brush. Hold your hand around 30cm (12in) above the painting and relax your wrist. Make a firm flicking motion to spatter the surface with your paint.

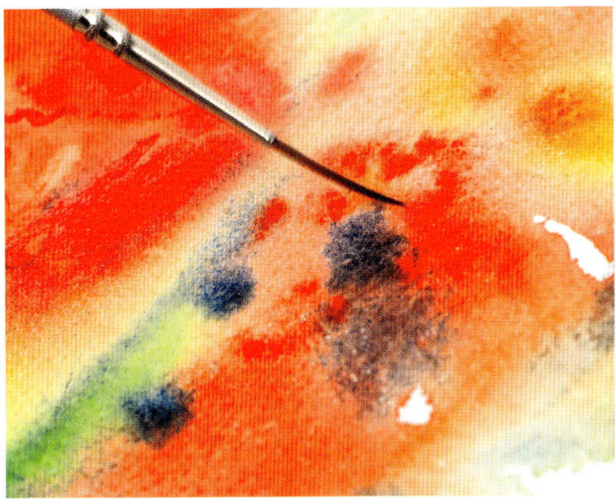

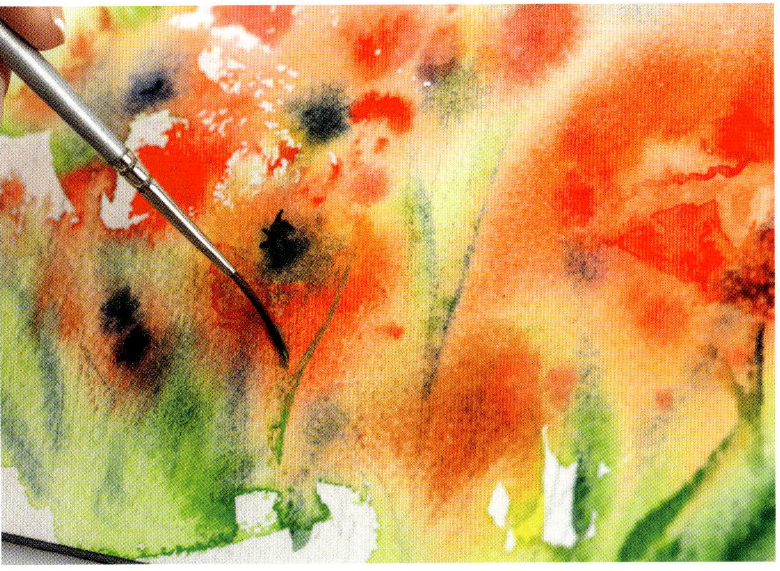

7 Allow the painting to dry completely, then bring the foreground poppies into focus, by using the tip of the small brush to add structure with wandering marks and strokes of vermilion and rose madder. For very dark red areas, add Schmincke violet, but be sparing.

8 Use the dark mix (French ultramarine and burnt umber) to develop the foreground poppy centres, and May green alongside French ultramarine for the stems and grasses.

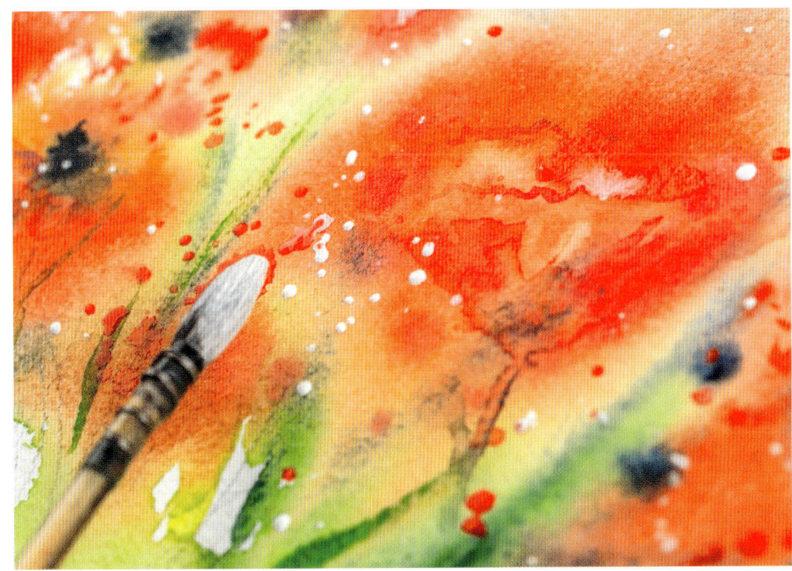

9 Use the medium brush to spatter vermilion onto the dry surface, then repeat with white acrylic ink. The larger brush will make larger marks, so be careful not to over-do things.

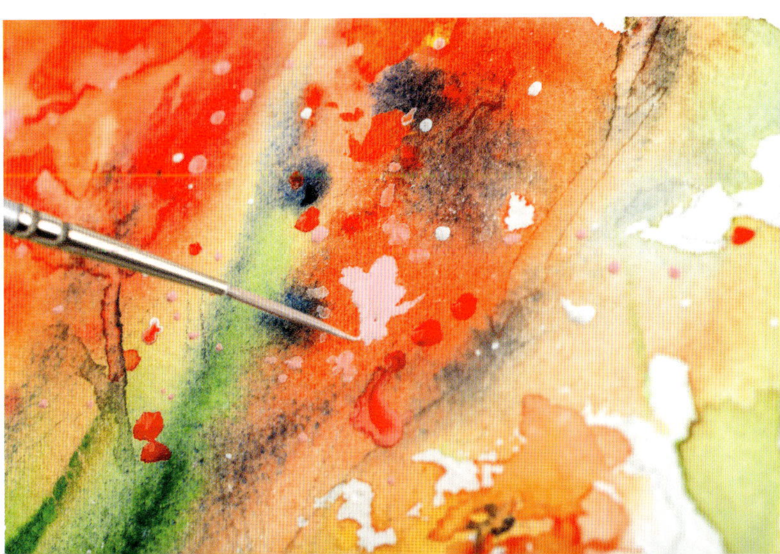

10 You can combine watercolour with inks – let's add some rose madder to the white ink to make a pink, and spatter that on the foreground using the small brush. You can use the same mix to add some small pink flowers for variety, too. Remember that acrylic inks need to be washed off your brushes immediately.

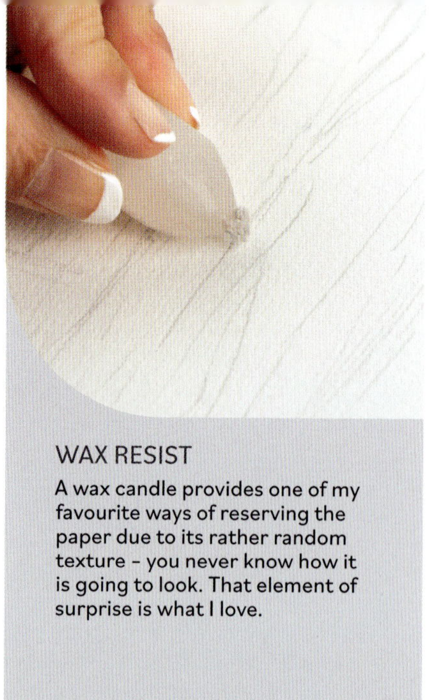

Bluebell wood

A visit to a bluebell wood is so therapeutic. Being out in the fresh air is good for our lungs; though when you see the most beautiful carpet of blues, purples, and pinks of the flowers, it really takes your breath away again – in a good way, of course!

WAX RESIST
A wax candle provides one of my favourite ways of reserving the paper due to its rather random texture – you never know how it is going to look. That element of surprise is what I love.

Using wax resist

Apply wax simply by using the candle like a wax crayon: just draw it on where you want light in the finished painting.

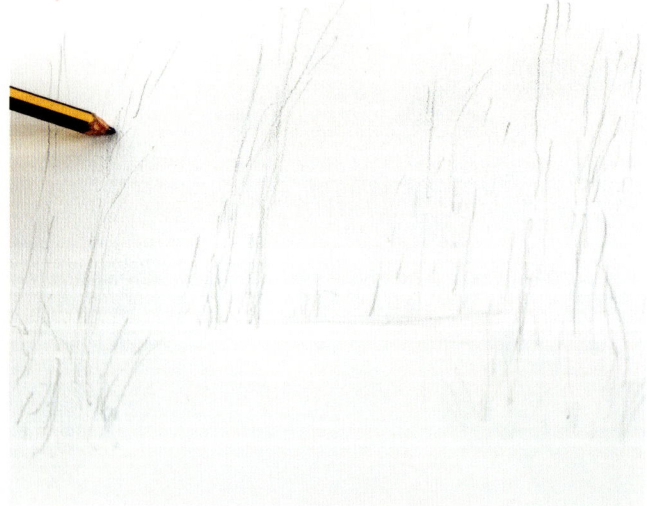

1 Make a light sketch with the HB pencil to establish the horizon line and a few main elements. Use the sketch to guide your placement of the wax, applying it mainly to the foreground trees.

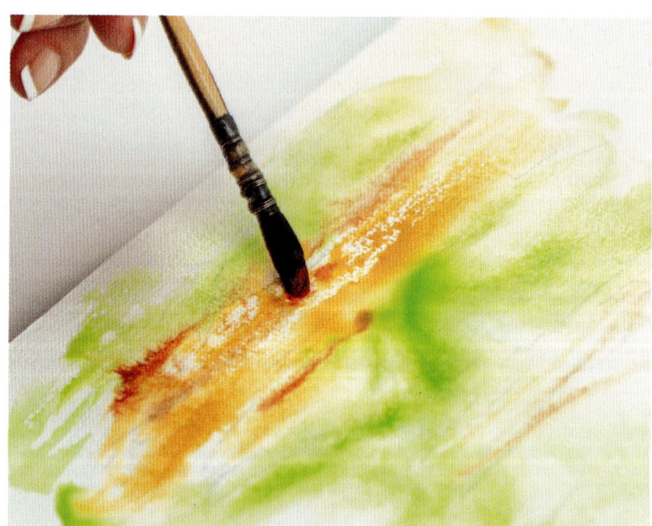

2 Apply clean water over the whole painting using the large brush, then add yellow ochre over the trees. You'll see the paint collect into beads and retreat from the waxed areas. Add May green in between the trees.

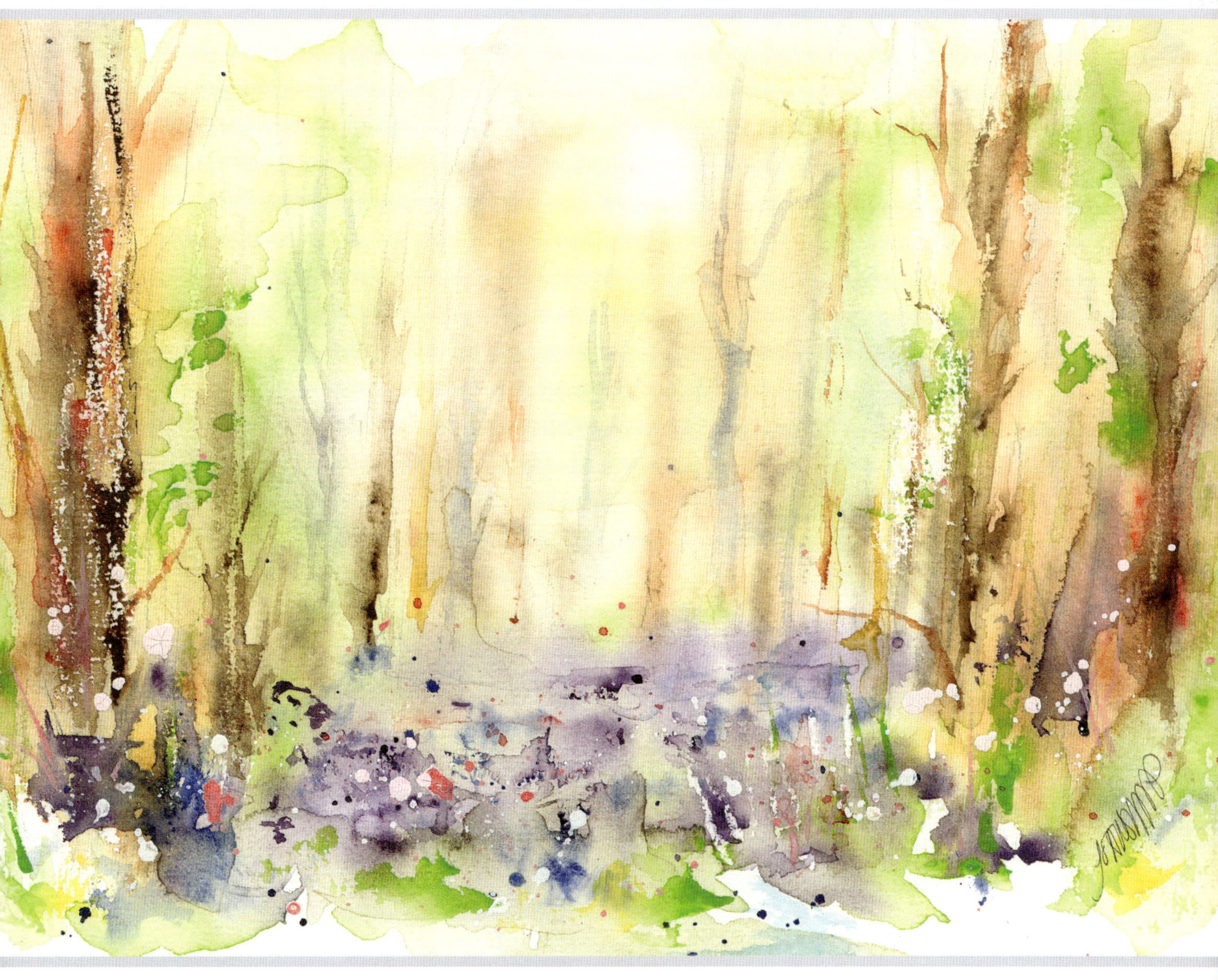

BLUEBELL WOOD
25.5 x 18cm (10 x 7in)

I have done quite a few paintings of bluebell woods and stumbled across this one when visiting Clevedon in Somerset, UK, with my husband. Of course, lot of photographs were taken, as I will never tire of painting such a stunning scene.

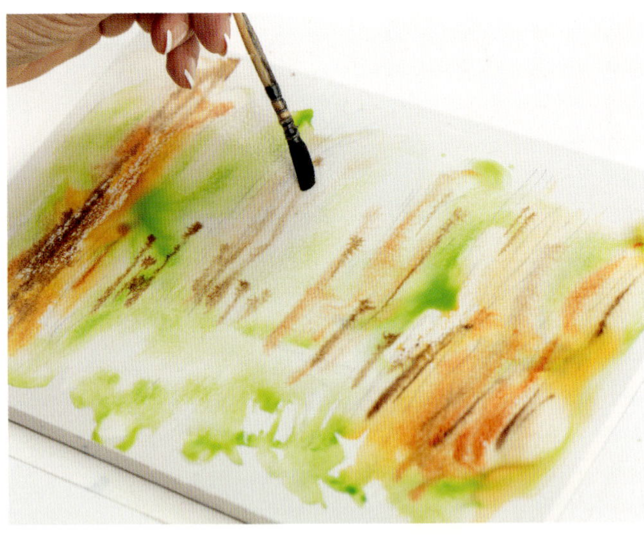

3 Continue building up colour over the painting; adding May green in the centre and in the foreground. Leave white areas for clear gaps. Change to the medium brush to add strokes of burnt sienna and burnt umber for smaller saplings and branches.

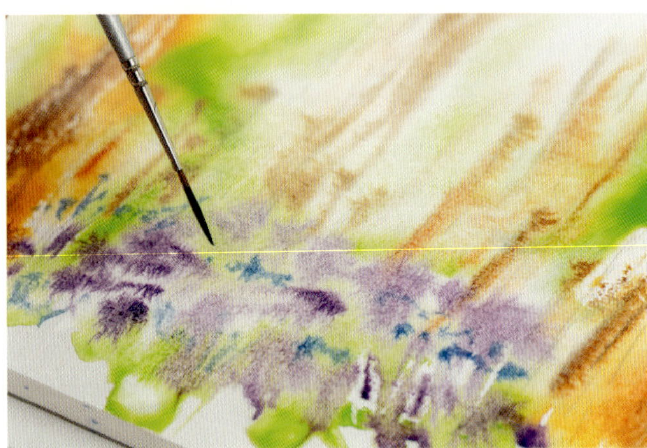

4 Begin building up the bluebells in the midground using Schmincke violet, then add smaller marks with French ultramarine wet into wet.

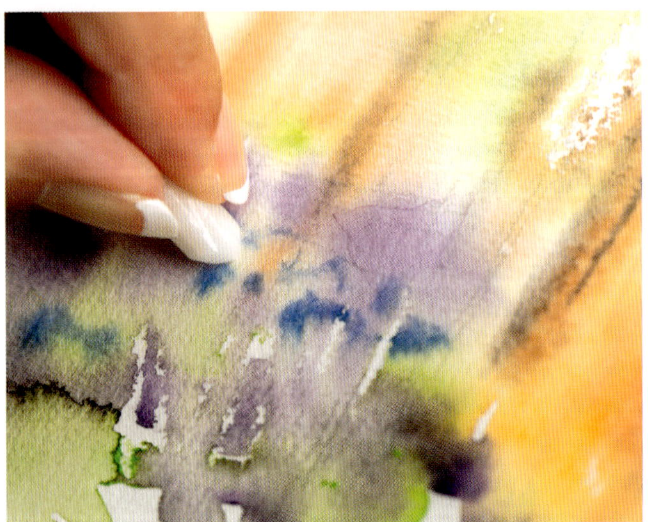

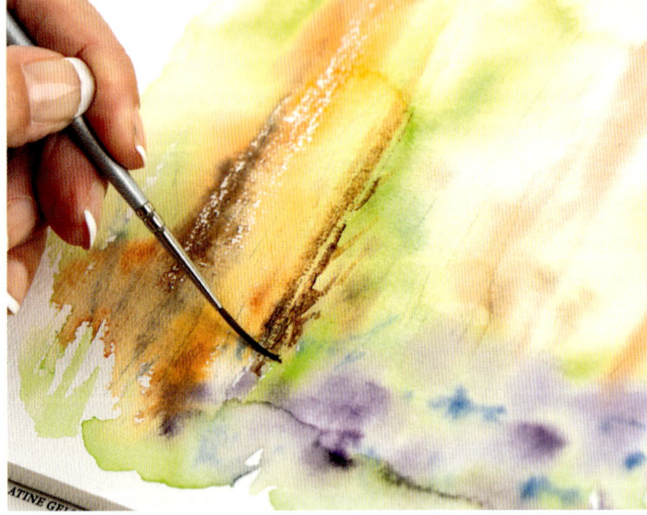

5 Once the painting is completely dry, use a thinner piece of wax to add more resist on the distant bluebells and midground trees. Rather than keeping the area white, it will preserve the existing colour.

6 Use burnt umber to work over the midground trees with the small brush. Apply the same colour to the foreground trees for shadow, too.

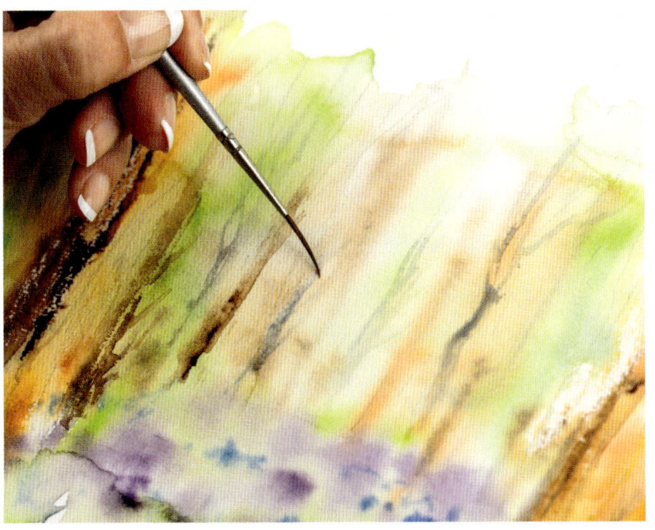

7 Make a neutral grey mix by diluting French ultramarine and burnt umber and use this to add the suggestion of distant trees.

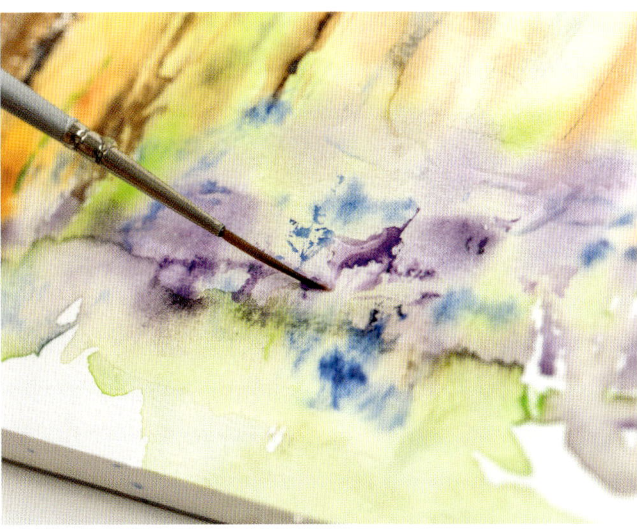

8 Hint at individual flowerheads in the mass of bluebells by using the tip of the small brush to add touches of Schmincke violet and French ultramarine.

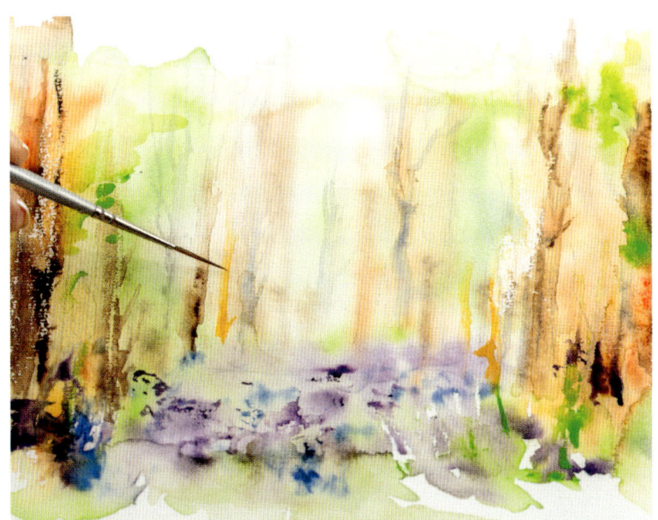

9 Add some warming touches to the foreground by adding subtle hints of vermilion to the trees, and yellow ochre in amongst the bluebells.

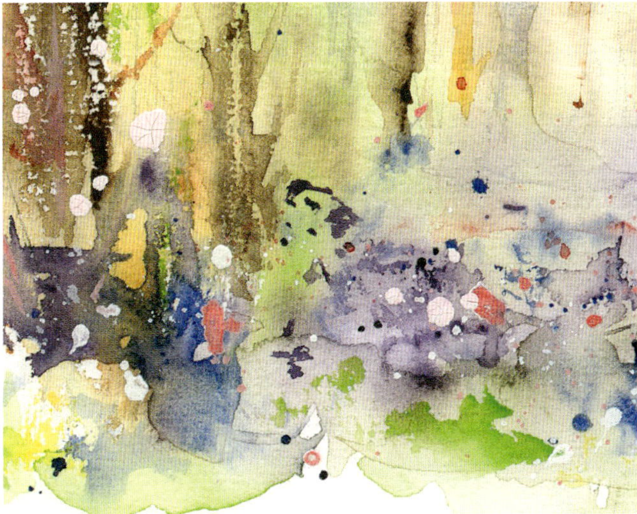

10 Tint white acrylic paint by mixing it with some of the mixes left in your palette and add some spattering (see page 116) for a little extra detail around the foreground woodland floor. Acrylic paints work well for detail in paintings like this, as unlike watercolour, the marks will sit on top of the resist.

Foxgloves

Extremely poisonous, foxgloves can be deadly if ingested – but an extract is used to make the drug digoxin, used in medicine to treat heart conditions. Happily, painting these beautiful, highly structured flowers brings no risks at all!

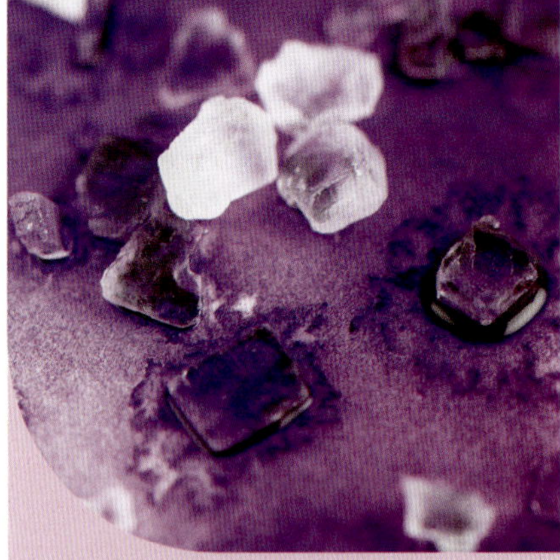

SALT

You can use any sort of salt for this technique. Fine-grained table salt will give small sparkles, while larger rock salt – as shown above – will result in more definite texture.

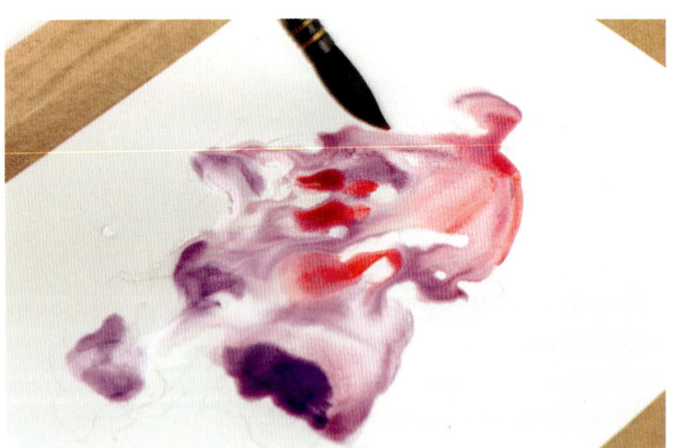

1 Begin with a light sketch made with an HB pencil. Wet the area with clean water and a large brush, then drop in rose madder and Schmincke violet, allowing the colours to mix and merge on the paper.

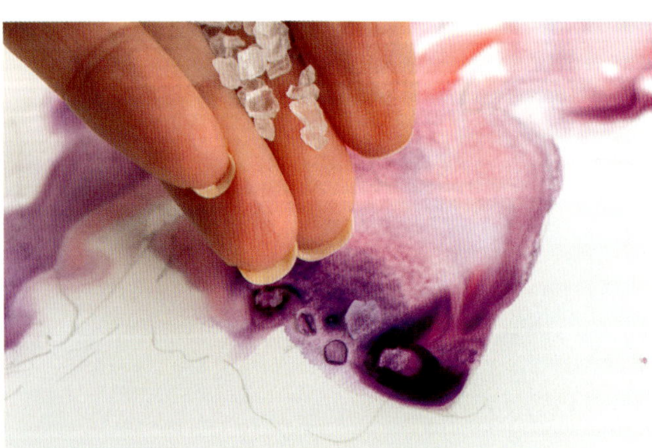

2 While the paint is wet, sprinkle on the salt. Don't scatter it randomly; aim for the areas where you want to final effect to be – in this case, the lighter areas of the inside of the petals.

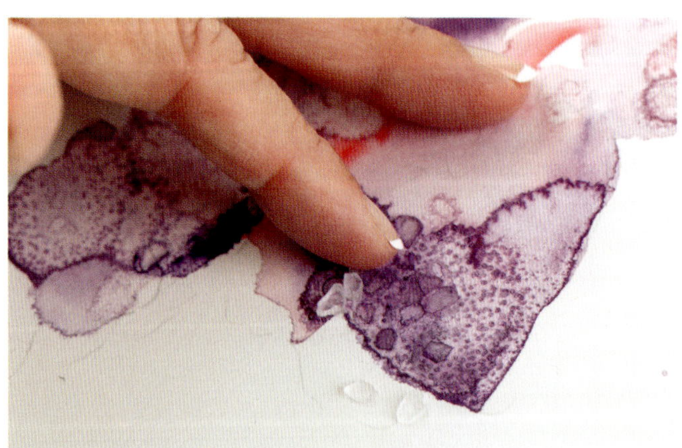

3 As long as you avoid the areas where the salt is, you can add more depth of colour by working wet into wet. Once you're happy, leave it to dry completely, then gently brush the salt away with a clean finger to reveal the effect.

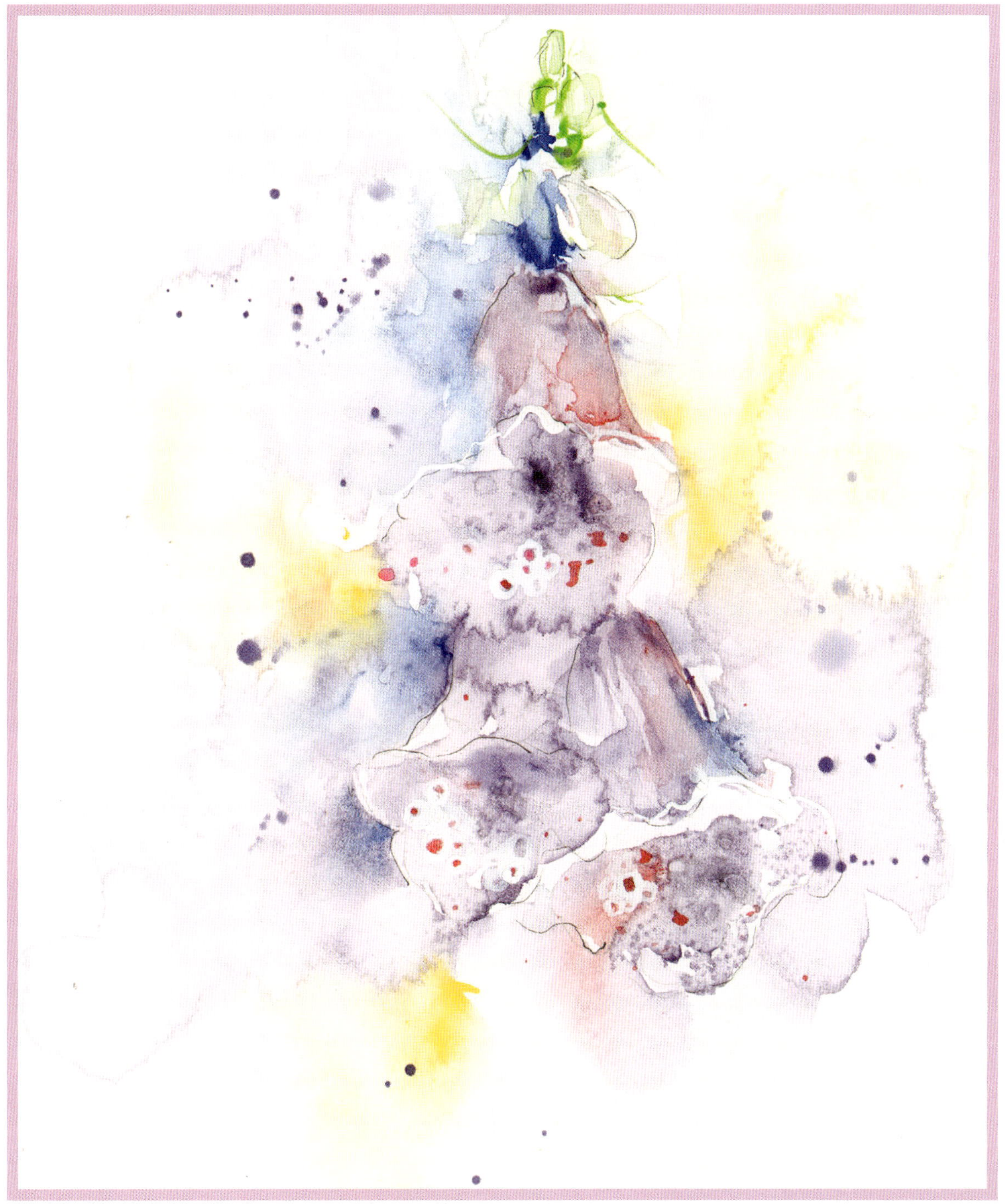

FOXGLOVES
14.5 x 21cm (5¾ x 8¼in)

I've found that the salt effect works best on Hot-pressed (HP)
paper, as the smooth surface means the effect stands out
clearly. Some textured papers can minimize the effect.

Some yellow was added in the background to the end result
as it is complementary to the purple flowers.

Rosebud

A yellow rose was my nan's favourite flower and so my mum would always ask for a single one in any bouquet she bought, too. I love this flower for these very reasons and so here we have two – one named in memory of my mum, Susan, and one named after my nan, Hilda.

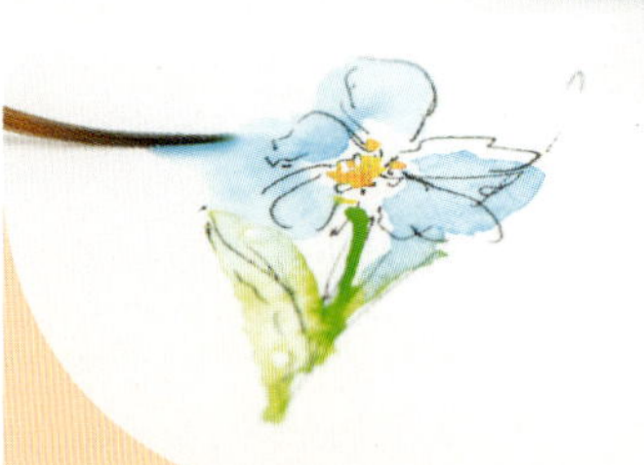

PEN AND WASH

I use pens like the Micron 005, Faber Castell XS and Staedtler Triplus Fineliner, which all have very fine points.

Using fineliner pens

Permanent fineliner pens are water resistant, so you can draw out your flower, then lay in a wash over it to add colour and movement. Note that there's no need to paint within the lines - in fact, part of the fun of pen and wash (also called line and wash) is the freedom it gives you.

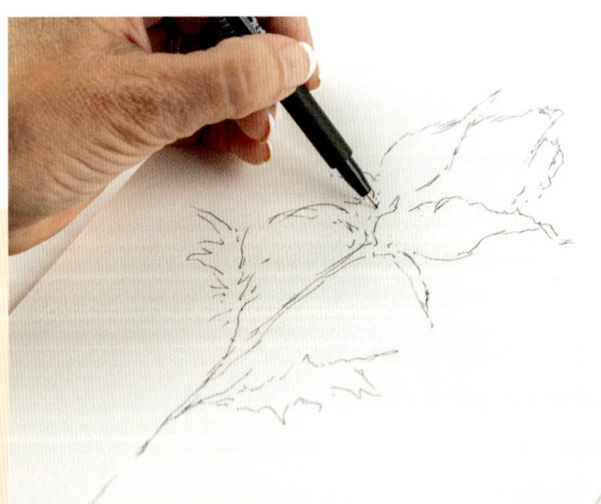

1 Start sketching with your pen. Be bold, not hesitant. If you make an error, just correct that part or move straight on - this will add to the overall liveliness and dynamism of the painting.

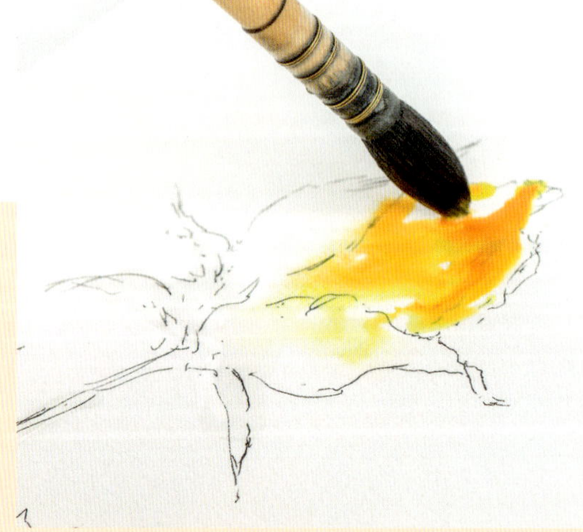

2 Wet the rosebud, the stem and the leaves with the large brush and clean water, then drop in vandium yellow on the rosebud, and add a touch of vermilion wet into wet.

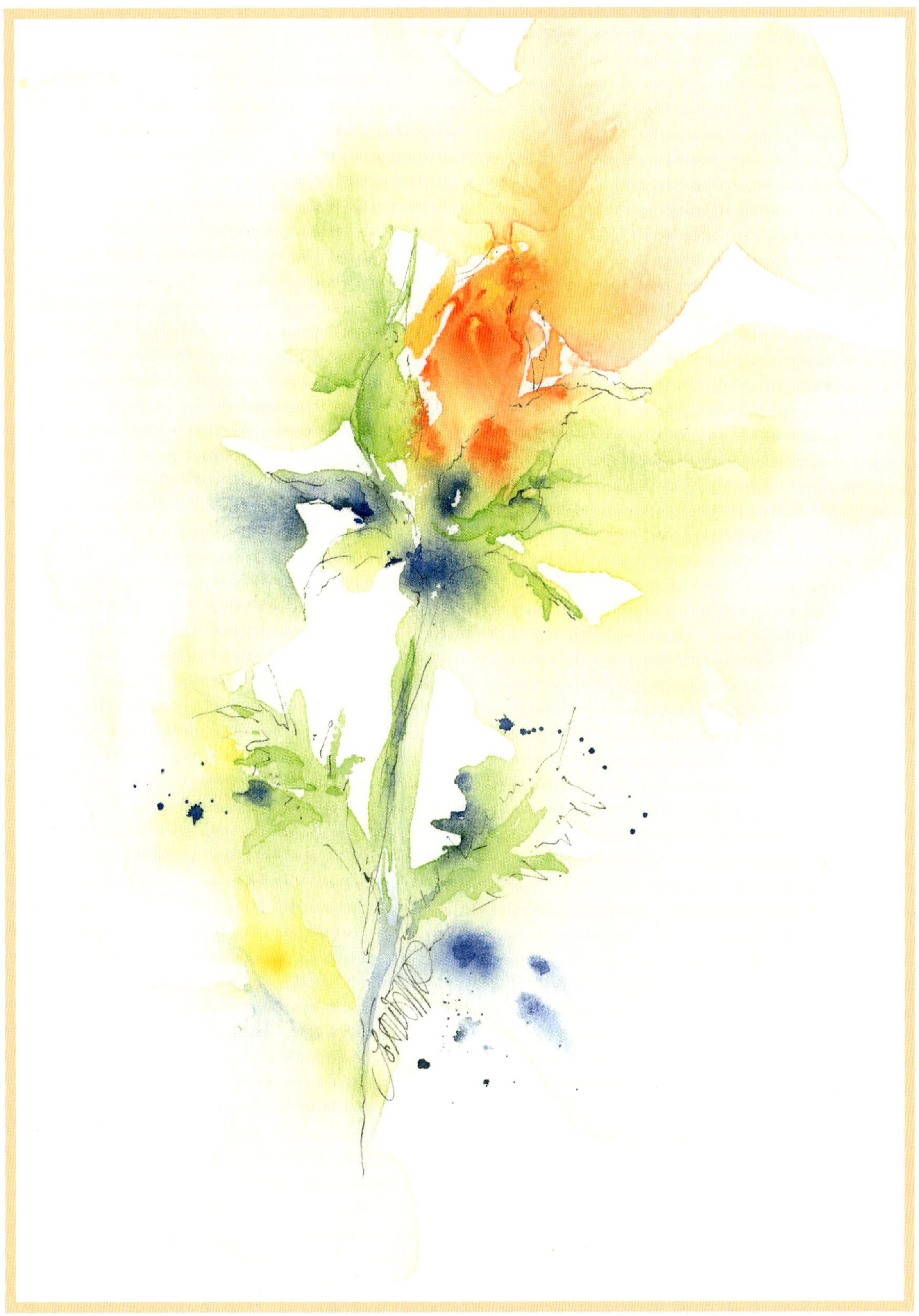

A YELLOW ROSE FOR HILDA
18 x 25.5cm (7 x 10in)

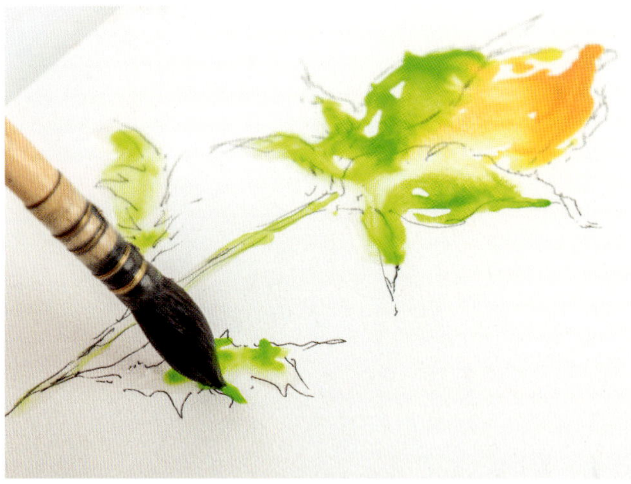

3 Use the tip of the large brush to add May green to the stem and leaves.

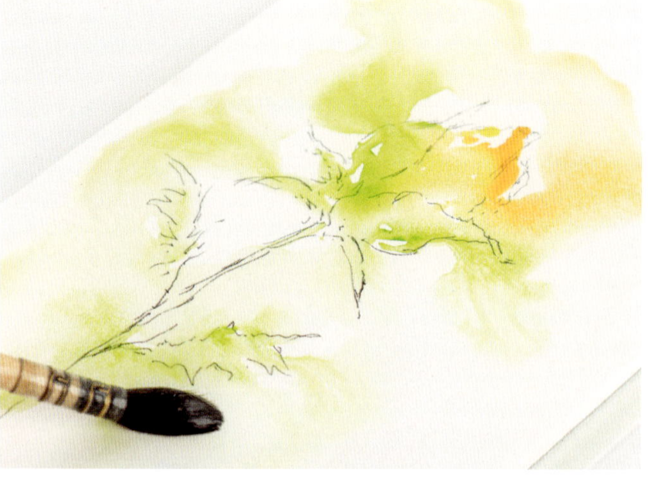

4 Rinse the brush, then use it to apply clean water to the background, drawing it in from the edges and just letting the water tickle the wet paint – you'll see it flow out and create a subtle background.

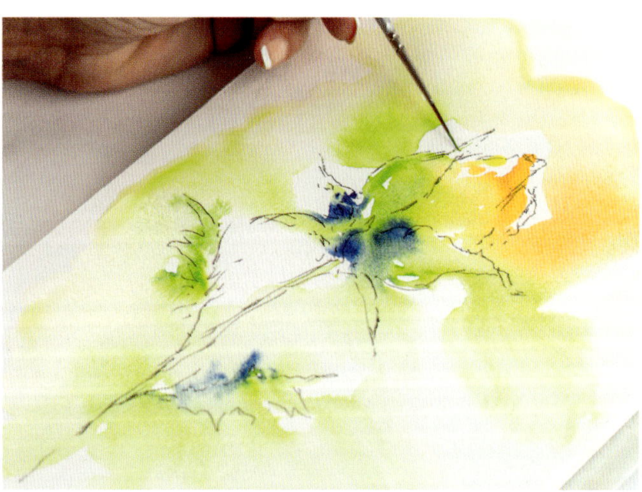

5 Add French ultramarine and May green to strengthen the green and suggest shaping through shadow.

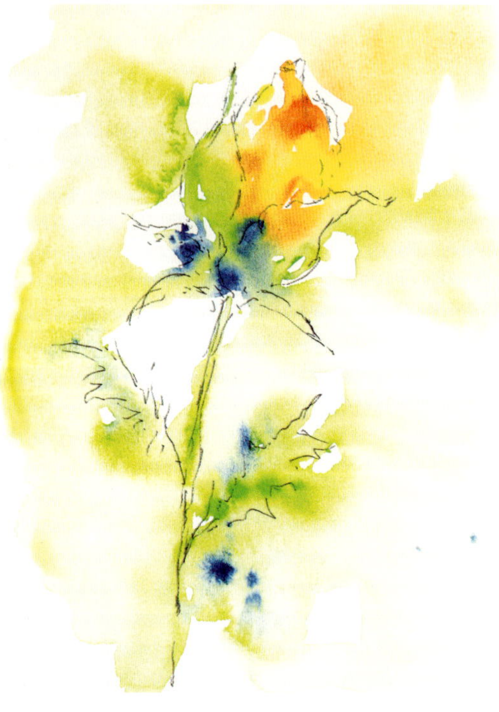

6 Optionally, you can add some spattering using a mix of French ultramarine and May green to add some further movement – it contrasts well with the clear lines created by the pen.

Using watersoluble pens

While traditional pen and wash work seeks to preserve the lines – fineliner pens are an easy way to add the detail that loose washes lack – you can also try using watersoluble pens.

Ink lines made with these pens will reactivate when wetted, a bit like watercolour, so you can break up hard lines and get a little more atmosphere in your finished piece.

When working over the top, work with a light, loose touch – otherwise you'll simply smear or wash away the line entirely.

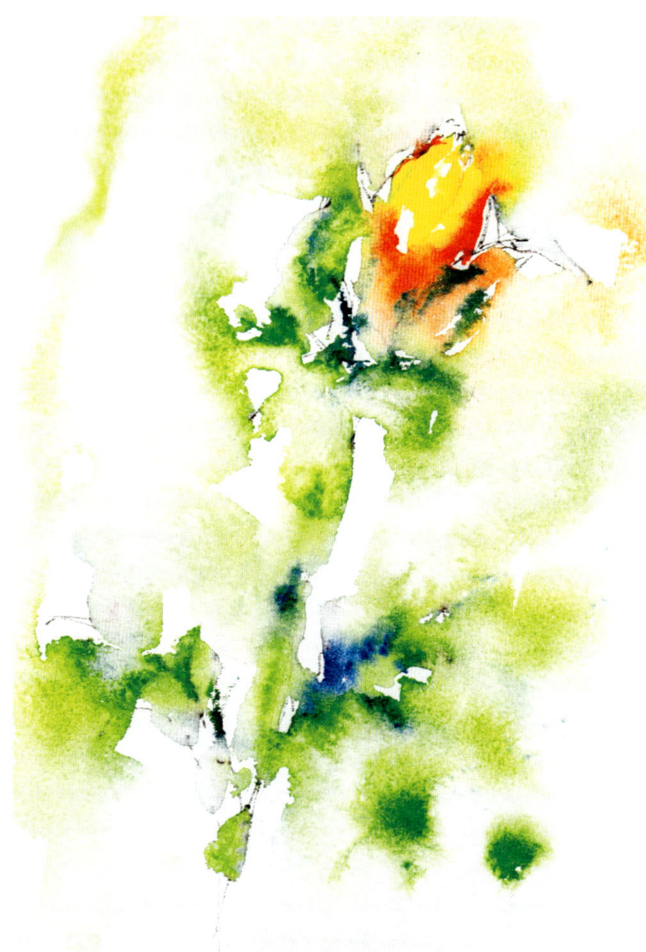

A YELLOW ROSE FOR SUSAN
18 x 25.5cm (7 x 10in)

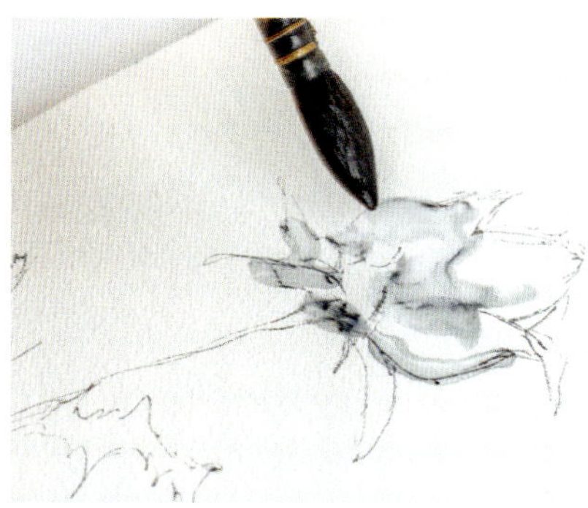

BLEEDING INTO WATER

Using my large brush (daddy) I will gently touch the pen lines to get some subtle grey tones from the pen. I am careful to leave some untouched so that there is a combination of looser and more defined edges, too.

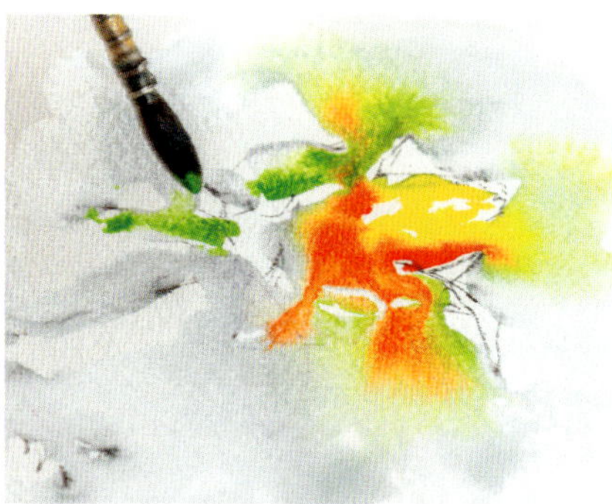

ADDING WATERCOLOUR WET INTO WET

Swapping to my medium brush (mummy) I ensure that the brush is very clean before picking up my chosen watercolours. I then drop them into the wet areas before pushing clean water up to all areas from outside in to allow the flower colours to spill back into the background areas.

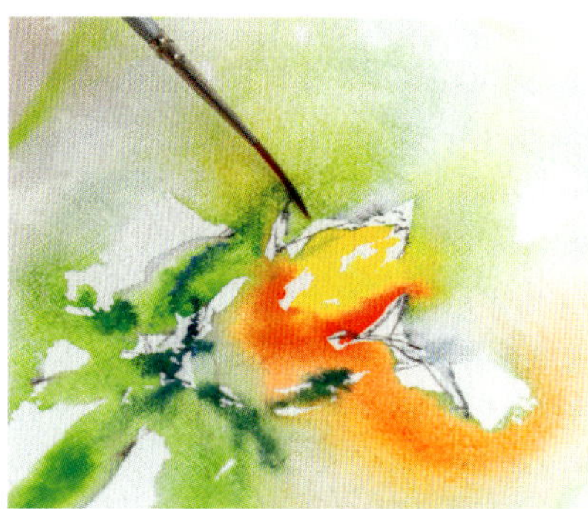

FINISHING TOUCHES

Finally, using my tiny rigger brush (baby) I will tap in some additional strengths and more defined marks, still keeping it loose by ensuring that I work wet into wet with plenty of water.

Which of the two finished paintings do you prefer? I love them both!

Mixed bouquet

Handmade paper acts differently to our usual watercolour paper, which is 'sized' (primed) to allow the water and colour to absorb at a slower pace. Many handmade papers instead act more like blotting paper, giving a completely different experience. I like to experiment with various papers from time to time so that I can come out of my comfort zone.

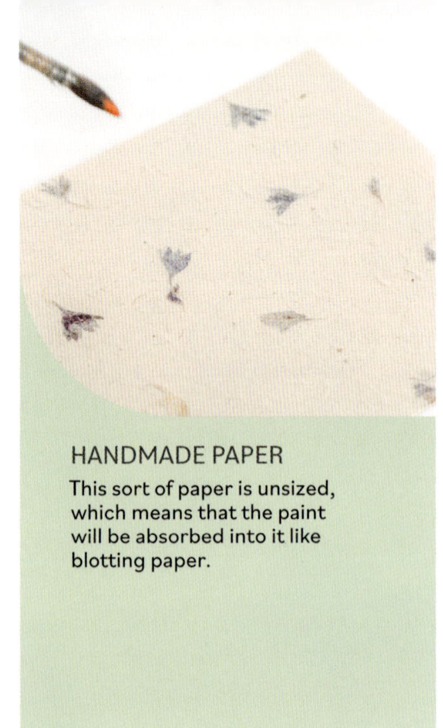

HANDMADE PAPER
This sort of paper is unsized, which means that the paint will be absorbed into it like blotting paper.

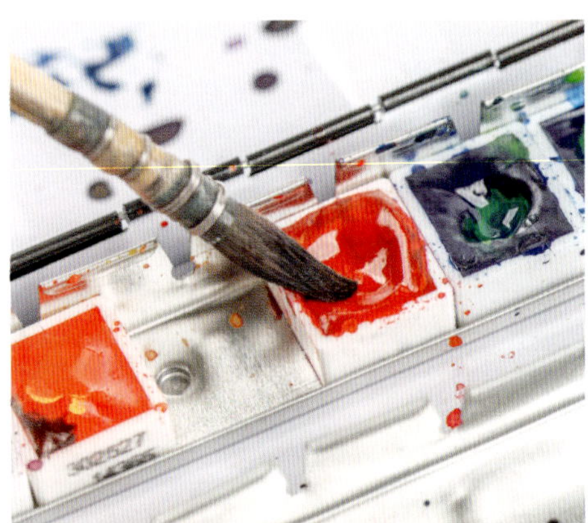

AVOID THE SPREAD
Use less water than usual when preparing your paints – otherwise the paint will simply spread out of control. Drybrush techniques and strong mixes will work well on surfaces like this.

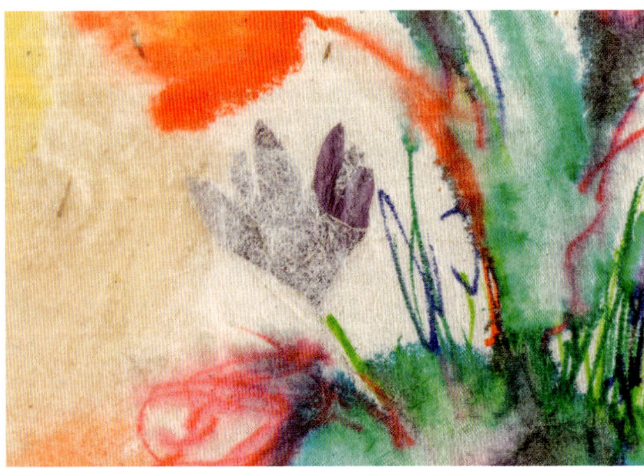

INCORPORATE ELEMENTS
Many handmade papers include petals or seedheads. You can build these into your composition.

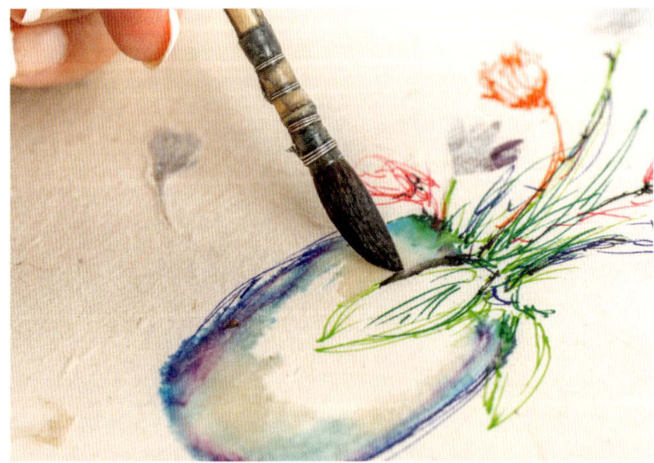

EXPERIMENT
Trying out handmade papers is a great opportunity to try combining different techniques. Here I'm using watersoluble pens (see pages 82–85) to complement my watercolours.

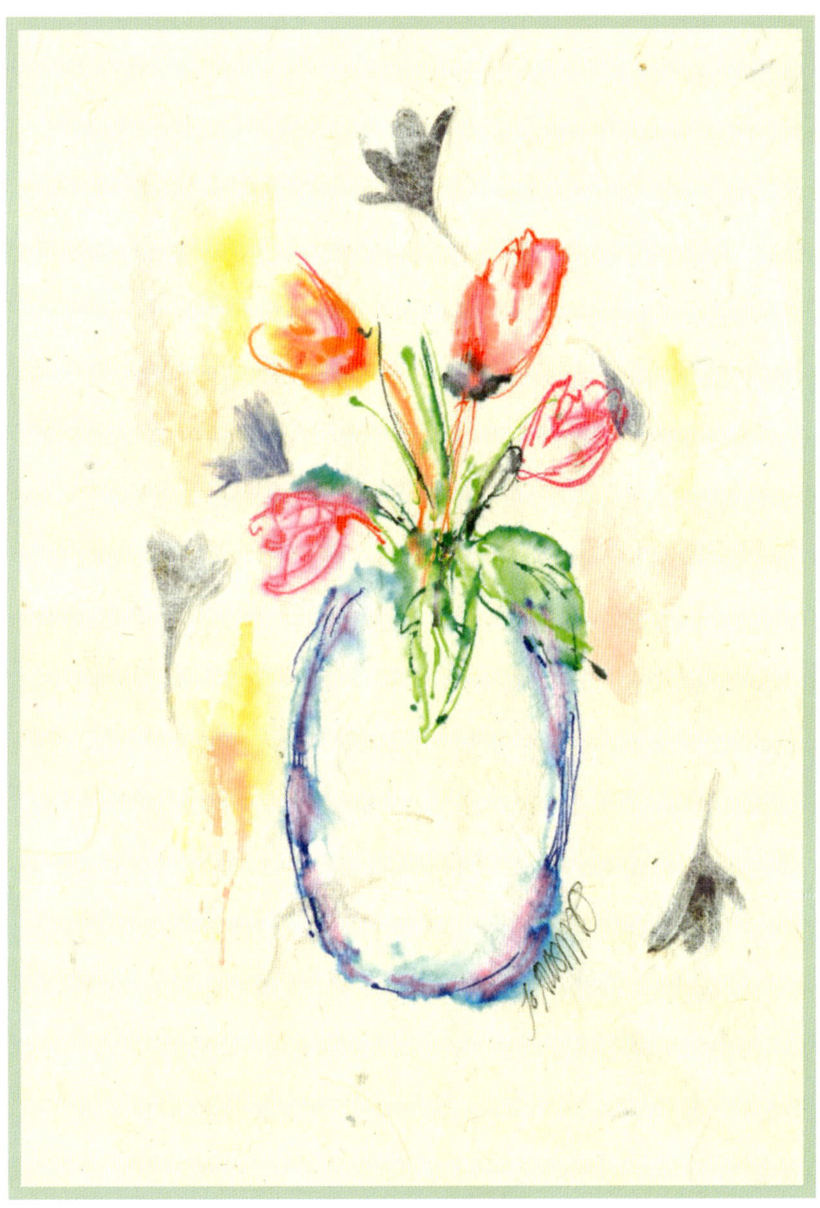

MIXED BOUQUET
9 x 13cm (3½ x 5in)

I've kept this composition small, so the petals in the handmade
paper match those I have added with watersoluble pen.

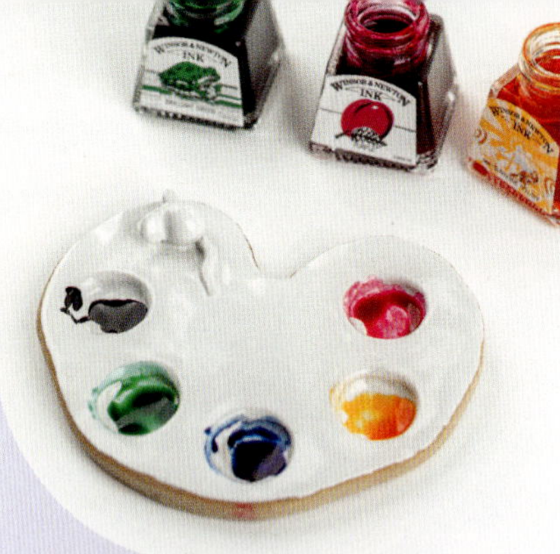

Lavender

I personally love the smell of this flower and seemingly the bee loves it just as much. Insects are attracted both to the scent and the wonderful blue and purple colours of the flower – as am I! The smell of lavender is calming, and is believed to aid sleep and reduce stress.

The inks I used in this painting are all Winsor & Newton calligraphy inks: brilliant green, purple, black Indian ink, ultramarine, sunshine yellow and deep red.

CALLIGRAPHY INKS

Calligraphy inks are formulated to be thicker than other types of ink so they can be used more precisely to create consistent marks.

Whatever the brand, inks are typically more vibrant than watercolours, but can otherwise be used with the same techniques.

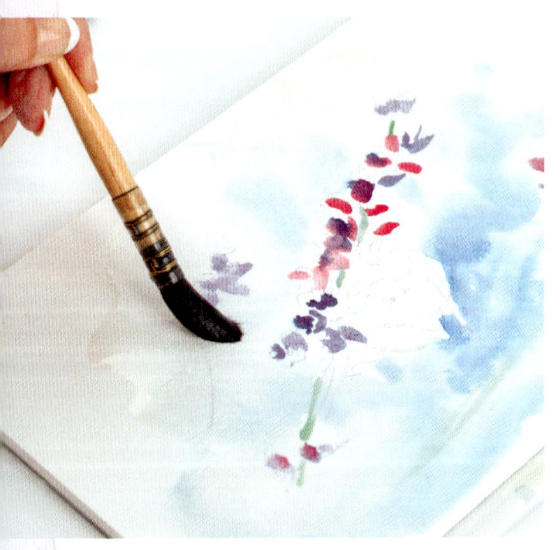

1 Make a light sketch with an HB pencil, and use the medium brush to add small marks of purple (actually quite a vibrant pink) and ultramarine; and then longer strokes of brilliant green.

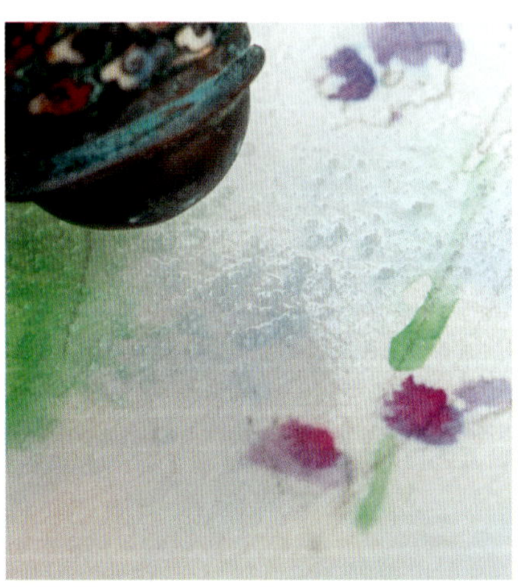

2 The inks will dry quickly. Use the large brush to overlay the background with clean water, and drop in ultramarine. Quickly add some table salt.

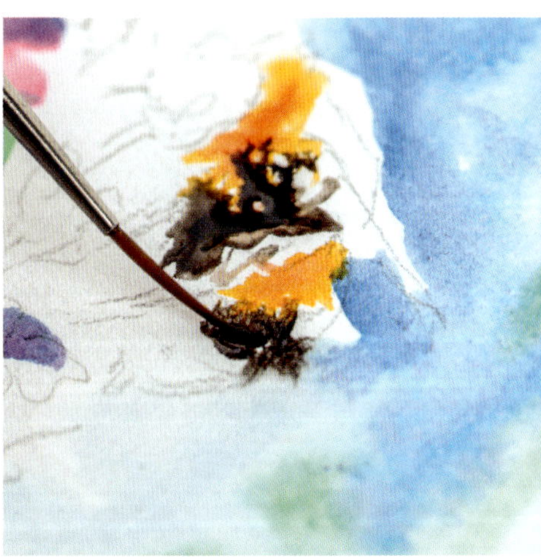

3 While the salt develops, paint the bee using sunshine yellow and a tiny hint of deep red for shading, then add the black stripes with Indian ink.

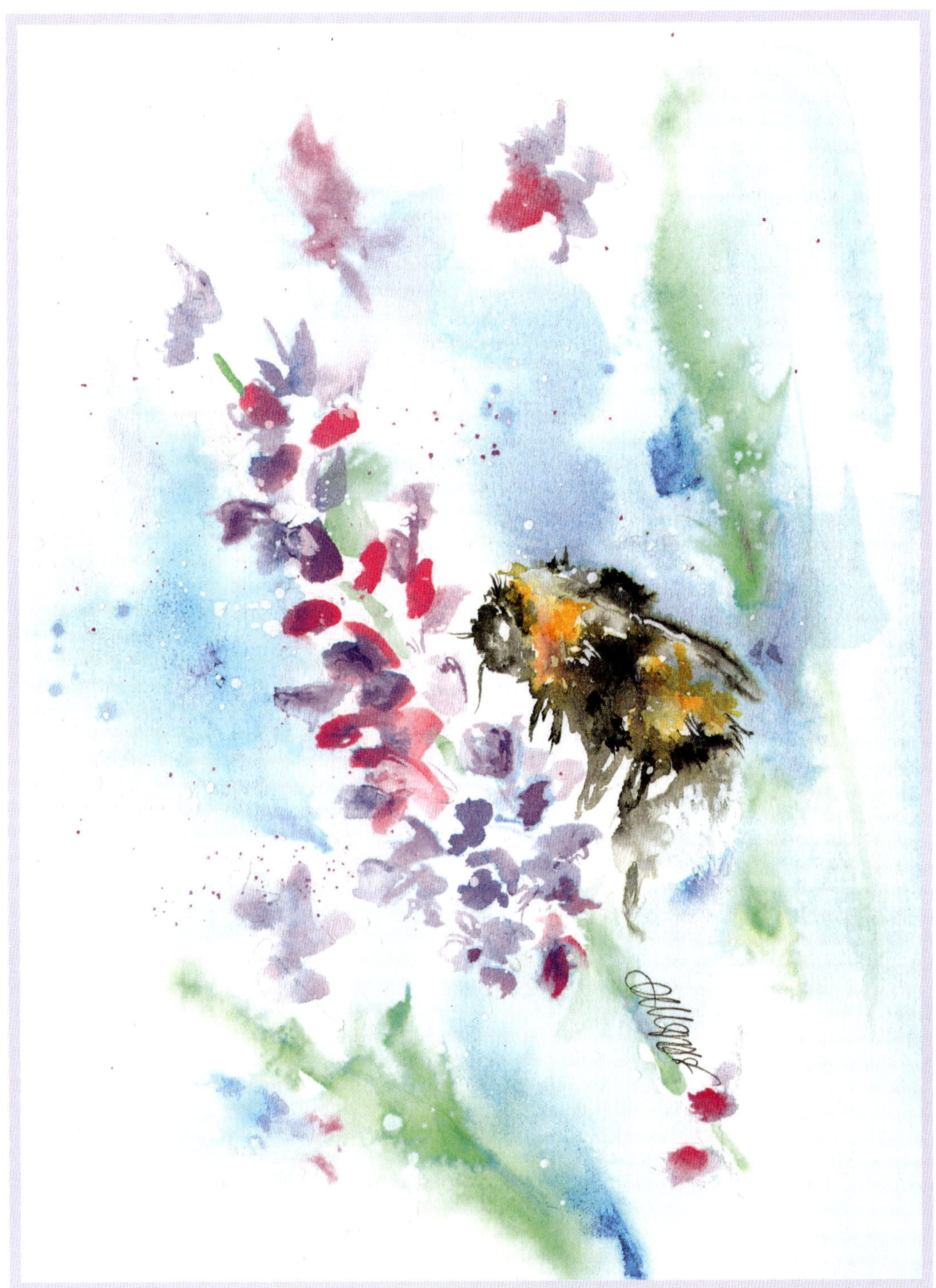

LAVENDER WITH BEE IN INKS
18 x 25.5cm (7 x 10in)

You can wait for the first layer to dry before adding the black Indian Ink to the bee. I opted to work while the yellow was wet, and you can see that you get wonderful interactions, quite different in character to those made with watercolour.

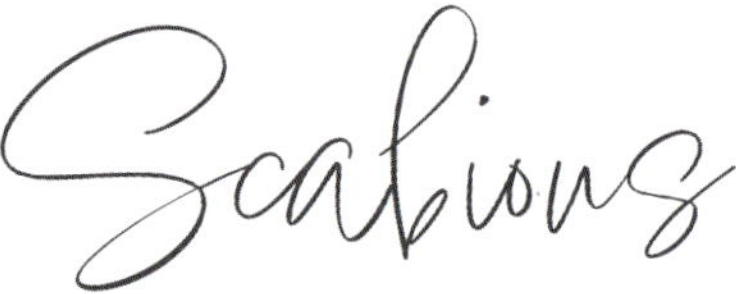

Scabious

Scabious (Scabiosa) is also known as 'pincushion flower' due to its appearance. It attracts a wide range of pollinators, so I felt that this blue butterfly would be perfect to accompany this flower.

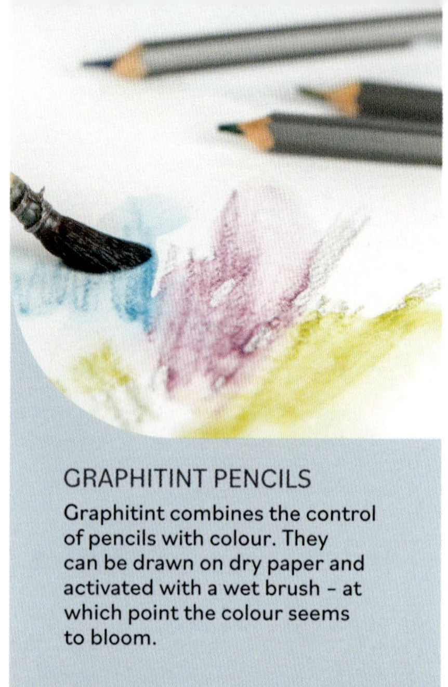

GRAPHITINT PENCILS
Graphitint combines the control of pencils with colour. They can be drawn on dry paper and activated with a wet brush – at which point the colour seems to bloom.

Using Graphitint pencils

Some students find it easier to draw than use a brush, and these pencils, which can be wetted to release their colour selectively – are an ideal 'safe step' into watercolour if you're just starting out. They are also a wonderful way to experiment even if you know watercolour inside-out.

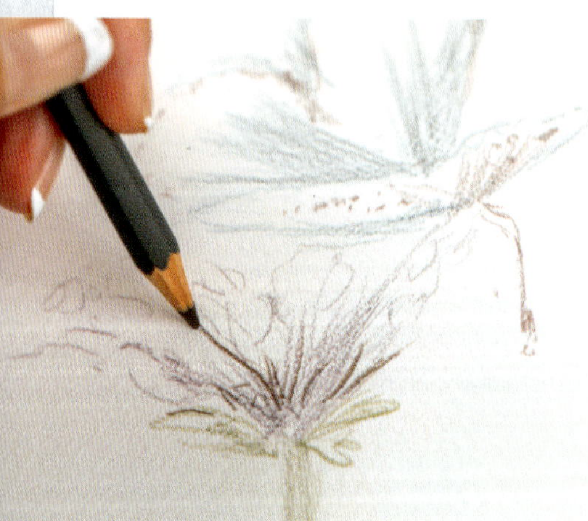

USE THEM LIKE PENCILS
You can use any pencil techniques with these: hatching, cross-hatching, pointillism, scribbles, curving strokes... you've got complete freedom.

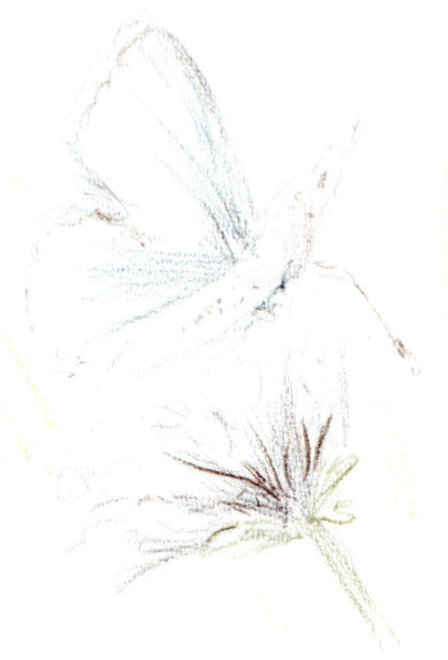

SUBTLE COLOURS
These pencils are very different to watercolour pencils. Less vibrant and colourful, they lend themselves to subtle effects.

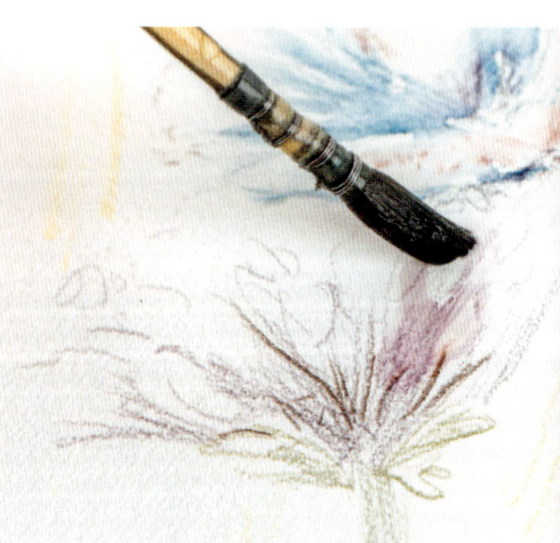

ADDING WATER
When wetted, the pigment bursts forth – as soon as you touch a wet brush to them, the colour becomes apparent.

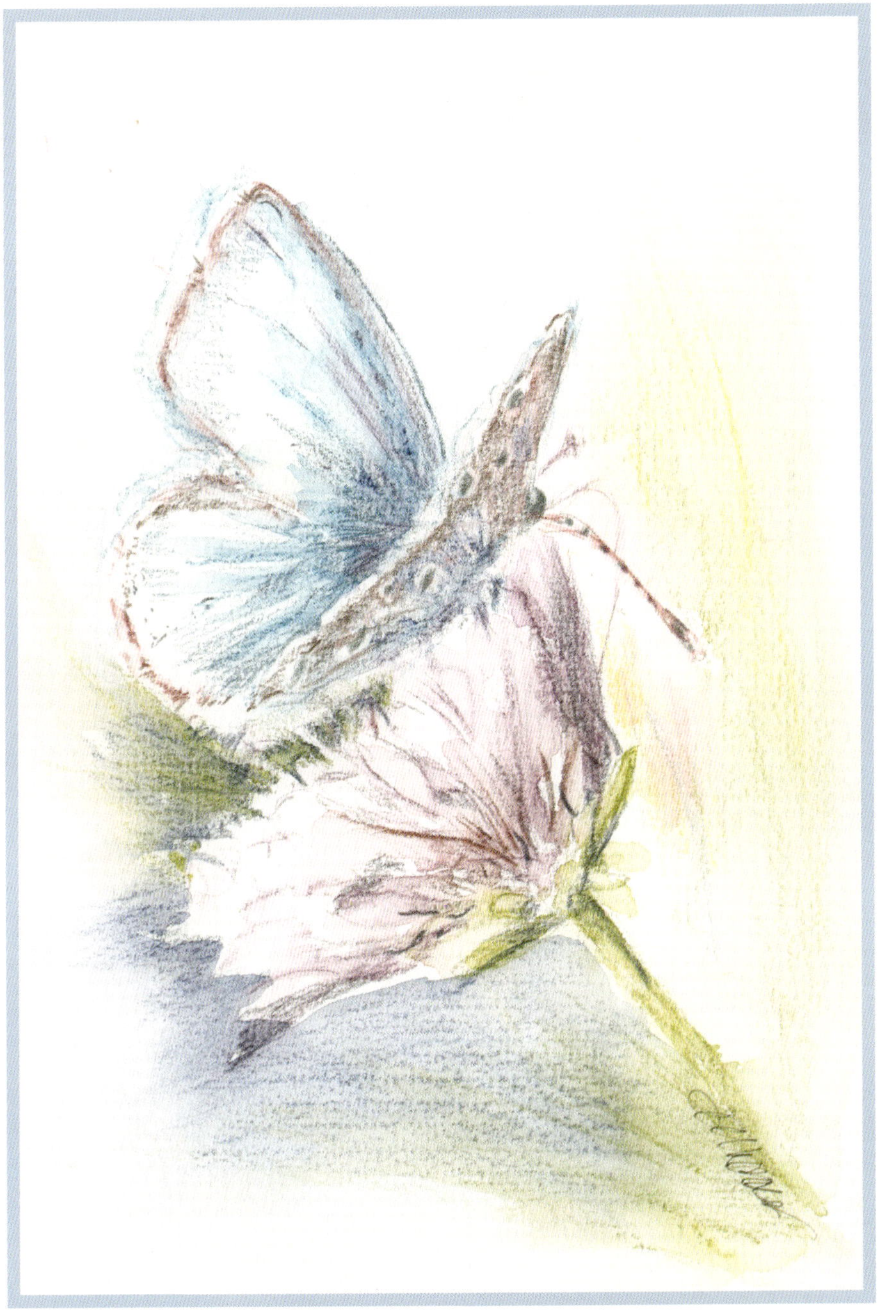

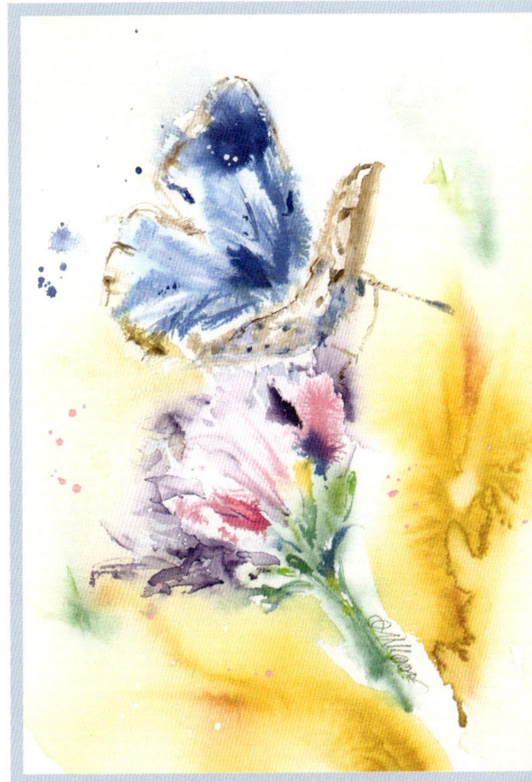

VIVID INKY BLUE BUTTERFLY
20 x 28cm (8 x 11in)

SCABIOUS WITH BLUE BUTTERFLY
20 x 28cm (8 x 11in)

Compare this delicate rendition of the scabious with the bolder version made with inks shown to the right. An identical subject, but very different results achieved through the use of different media.

Delphiniums

Sometimes known as larkspur, delphiniums can reach a great height of 1.8m (6ft) tall, and are very toxic to both humans and animals. I wanted to paint these elegant blooms as I love both the colour and the shape of the petals. Along with the waterlily, delphiniums are also the birth month flower of July, which is when my birthday falls. I just had to include both in this book!

ISOPROPYL ALCOHOL
Rubbing alcohol is used to clean and sterilize wounds, but it also unlocks interesting artistic effects.

Because alcohol evaporates much more quickly than water, it interacts differently with the pigment in the paint.

Using isopropyl alcohol

When sprayed into wet paint, beautiful mottled effects can be created. You can also spray the alcohol on the surface before you begin, which gives a darker result to the finished painting.

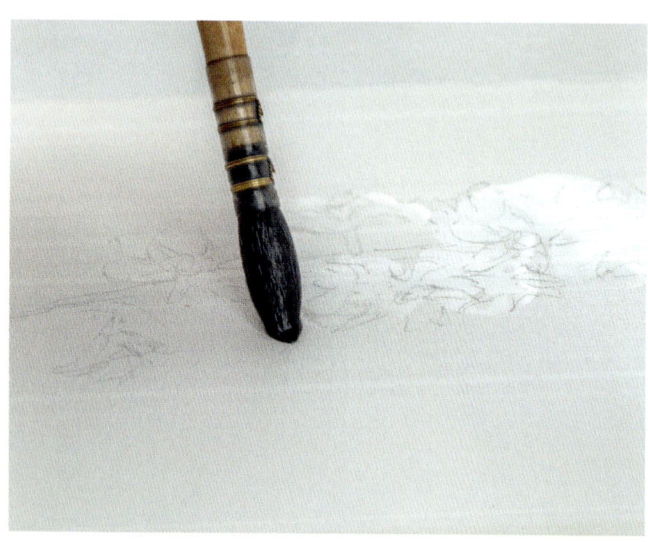

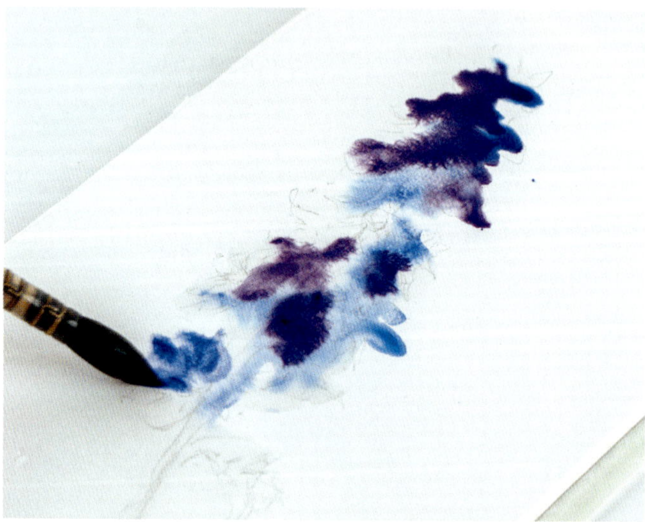

1 Lightly sketch out your initial drawing using an HB pencil. Wet the flowers using the large brush and clean water. Be careful to leave some white spaces for later sparkle.

2 Drop in French ultramarine and Schmincke violet with short, sweeping strokes away from the stem.

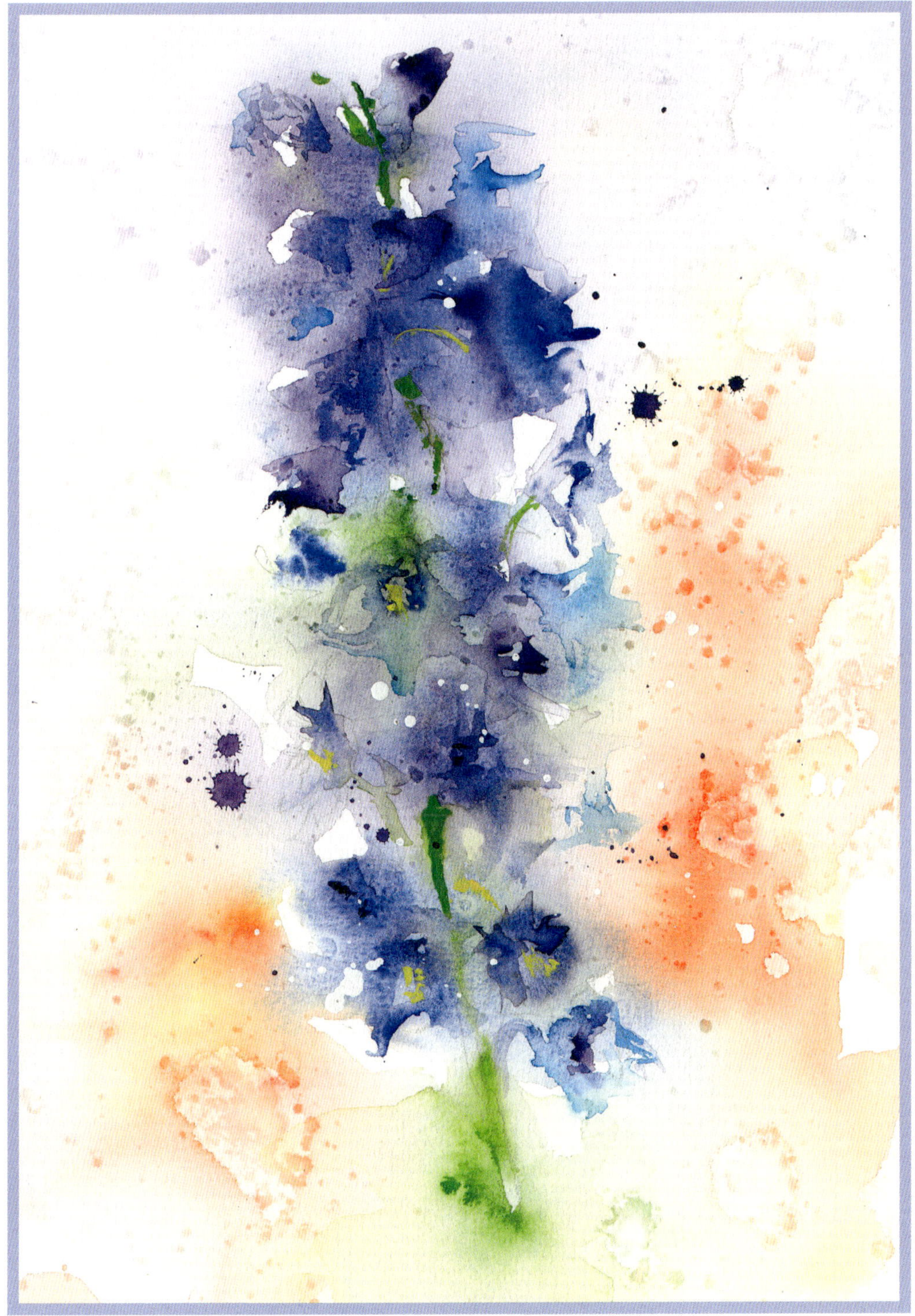

DELPHINIUMS IN WATERCOLOUR WITH ALCOHOL, INK AND ACRYLIC
18 x 25.5cm (7 x 10in)

I decided to use isopropyl for the background to give
the effect of movement, as though this tall flower is
swaying a little in the breeze.

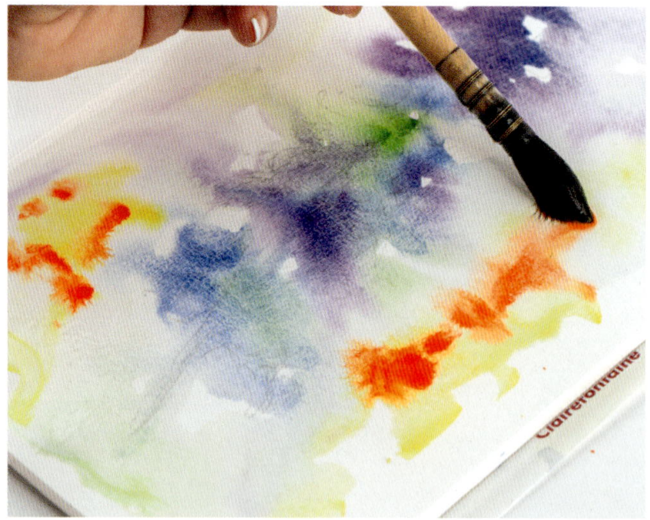

3 Hint at the stem with May green roughly halfway down, then wet the background and drop in vanadium yellow and vermilion.

Adding texture with isopropyl alcohol

I most often use isopropyl alcohol for adding a mottled texture to my background washes. It's a quick way to vary a wash and add interest.

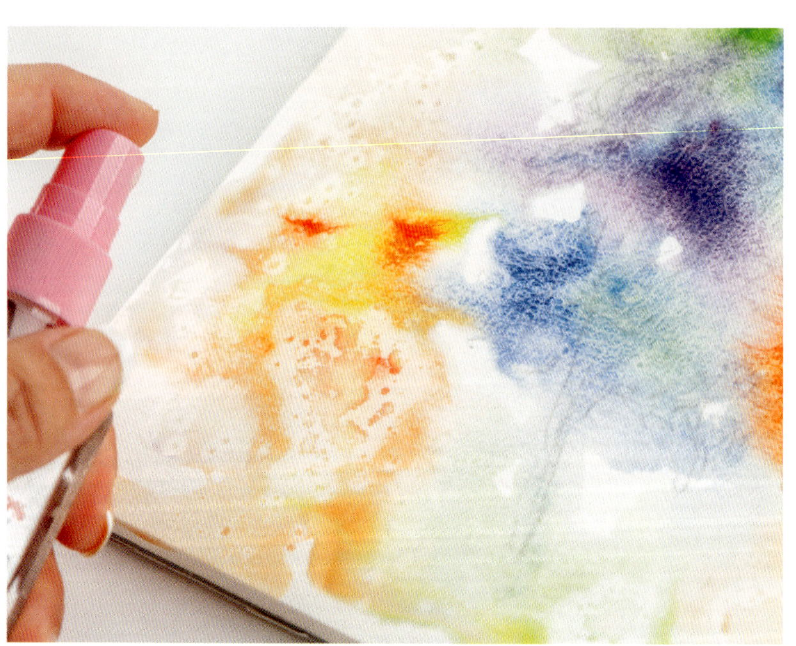

4 Use a spritzer to spray the alcohol directly onto the wet surface, working from about a hand's span from the surface. The alcohol will evaporate faster than the water, and push the pigment around.

5 While some areas remain wet, swap to a small brush and drop in touches of a dark mix of French ultramarine and burnt umber.

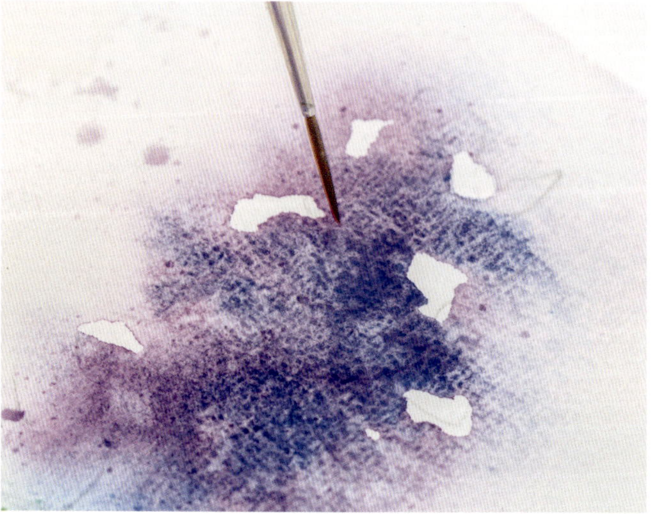

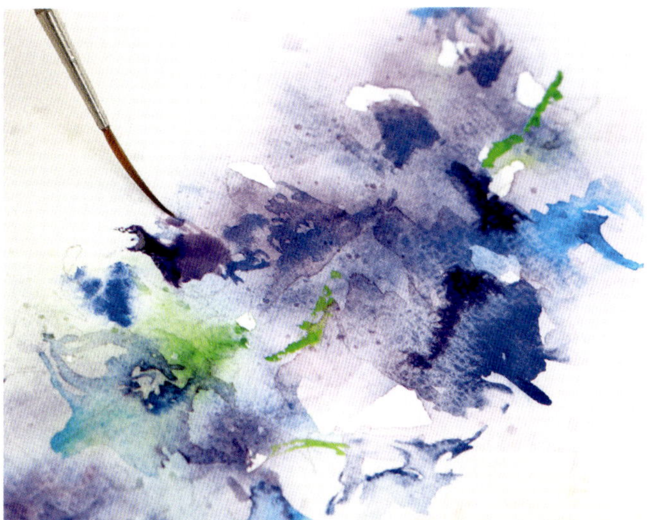

6 Once the painting has dried, pick out finer darks with small touches.

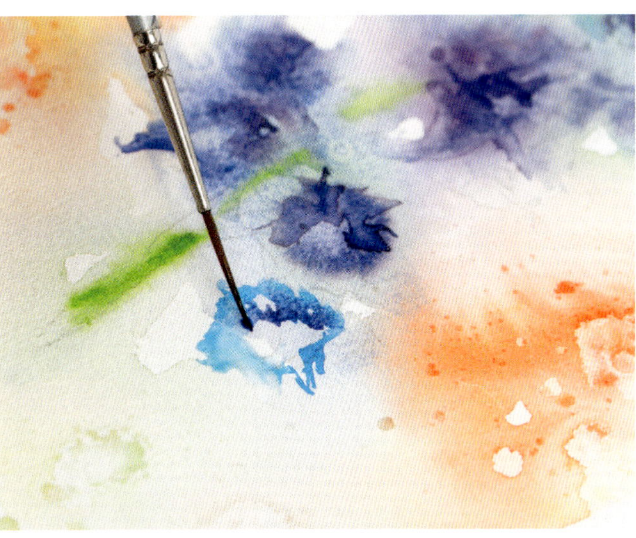

7 Still using the small brush, add helio cerulean for brighter touches, and Schmincke violet for deeper areas.

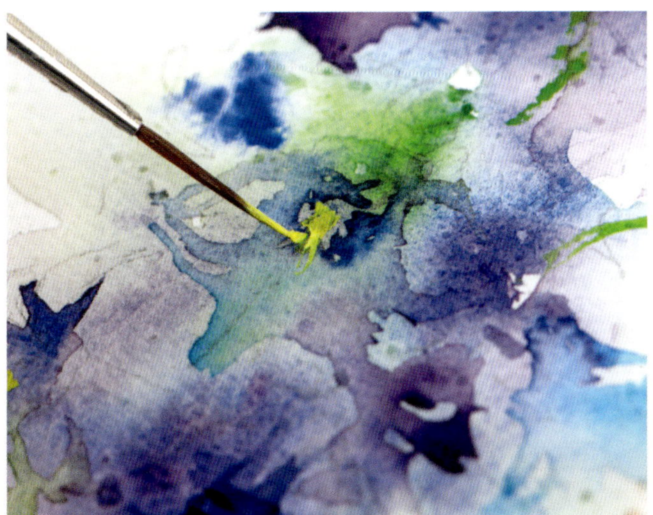

8 Touch in nearly pure (no water added) vanadium yellow for the flower centres. This colour is quite opaque when used like this, and will cover the darks effectively in small areas.

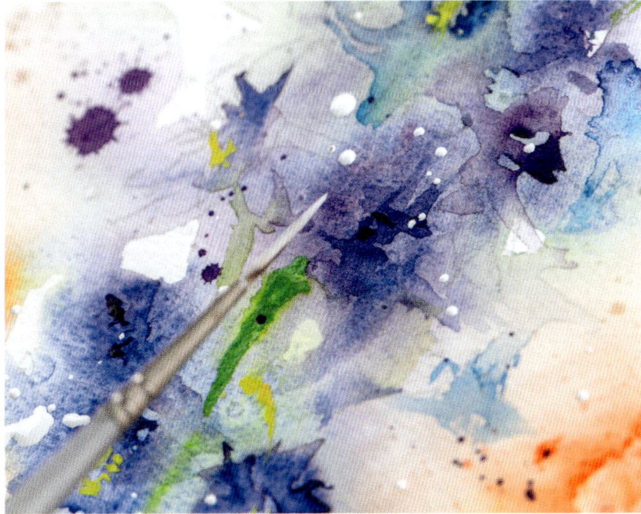

9 Add some spattering with Schmincke violet and white acrylic ink. These small dots really complement the speckles and marks created with the alcohol spray.

Marigold

Due to the complex head of this flower, I thought that the food wrap would work perfectly to suggest the folds in the petals.

Watercolour normally dries very quickly, but it takes much longer under plastic food wrap – patience is required for these effects.

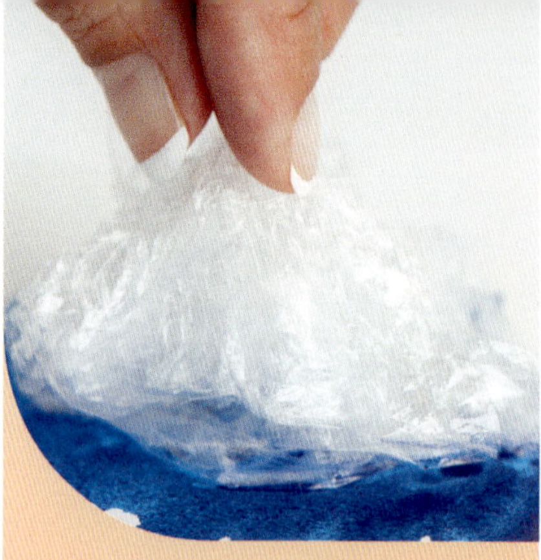

PLASTIC FOOD WRAP
This pliable, clear plastic gives you a simple way to create beautiful textures that would be impossible to make with a brush. The technique works best over bold colours applied strongly, because you need plenty of pigment to gather.

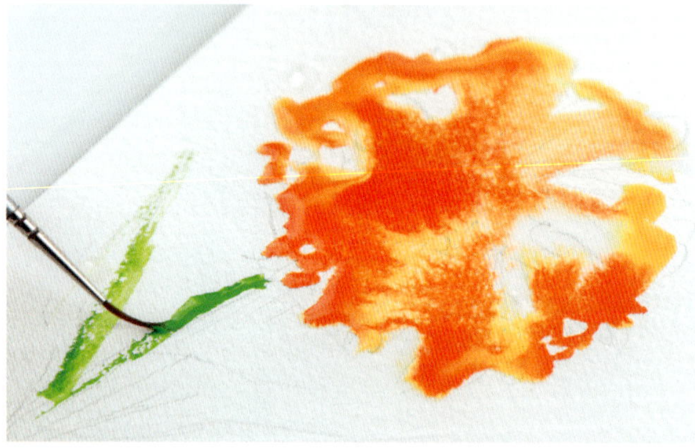

1 Lay in plenty of your colours - I've used vanadium yellow and vermilion wet into wet to make a warm orange for the marigold, and used May green for the stem and leaves.

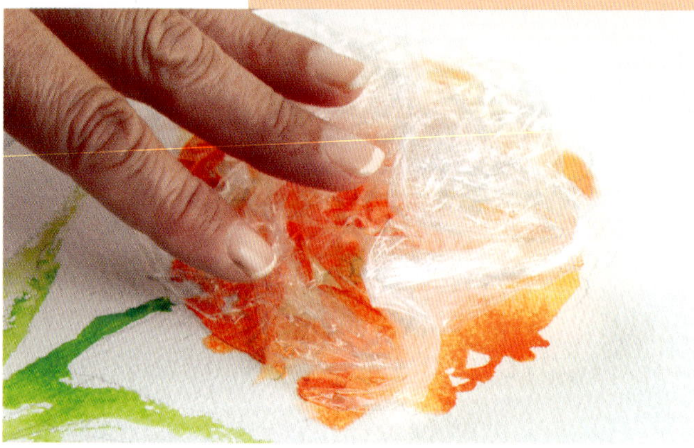

2 Scrunch up the plastic food wrap into a loose ball, then gently place it over the marigold. Lightly pat it down, then leave it well alone.

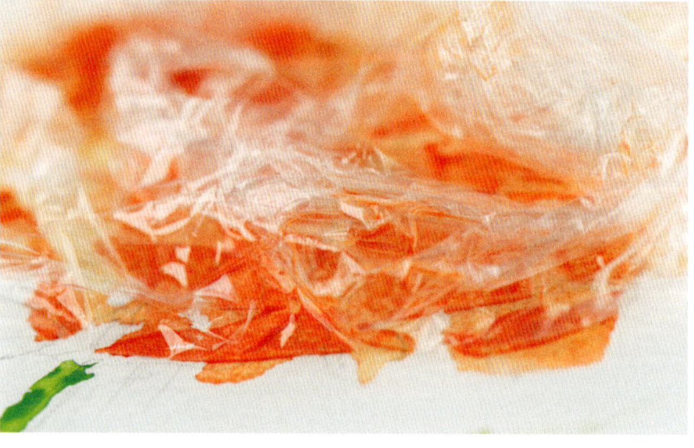

3 Leave to dry completely: preferably overnight, as the paint will take longer to dry with this technique. Don't be tempted to peep!

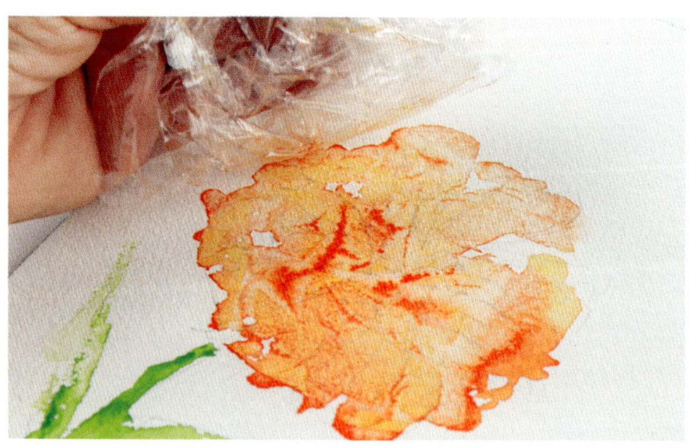

4 Gently lift away the plastic wrap to reveal the effect.

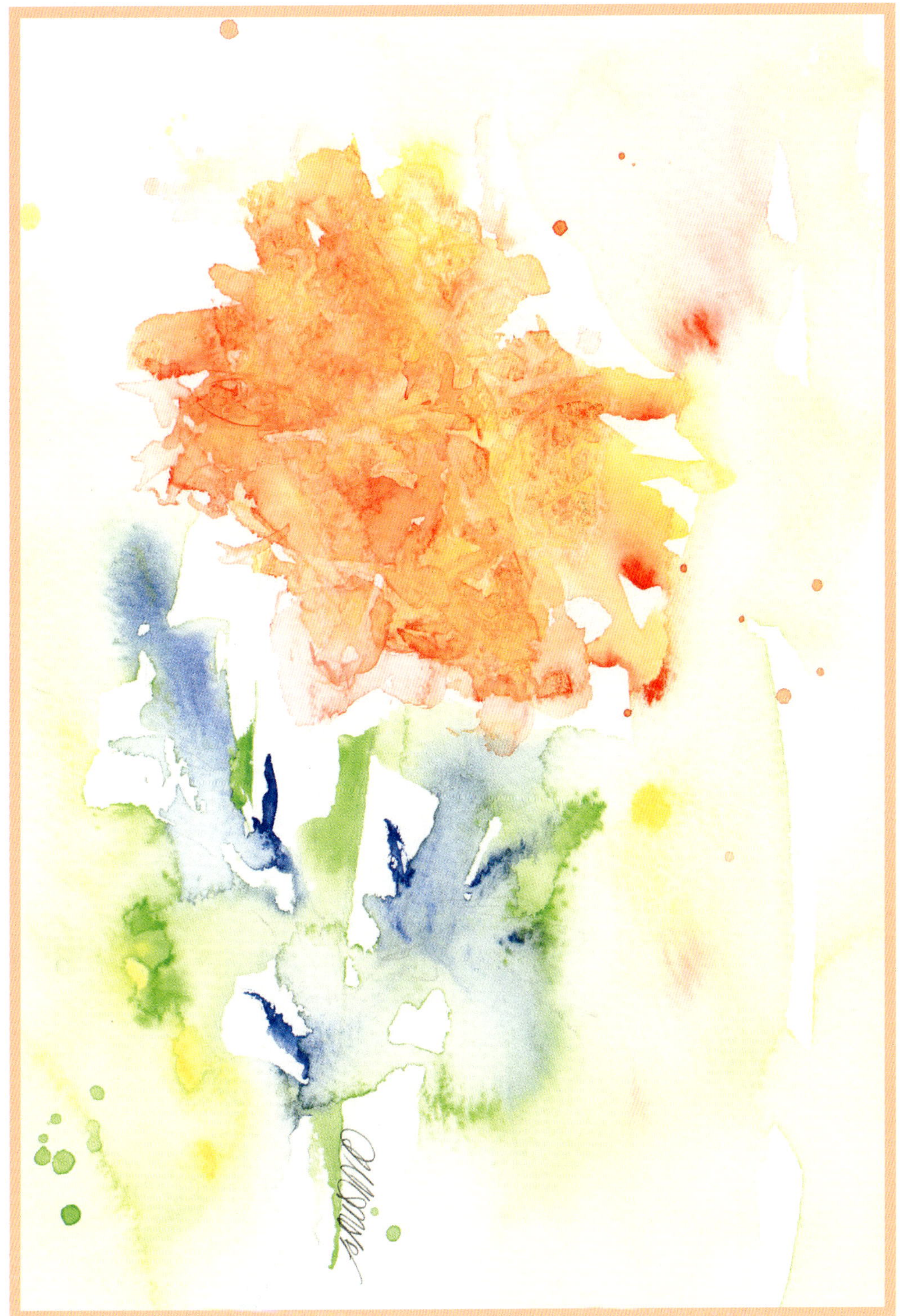

BRIGHT MARIGOLD
15 x 23cm (6 x 9in)

In this example, I used additional brush strokes and more
strength of colour to accentuate and pick out some of the
marks made by the food wrap.

Afterword

I have thoroughly enjoyed writing this book and putting together a wide selection of beautiful flower paintings for you to enjoy. I hope that I have enlightened you on how to achieve a looser way of painting with the advice and topics for you to practise.

Art is such great therapy, and not only does it bring us such joy, but others can appreciate this too. Look around you, there's a world full of painting opportunities for you to explore. Remember though, please do it for you: there should be no pressure and you can do everything at your own pace.

We all love to learn, and I sincerely believe we can all achieve great art. I hope the suggestions in this book have given you lots of ideas to try and that, like me, you never tire of learning more. Long may our painting adventures continue!

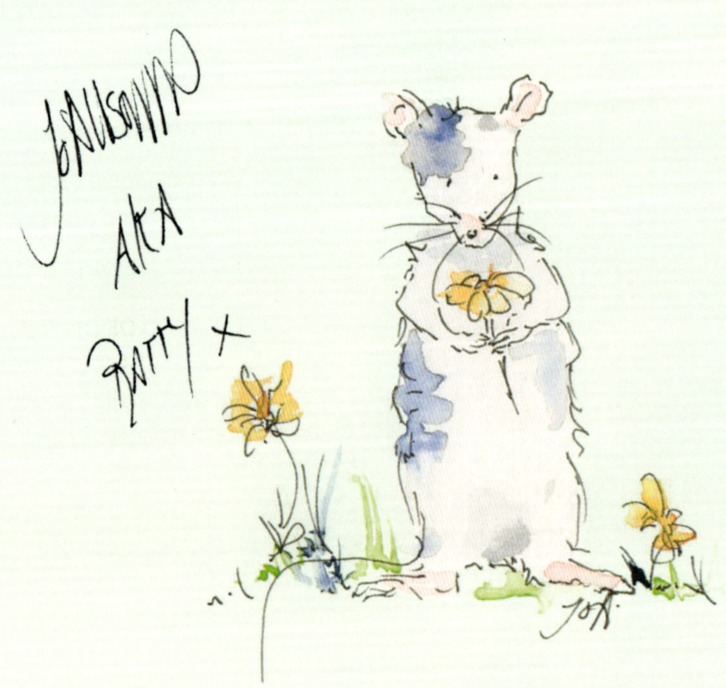

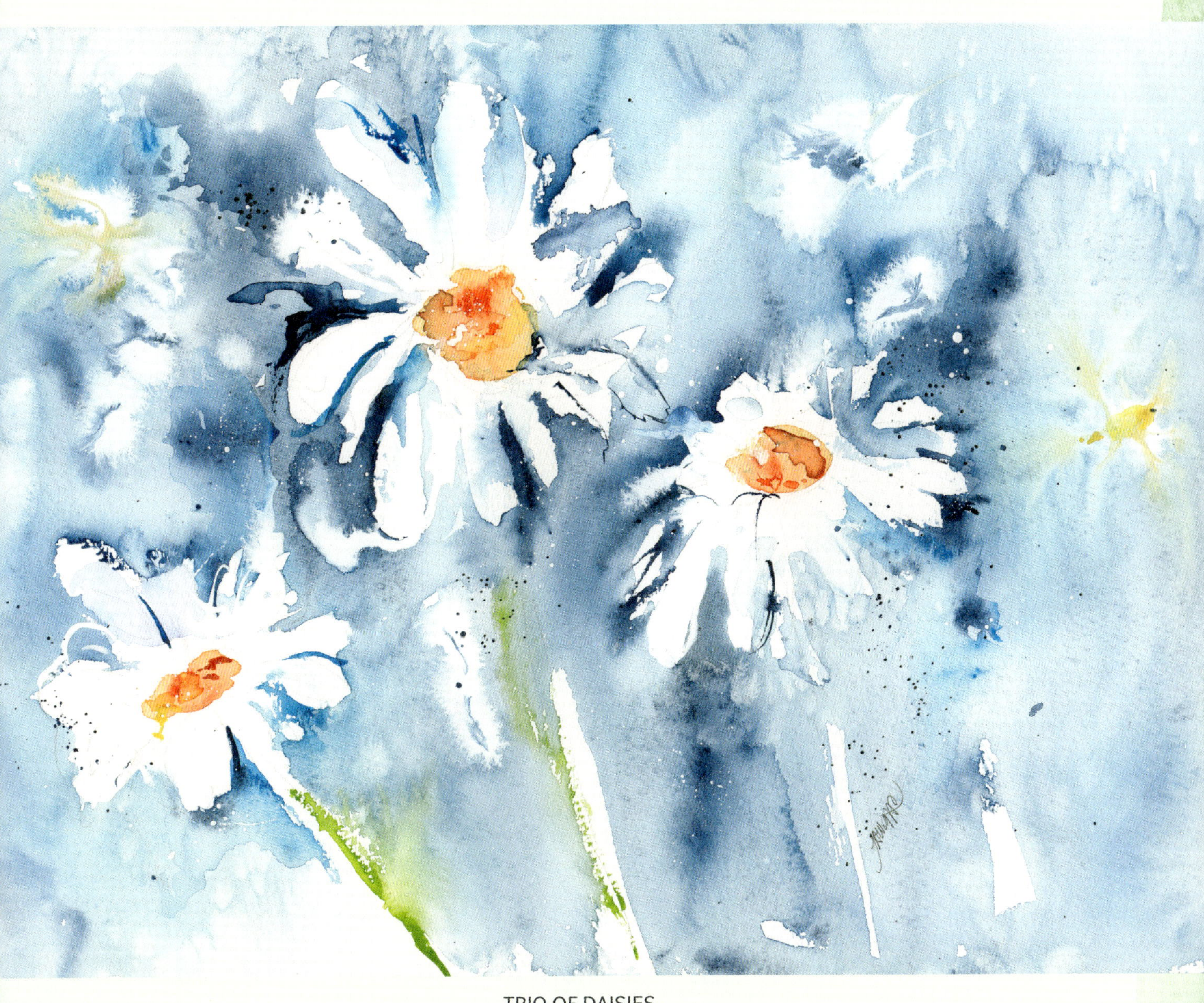

TRIO OF DAISIES
30.5 x 25.5cm (12 x 10in)

Watercolour with the inclusion of white acrylic.

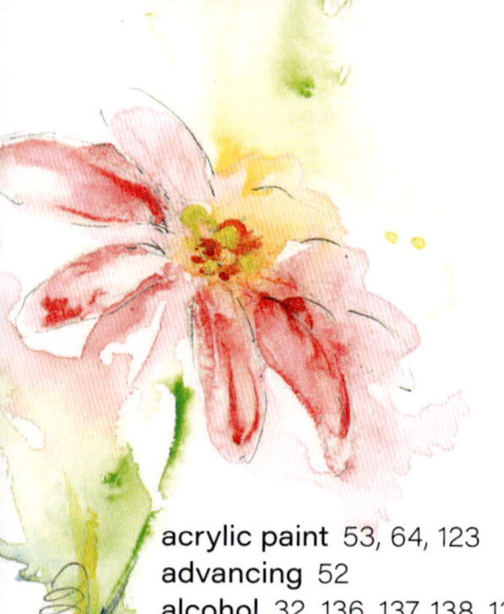

Index